Security, Society and the State in the Caucasus

The Caucasus, including the South Caucasus states and Russia's North Caucasus, continues to be an area of instability and conflict. This book, based on extensive original research, explores in detail, at both the local and regional levels, the interaction between state and society and the impact of external actors' engagement in the region within a conceptual framework linking security and democracy. Unlike other books on the subject, which tend to examine the issues from a Western political science perspective, this book incorporates insights from sociology, geography and anthropology as well as politics and contains contributions from scholars who have carried out extensive research in the region within a European Commission-funded Seventh Framework Programme project.

Derek Averre is a reader at the Department of Political Science and International Studies, University of Birmingham.

Kevork Oskanian is a lecturer at the Department of Political Science and International Studies, University of Birmingham.

BASEES/Routledge Series on Russian and East European Studies

For a full list of available titles please visit: www.routledge.com/BASEES-Routledge-Series-on-Russian-and-East-European-Studies/book-series/BASEES

Series editors: sociology and anthropology: Judith Pallot (President of BASEES and Chair), University of Oxford economics and business: Richard Connolly, University of Birmingham media and cultural studies: Birgit Beumers, University of Aberystwyth politics and international relations: Andrew Wilson, School of Slavonic and East European Studies, University College London history: Matt Rendle, University of Exeter.

This series is published on behalf of BASEES (the British Association for Slavonic and East European Studies). The series comprises original, high-quality, research-level work by both new and established scholars on all aspects of Russian, Soviet, post-Soviet and East European Studies in humanities and social science subjects.

122. Inside the East European Planned Economy
State Planning, Factory and Manager
Voicu Ion Sucală

123. Ideology and Social Protests in Eastern Europe
Beyond the Transition's Liberal Consensus
Veronika Stoyanova

124. Belarus under Lukashenka
Adaptive Authoritarianism
Matthew Frear

125. Class Cultures in Post-Socialist Eastern Europe
Dražen Cepić

126. Belarus – Alternative Visions
Nation, Memory and Cosmopolitanism
Simon Lewis

127. Russian Culture in the Age of Globalization
Edited by Vlad Strukov and Sarah Hudspith

128. Security, Society and the State in the Caucasus
Edited by Derek Averre and Kevork Oskanian

Security, Society and the State in the Caucasus

Edited by
Derek Averre and Kevork Oskanian

LONDON AND NEW YORK

First published 2019
by Routledge
2 Park Square, Milton Park, Abingdon, Oxon OX14 4RN

and by Routledge
52 Vanderbilt Avenue, New York, NY 10017

Routledge is an imprint of the Taylor & Francis Group, an informa business

© 2019 selection and editorial matter, Derek Averre and Kevork Oskanian; individual chapters, the contributors

The right of Derek Averre and Kevork Oskanian to be identified as the authors of the editorial material, and of the authors for their individual chapters, has been asserted in accordance with sections 77 and 78 of the Copyright, Designs and Patents Act 1988.

All rights reserved. No part of this book may be reprinted or reproduced or utilised in any form or by any electronic, mechanical, or other means, now known or hereafter invented, including photocopying and recording, or in any information storage or retrieval system, without permission in writing from the publishers.

Trademark notice: Product or corporate names may be trademarks or registered trademarks, and are used only for identification and explanation without intent to infringe.

British Library Cataloguing in Publication Data
A catalogue record for this book is available from the British Library

Library of Congress Cataloging-in-Publication Data
A catalog record has been requested for this book

ISBN: 978-0-815-35388-1 (hbk)
ISBN: 978-1-351-13483-5 (ebk)

Typeset in Times New Roman
by Taylor & Francis Books

Contents

List of figures and tables	vii
List of contributors	viii
Acknowledgements	xii

Introduction: security and democracy in the Caucasus: the interaction of state and society   1
LAURE DELCOUR, KEVORK OSKANIAN AND DEREK AVERRE

1 The tip of the democratisation spear? Role and importance of the Georgian Armed Forces in the context of democratisation and European integration   13
MARION KIPIANI

2 Russian governance of the North Caucasus: dilemmas of force and inclusion   37
JULIE WILHELMSEN

3 Overcoming the status quo in the unrecognised states of the South Caucasus: internal and external limitations   56
ROXANA ANDREI

4 Transformation policies and local modernisation initiatives in the North Caucasus   78
V.A. KOLOSOV, O.I. VENDINA, A.A. GRITSENKO, M.V. ZOTOVA, O.B. GLEZER, A.A. PANIN, A.B. SEBENTSOV AND V.N. STRELETSKII

5 The making of groups, boundaries and cleavages in the South Caucasus: from macro to micro dynamics   102
GIULIA PRELZ OLTRAMONTI

vi *Contents*

6 Arctic labour migration, vulnerability, and social change in the
   South Caucasus: the case of Azerbaijanis in the polar cities of
   Murmansk and Norilsk   120
   SOPHIE HOHMANN

7 Armenian volunteer fighters in the Nagorno-Karabakh conflict:
   an eye on narrative trajectories in a no-war no-peace situation   145
   AUDE MERLIN AND TALINE PAPAZIAN

8 'Exorcism of cultural otherness': refugee women in post-Soviet
   Armenia   167
   EVIYA H. HOVHANNISYAN

   Index   183

List of figures and tables

Figures

4.1 "Anchor" investment projects in the North Caucasus	91
4.2 Nodal modernisation in the North Caucasus	93
6.1a Nodal modernisation in the North Caucasus	121
6.1b Net migration rate per 1,000 persons, Azerbaijan	121
6.2 Number of migrants who left Azerbaijan per period (in thousands)	124
6.3 Ethnicity according to Russian or foreign citizenship of the CIS countries	124
6.4 Foreign citizens on the territory of the Russian Federation (aggregate data)	124
6.5 Number of Azerbaijani inhabitants in various regions of Russia according to censuses (Rosstat). www.gks.ru/free_doc/new_site/ (for censuses 2002 and 2010)	129
6.6 Ethnic groups from Caucasus and Central Asia in Murmansk oblast according to censuses (Rosstat). www.gks.ru/free_doc/new_site/ (censuses 2002 and 2010)	129
6.7 Distribution of Azerbaijani inhabitants, by cohort (year of move) and nationality (Russian or Azerbaijani) in Murmansk, Apatity (the second largest city in the region) and two monocities (Monchegorsk and Olenegorsk, both in Kola Peninsula)	130
6.8 Nationalities from Southern Caucasus and Central Asia living in Norilsk and its satellites (Census 2010)	130
6.9 Level of educational attainment among Azerbaijani inhabitants of Murmansk city (Census 2010)	131

Tables

4.1 Do you think the level of corruption in your region is decreasing, increasing, or not changing?	94

Contributors

Derek Averre is a reader in Russian Foreign and Security Policy and former Director of the Centre for Russian, European and Eurasian Studies at the Department of Political Science and International Studies, University of Birmingham. His main research interests focus on Russian foreign and security policy, Russia–Europe relations and arms control/non-proliferation issues. He has co-edited a book and journal special issues and written numerous journal articles and book chapters, as well as organising a series of policy and academic conferences and presenting widely in the US and Europe on these topics. He is a member of the Editorial Board of the journal *European Security*.

Kevork Oskanian is a lecturer at the University of Birmingham's Department of Political Science and International Studies (POLSIS); he obtained his PhD at the London School of Economics' Department of International Relations and has previously taught at the LSE and at the University of Westminster. His latest monograph, *Fear, Weakness and Power in the Post-Soviet South Caucasus* (Springer, 2013), analyses security in the region from a Copenhagen School perspective; his current research interests include post-colonial perspectives on contemporary Eurasian politics, the role of liberal ideology in the shaping of Western policies towards the former Soviet Union, and securitisation-based approaches to state weakness.

Roxana Andrei is a PhD candidate at the University of Coimbra, Portugal and has more than ten years' experience in the field of conflict management and human rights, with a keen focus on post-conflict developments in the Balkans and in the Caucasus. Between 2008 and 2013, she worked for the European Court of Human Rights of the Council of Europe. She is a fellow of the OSCE Documentation Centre, Prague and of the Foundation for Science and Technology, Portugal. Her current research focuses on cooperation and conflict dynamics in the energy field of the Caspian–Black Sea region.

Laure Delcour is a visiting professor at the College of Europe and Research Fellow at the Fondation Maison des Sciences de l'Homme, Paris. She was previously scientific coordinator of the EU-funded FP7 project 'Exploring the Security-Democracy Nexus in the Caucasus' at the Fondation Maison des Sciences de l'Homme. Her research interests focus on the diffusion and reception of EU norms and policies as part of the European Neighbourhood Policy, as well as region-building processes in Eurasia. Her publications include *The EU and Russia in Their 'Contested Neighbourhood': Multiple External Influences, Policy Transfer and Domestic Change* (Routledge, 2017), and 'Beyond geopolitics: exploring the impact of the EU and Russia in the 'contested neighborhood' (special issue co-edited with E. Ademmer and K. Wolczuk), *Eurasian Geography and Economics* (57)1, 2016.

O.B. Glezer is a leading research fellow at the Department of Social and Economic Geography, Institute of Geography, Russian Academy of Sciences, Saint Petersburg.

A.A. Gritsenko is a research fellow at the Laboratory of Geopolitical Studies, Institute of Geography, Russian Academy of Sciences, Saint Petersburg.

Sophie Hohmann is a lecturer at the French Institute for Oriental Studies (INALCO, Paris) in the Department of Eurasian Studies. She has also been an associate researcher at the Centre for Russian, Caucasian and East-European Studies (CERCEC, EHESS/CNRS) and at the Fondation Maison des Sciences de l'Homme, both in Paris. She holds a PhD in social sciences from the EHESS (School of Advanced Studies in Social Sciences) in Paris. Her research focuses on demographic trends and migration issues in and from South Caucasus and Central Asia to Russia's Arctic cities. She has published numerous papers and her latest book is *Pouvoir et Santé en Ouzbékistan* (Editions Petra, 2014).

Eviya H. Hovhannisyan is a PhD candidate in the Department of Anthropology at the European University at Saint Petersburg. Previously she was a junior researcher at the Codicology Department of the Mesrop Mashtots Institute of Ancient Manuscripts, Yerevan, and a visiting fellow within Ira.urban project at the Leibnitz Institute for Regional Geography, Leipzig. Her research interests include diaspora and refugee studies, identity and nationalism studies, anthropology of the Caucasus and Armenian studies. She is the author of 'Elitism among Refugees in the Rural Environment: Authority, Kinship, Social Networks and Economic Survival' in Y. Antonyan (ed.), *Elites and 'Elites': Transformations of Social Structures in Post-Soviet Armenia and Georgia* (Yerevan, 2016) and 'Phantom settlements: Study of the abandoned village Old Harzhis' in *From Private to Public – Transformation of Social Spaces in the South Caucasus* (Heinrich Böll Foundation, 2015).

Marion Kipiani has worked as a consultant on conflict transformation and post-conflict recovery in the South Caucasus and the Middle East, including five years of fieldwork in Georgia. She holds a Master's degree in Peace Studies from the University of Hagen in Germany and is currently

x *List of contributors*

pursuing further studies in international affairs and international security as a Fulbright student in the United States. Her research interests cover geostrategic competition in Eurasia and the wider Black Sea region as well as security and regional policy in the post-Soviet space.

V.A. Kolosov is Deputy Director of the Institute of Geography, Russian Academy of Sciences, Moscow, and Head of the Laboratory of Geopolitical Studies. He is also Past President of the International Geographical Union.

Aude Merlin is a lecturer in Political Science at the Université libre de Bruxelles (Brussels). She is a specialist in Russian and Caucasian Studies and a member of CEVIPOL (www.cevipol.be). She has worked extensively on the conflicts in Chechnya, including for various NGOs active in Chechnya. Her recent scientific work relates to the trajectories of war veterans of conflicts in the Caucasus. She has recently published the following: 'Remembering and forgetting in Chechnya today: using the Great Patriotic War to create a new historical Narrative?', in Anne Le Huérou, Aude Merlin, Amandine Regamey and Elisabeth Kozlowski (eds), *Chechnya at War and Beyond* (Routledge, 2014); with Ekaterina Gloriozova (eds), 'Sotchi 2014: la Russie à l'épreuve des Jeux, les Jeux à l'épreuve du Caucase', in *Connexe: les espaces post communistes en question(s)* (Brussels-Geneva, 2016); and with Anne Le Huérou, 'La Tchétchénie de Kadyrov, atout ou menace pour l'État russe?', in Isabelle Facon and Céline Marangé (eds), *Russie, le dilemme de sécurité (Défense nationale*, No. 802, 2017).

A.A. Panin is a senior research fellow at the Laboratory of Atlas Mapping, Faculty of Geography, Lomonosov Moscow State University.

Taline Papazian holds a doctorate in political science. Her PhD (2011, Institut d'Etudes Politiques, Paris) offered a reassessment of the Nagorno–Karabakh conflict on state-building in Armenia in the late Soviet and post-Soviet periods. After being adjunct lecturer at Sciences Po, Paris in political science, international relations, Soviet and post-Soviet studies and European studies, she now is a fellow at the University of Southern California, Institute of Armenian Studies in Los Angeles. She has been working on comparative politics and armed conflicts in the South-Caucasus (Azerbaijan, Georgia, Armenia) as well as, more recently, in Israel. Within the framework of the Cascade programme, her work focused on trajectories of war veterans and post-conflict societies and institutions. Her most recent publications include *L'Arménie à l'épreuve du feu. Forger l'Etat à travers la guerre* (Karthala, 2016) and 'Engagement militaire et droits politiques des Arméniens: la Légion d'Orient, un exemple de négociations entre une nationalité non souveraine et ses Alliés européens', in *Revue des mondes musulmans et de la Méditerranée*, December 2017.

Giulia Prelz Oltramonti is a post-doctoral researcher in political science at the Université libre de Bruxelles and a lecturer in international relations and humanitarian aid at the Université Catholique de Louvain. Her research focuses on political economies of conflict protraction in the Caucasus, processes of informality, and border/boundary dynamics. Her latest publications are 'Conflict protraction and the illegality/informality divide', *Caucasus Survey* (4)1, 2017; 'Securing disenfranchisement through violence and isolation: the case of Georgians/ Mingrelians in the district of Gali', in *Conflict, Security and Development* (16)3, 2016; 'Southbound Russia: processes of bordering and de-bordering between 1993 and 2013', in *Connexe* (2), 2016; and 'The political economy of a de facto state: the importance of local stakeholders in the case of Abkhazia', in *Caucasus Survey* (3)3, 2015.

A.B. Sebentsov is Senior Research Fellow at the Laboratory of Geopolitical Studies, Institute of Geography, Russian Academy of Sciences, Saint Petersburg.

V.N. Streletskii is the Head of the Department of Social and Economic Geography, Institute of Geography, Russian Academy of Sciences, Saint Petersburg.

O.I. Vendina is a leading research fellow at the Laboratory of Geopolitical Studies, Institute of Geography, Russian Academy of Sciences, Saint Petersburg.

Julie Wilhelmsen is a senior research fellow at the Norwegian Institute of International Affairs (NUPI), Oslo. She holds a PhD in Political Science and conducts research in the fields of critical security studies, Russian foreign and security policies and the radicalisation of Islam in Eurasia. The two post-soviet Chechen wars have been a constant focus in her research. Wilhelmsen is an editor of the journal *Internasjonal Politikk* and has a wide outreach to the Norwegian public on issues related to Russia and Eurasia. Her most recent publication is *Russia's Securitization of Chechnya: How War Became Acceptable* (Routledge, 2016).

M.V. Zotova is Senior Research Fellow at the Laboratory of Geopolitical Studies, Institute of Geography, Russian Academy of Sciences, Saint Petersburg.

Acknowledgements

Original research for this edited volume has received funding from the European Union's Seventh Framework Programme for research, technological development and demonstration under the European project CASCADE, GA No. 613354, led by Professor Laure Delcour of FMSH Paris. The editors would like to acknowledge the support and encouragement of Laure and her very able team at FMSH.

Introduction

Security and democracy in the Caucasus: the interaction of state and society

Laure Delcour, Kevork Oskanian and Derek Averre

Introduction: security and democracy in the Caucasus

Both academic and policy writing have revealed the complexities and tensions that beset any investigation into issues related to security and democracy in the Caucasus. The break-up of the USSR opened up multiple fissures, both intra- and inter-state, and set in motion political, economic and social processes that have generated instability and insecurity in the region (Cheterian, 2008; Coppieters, 1996; Zürcher, 2007). The armed conflicts that erupted as the former Soviet republics sought independence from Moscow – particularly those involving Abkhazia, South Ossetia and Nagorno-Karabakh, all now *de facto* state-like entities – continue to pose unresolved threats and challenges to regional stability. The polities in the South Caucasus states have remained at best 'hybrid' regimes (Levitsky & Way, 2002), combining formal elements of democratic governance with deeper-seated informal and/or illiberal practices common to authoritarianism, which are to varying degrees detached from society. Ethnic unrest in the North Caucasus has been dealt with using repressive methods which have called into question Russia's commitment to the rule of law (Hughes, 2007; Sanders, Tucker, & Hamburg, 2004), and has recently acquired features of an Islamist insurgency (Youngman, 2016). Local conflicts have, over time, intersected with the actions of external state or non-state actors: while the Caucasus may be viewed as a regional 'security complex', the broader context of local developments must be kept firmly in mind.

The South Caucasus became part of Europe's 'neighbourhood' shortly after the establishment of the EU's European Neighbourhood Policy in 2004. Only a few years later, the region's states were incorporated into the EU's Eastern Partnership policy framework, which promised 'a step change in relations with these partners... responding to the need for a clearer signal of EU commitment following the conflict in Georgia and its broader repercussions' and a greater role for the EU in region of strategic importance for it (European Commission, 2008). This raised immediate challenges for the EU; the assumption that Europe's own security can largely be ensured by the projection of its norms beyond its borders (Kirchner and Sperling, 2007, p. 13; Lavenex, 2004) and the self-conception of the EU as 'an agent of international democracy promotion in its

2 *Laure Delcour, Kevork Oskanian and Derek Averre*

neighbourhood' (Lavenex and Schimmelfennig, 2011, p. 885), came up against the realities of a region marked by disputed borders and territorial conflicts, weak or immature institutions, little historical experience of democracy, imperfectly modernised economies characterised by elites' dependence on resources/rents, and population movements/migration (Nodia and Stefes, 2015, pp. 11–14). The security environment on Europe's eastern periphery has highlighted the difficulties faced by the EU in promoting democracy and raised fundamental questions about the complex connection between democracy and security.

These external developments have attracted the increasing attention of scholars and policy communities in the light of the geopolitical and normative challenges posed by Russia to the European Union (EU) and the states in the EaP, particularly since the war between Russia and Georgia in 2008 and the crisis in Ukraine in 2014. At the regional level, Russia's increasingly assertive policies, combining military intervention and the offer of alternative political and economic models, appear designed to counter any nascent democratisation in the South Caucasus states (Tolstrup, 2009; Christou, 2010; Cadier, 2014). Russia perceives Western-inspired democratisation both as a threat to stability in the region and as part of a broader Western expansionist agenda (Delcour and Wolczuk, 2015). In fact, faced with a democratic deficit and indeterminate political change in the South Caucasus, the Eastern Partnership has focused less on promoting democracy and more on governance projects, whose immediate goal is to stabilise state institutions rather than decentralise political power through direct support for longer-term political reforms. Recent ENP documents are explicit: the 'daunting political, economic and social challenges' in the neighbourhood 'leav[e] policy-makers little time to focus on medium- and long-term reforms' which can only be carried out by elected politicians and citizens in the neighbourhood countries (European Commission, 2013, pp. 2, 4). On the one hand the EU emphasises the need for closer engagement with these countries on security, rule of law and civilian crisis management through Common Security and Defence Policy (CSDP) instruments, and support for a greater role for civil society in democratic and socio-economic reform (which was stepped up in the EaP, albeit with limited results; see Börzel and Lebanidze, 2015, p. 20). On the other hand, despite the understanding that 'the emergence of alternative regional integration schemes in the Eastern neighbourhood presents a new challenge' (European Commission, 2013, p. 22) – a clear reference to the Russian-led Eurasian Economic Union (EEU) – the EU has produced no clear political response in terms of closer security engagement with the neighbourhood. Indeed, the 2015 ENP review document states that, while continuing to work with governments, civil society and citizens on human rights and democracy issues, 'The new ENP will take *stabilisation* as its main political priority in this mandate' (European Commission, 2015, emphasis added).

Yet this approach pays less attention to how societal pressures and demands impact on the stability and legitimacy of institutions. In post-conflict societies, institutional imbalances may stifle local voices and even result in the maintenance of existing political hierarchies and belief systems. Investigating internal, or intra-state, processes is crucial to a fuller understanding of security/insecurity and democracy/authoritarian dynamics in the Caucasus. A lack of knowledge about democratic culture and citizenship, and a low level of social participation, prevents people in the region from exercising their rights and participating in decision-making appropriate to a genuine democratic system of governance (Large and Sisk, 2006, pp. 29–30). Shifting patterns of economic dependence and social change across the region – an 'open-ended and contested process of social transformation' within communities (Flockhart, 2005, p. 35) – pose new problems for the region's governments and, indeed, add to the EU's challenges in promoting democratic governance. In Russia's own North Caucasus, the use of paramilitary forces and co-optation of local leaders by Moscow, establishing top-down governance and centralised power aimed at suppressing ethno-nationalist separatism and Islamist militancy and preserving Russia's territorial integrity, have provoked 'instability and backlash' (O'Loughlin, Kolossov and Toal, 2014, p. 427). Expectations of a 'transition' to prosperous and stable democracies across the region, aided by the EU's 'transformative' external policy aimed at ameliorating the security environment, have largely been disappointed.

An immediate problem is that the conceptual framework for study of the region has often been shaped by European approaches, which take insufficient account of these local dynamics. The divergences between external and local actors' perceptions of what constitutes security and democracy, and the importance of widening perspectives beyond state-dominated narratives, prompt consideration of a number of problems: the impact of weak domestic governance on decision-making processes; the tendency of undemocratic regimes to manipulate popular opinion and securitise issues in order to justify illiberal policies; local-level practices of citizenship, social inclusion/exclusion and interaction between ethnic/religious minorities; and security sector reform and external assistance for conflict resolution.

The project[1] on which the present volume is based originated in the EU's Seventh Framework Programme, which called explicitly for 'a deeper understanding not only of the security problems and their root causes, but also of the potential for democratization in the [Caucasus] region', with a particular focus on the link between intra-state democratisation and regional security (see EuroEast, 2012). The project from the outset tackled an ambitious agenda of multidisciplinary research on a complex region where democracy has put down only shallow roots and underlying drivers of insecurity – poverty, inequality, corruption, nationalism – remain present. It aimed to investigate the reception, ownership and assimilation by local actors of externally promoted democracy processes, and the extent to which key external actors – in particular the EU, but also Russia – engage with the perceptions and priorities of local actors. This volume is composed of contributions that examine in detail the local and regional aspects of security and democracy and – using field work carried out in the states of the region, including

4 *Laure Delcour, Kevork Oskanian and Derek Averre*

Russia's North Caucasus – dig down to the societal level to gain a fuller understanding of the issues explored. The chapters gathered in this volume highlight the interconnections between different levels of security. As shown by several contributions, these linkages play out differently. External actors can be both drivers of security and insecurity (e.g. by playing a role in the spill-over of conflicts) for Caucasian states and societies, as well as inter-state relations. In a similar vein, the state (which retains its hold over key attributes of security) can also be a source of insecurity for its own citizens, either when it relies upon violence and coercion or when it fails to deliver effective socio-economic policies.

Security governance and democracy in the Caucasus

The conflict dynamics in the Caucasus, influenced by external actors, state weakness and societal cleavages, do not lend themselves to easy solutions. The exploitation of the 'frozen' or 'simmering' conflict environment by political groups on the one hand, and the survival of local peoples through adaptation to that environment on the other, are two sides of the debased coinage of conflict resolution. The provision of security and welfare in a divided and largely poor region often stumbles against political obstacles. The EU's approach to involvement in conflict-affected countries – focusing increasingly on top-down governance reforms at the expense of dealing with local power relations that underlie and fuel conflicts – has failed to make a substantial impact on the South Caucasus' regional security agenda and could even contribute to a wider process of destabilisation around the regional conflicts. Russia, in terms both of its policies in the North Caucasus and of its evolving relations with Abkhazia and South Ossetia, has prioritised stabilisation, or 'normalisation', through a combination of sponsoring local security actors and bureaucratic solutions to local development.

How do the policies of state actors in the region address the problems of security governance and what channels exist for the expression of the views and perceptions of local societal actors? How do state actors use political, diplomatic and military engagement to mitigate conflict dynamics and alter the status quo? How might democratic reform, particularly of security and defence institutions, enhance the prospects for security? The likely weakening of regional links stemming from the integration of the South Caucasus into competing EU and EEU economic systems is not confined to high politics but risks deepening intra-regional political fault lines through the creation of 'harder' local borders within the region. Given this context, what are the prospects of reducing the destabilising aspects of EU-Russia competition, when Russia's Treaty on Alliance and Strategic Partnership with Abkhazia and its Alliance and Integration Treaty with South Ossetia threaten to entrench their separation from Georgia, and when Armenia's accession to the EEU is seen by Azerbaijan as tantamount to the integration of the Nagorno-

Karabakh economy into the EEU along with Armenia, thereby consolidating the conflict?

The first three chapters in this volume focus on various aspects of EU and Russian approaches to security governance in the Caucasus region. Marion Kipiani's chapter focuses on security sector reform (SSR) in Georgia and how its defence and security institutions have been transformed from a site of corruption, crime and poor governance – which had a deleterious effect on the country's civil and ethno-political conflicts – to a much more professionalised institutional structure that has even played a role in multilateral (NATO- and EU-led) military missions. Nevertheless, there are tensions between security and democracy imperatives: the evolution of democratic, independent and transparent oversight over the defence sector has generally lagged behind the modernisation and professionalisation of its institutions, which contributed to the outbreak of war between Georgia and Russia in 2008.

This has implications beyond the Georgian governing elite's exercise of political power and approach to human rights: it is an important development in terms both of domestic governance and of the development of Georgia's broader integration into the Euroatlantic security culture. As Kipiani argues, the improbability that Georgia, despite its pursuit of a Membership Action Plan with NATO and its status as star pupil of the EU within the Eastern Partnership, will be offered membership status in NATO and the EU means that sustaining SSR and addressing deficiencies in security governance will require new formats of cooperation and assistance: rather than large-scale 'hard' military assistance, it will need targeted advice on parliamentary and independent oversight, continuing support in dealing with human rights issues and help in tackling emerging security challenges. Institution-building is a crucial prerequisite for effective and legitimate crisis management, in order to support efforts to bring peace and security to the hostile regional environment of the South Caucasus. Whether the political will of the Georgian government, beset by concerns over state sovereignty, which has been fundamentally challenged by its separatist entities, and potentially facing further externally induced destabilisation by Russia, can be sustained in the longer term remains open to question.

Julie Wilhelmsen analyses Russia's efforts to strike a balance between security and political freedoms in the context of its restive North Caucasus, looking both at Moscow's approaches in the period since Vladimir Putin came to power and at the potential for mobilisation against Russian rule in the North Caucasus. Her analysis is guided by the assumption that the state needs to cater for a broad and complex set of needs in the societies of the region in order to achieve efficient governance and legitimise its rule, balancing security and economic welfare and articulating an inclusive identity from the top down while allowing for a local voice in the system from the bottom up. These needs are particularly important in sustaining legitimate governance in areas such as the North Caucasus that are ethnically and religiously

6 *Laure Delcour, Kevork Oskanian and Derek Averre*

diverse. Even if conscious efforts have been made to complement a robust security policy with socioeconomic development (a theme dealt with from a human geography perspective by Kolosov et al later in this volume), inclusive identity articulation in official rhetoric has diminished, along with opportunities for North Caucasus populations to have meaningful representation in local political governance. This situation creates fertile ground for illegal economic practices and – of considerable concern in terms of regional security – the emergence of alternative political entrepreneurs, including extremist Islamists, who claim to offer security from state repression and alternative visions of where the North Caucasus populations belong.

The chapter by Roxana Andrei examines the role of Russia and international organisations – in particular the EU – in the conflict resolution and peace-building process in Abkhazia, South Ossetia and Nagorno-Karabakh. The challenges of building peace in these unrecognised states depends on the approach of external actors (Russia and EU) as well as on structural internal dynamics in these 'quasi-states', where there is a distinct preference for maintaining the conflict status quo. Andrei argues that, in terms of external limitations to conflict resolution, both Russia's and EU's engagement and their impact on the peace building process in the quasi-states have been limited and contributed to maintaining the status quo in the region. Although they do take into consideration the new security threats at intra-state and transnational level, the political focus of the external actors on peacebuilding is rather disengaged from the problems of post-conflict transformations at the society and community level. In addition to these external limitations, internal considerations further contribute to maintaining the status quo unaltered; the role of shadow economy entrepreneurs benefitting from the war and the post-conflict informal economy, the lack of trust in the peacekeeping operations and their actors, the functioning of the unrecognised states as 'normal' or *de facto* states and their further militarisation, maintains an environment of insecurity and tension. Andrei concludes by arguing that local actors' preferences should be a foremost consideration when engaging with the unrecognised states; engagement, even without recognition, in order to expand the degree of interaction with the wider democratic international community may allow the entities to move beyond the role of mere puppets dependent on external support.

The human and economic geography of the Caucasus

Part of the research agenda of CASCADE – an EU-funded FP7 project on the democracy-security nexus in the Caucasus – aims to reflect changing patterns of economic dependence and the growing role of regional development across the region. Poverty, isolation and backwardness of rural areas engender social polarisation and cleavages between social groups, militating against modernisation and forming major obstacles to democratisation and stability. The depopulation of mountain areas and uncontrolled urbanisation

Security and democracy in the Caucasus 7

are leading to the degradation of the natural environment in the North Caucasus, and land privatisation is shaped by informal practices; both of these trends lead to interethnic tensions and have the potential for conflict. Scholars have argued that the main trend in the North Caucasus points to pluralisation rather than democratisation – the lack of civil society institutions means that they are substituted by other forms of consolidation, which are mainly religious-based or centred on family networks.

Vladimir Kolosov and his co-writers focus their attention on the North Caucasus, Russia's most unstable region, characterised by ethnopolitical and territorial conflicts, economic crises, social turbulence and growing Islamist influence. Processes under way in the North Caucasus republics are analysed in terms of both 'modernisation' and 'demodernisation' trends. Issues of the region's development are central to the agenda of the federal and regional authorities but, at the same time, their opinions on opportunities for and ways of implementing development differ significantly: practically all regional elites emphasise the uniqueness of their own republic while the federal authorities, on the contrary, strive for solutions to local problems in a broader use of unified and politically neutral approaches to development. The authors of this chapter offer an evaluation of the results of administrative efforts to develop the regions of the North Caucasus Federal District (NCFD). They focus mainly on the analysis of processes that adapt the reforms being undertaken to regional specifics and on the symbiosis of the results of self-organisation of the population and federal and regional innovations, including so called large-scale 'anchor' projects. The analysis of the administrative policy in the North Caucasus is followed by a brief examination of the demographic situation in the region, which simultaneously creates opportunities for development while amplifying social instability. The authors also consider the influence of significant transformations of the ethnic structure in various areas on the 'modernisation' agenda. They use the data of four focus groups to analyse the relationship between traditional and 'modern' values shared by North Caucasians – their views on issues such as individual success, education, migration, gender and relations with family members.

The authors conclude that the rapid development of private entrepreneurial activities in the region coincides with the presence of local communities that maintain a deep attachment to traditional values and culture. This combination inevitably generates contradictions; in trying to resolve them, North Caucasus societies see a way out either in amplifying the regulatory role of the secular federal state and its programmes of regional development, or in various forms of Islam that are becoming increasingly popular, especially among young people. This raises the challenge of reconciling common points in opposing processes and making economic and cultural mechanisms of society work in unison.

The chapter by Giulia Prelz Oltramonti examines the production and interaction of different kinds of cleavages (national, political, social, economic) in the borderlands of the South Caucasus. If borderlands generally

8 *Laure Delcour, Kevork Oskanian and Derek Averre*

create 'energies and opportunities arising from the contrasts and dis-continuities that they both create and then police' (Jackson, 2008), it is crucial to identify and analyse the multi-dimensionality of the boundaries engendering them. The paper first identifies some of the cleavages that exist today in the South Caucasus; these may be based on identities (linguistic, religious, ethnic), economic and commercial frameworks, political and security structures, social realities (urban-rural divides, wealth and opportunity distribution) or legal frameworks (including citizenship status and ability to cross borders and migrate). They produce a fragmented regional map, a 'web of boundaries' that impact on trade and the mobility of people, their sense of identity and their coping strategies.

Oltramonti goes on to explore in depth specific cases from the areas of Abkhazia and the Georgian-Armenian borderland with the aim of investigating how some of these complex cleavages coincide or differ and how they affect each other. Formal processes of drawing new boundaries have occurred in the last few years, such as the implementation of Deep and Comprehensive Free Trade Agreement (DCFTA) with between the EU and Georgia and the establishment of the EU-Georgia Association Agreement; Armenia's accession to the Russian-led Eurasian Economic Union; and the recent Russia-Abkhaz Treaty on Alliance and Strategic Partnership. In part, they are the *de jure* formulation of economic and military trends that have been developing over a much longer period in terms of infrastructure, investments, passports, visa regimes and informal measures to promote or restrict trade – all the results of purposeful policy choices made by powerful actors. At the same time, however, they create new boundaries in an already highly fractured region. This paper explores how these new manifestations of 'us versus them' affect – and are in turn affected by – existing cleavages.

Ethnographic and sociological approaches

As outlined in the introduction to this chapter, the CASCADE project has aimed to assess the impact of conflict and economic dislocation on the marginalisation of societal groups, and on migration in terms of the challenges of demographic shifts, social mobility and security. Labour migration plays a major social and economic role, providing both a welfare safety net where the economic system fails to provide for the population's needs; also important is the role it plays in reinforcing social ties in a situation where the state authorities are regarded with mistrust. This is an essential aspect of human and societal security, which has been understudied in the region. An effective migration policy, involving visa facilitation and mobility partnerships, could be a major tool for strengthening the EU's impact in the South Caucasus, but it needs to be based on accountability and transparency and the EU should aim to strengthen social institutions in the region by promoting models that take into account local historical experiences. The challenges presented by migration are not confined to economics, however;

Security and democracy in the Caucasus 9

the movements of populations as a result of conflicts in the region, and the 'memory of war' that they bring with them, may be mobilised and used as a resource for building authority that can lead to resistance to efforts towards peace.

Sophie Hohmann argues in her chapter that, while numerous studies have been devoted to post-Soviet labour migration towards the main Russian cities (Moscow, Saint-Petersburg, Omsk, Novosibirsk), such migrations from the South Caucasus to Russia's Far North remains understudied. There are substantial communities of migrants from Azerbaijan in Russia's Arctic cities, albeit in smaller numbers than in central Russian cities. Migration flows from Central Asia are more recent and are more often considered in the context of post-colonial studies in accordance with a 'post-Soviet logic'. However, in order to understand better the historical conditions that created them, these migrations need to be considered in a longer-term perspective. Migration flows to the industrial Far North offer a unique opportunity to study new migrants' trajectories and to cross-refer these trajectories with the historical and socio-economic roots of such mobilities during the Soviet era. By focusing on migrants' professional niches, this article explores how migrants see their relationships to Arctic cities and to others nationalities in a special industrial environment and extreme climatic conditions. This analysis of polar migration provides new insights into the geography and sociology of Russian margins, showing how labour migration after the collapse of the USSR follows different logics from those prevailing during the Soviet era.

The issue of organisational strategies of migrants in the post-Soviet era (after 1991) is analysed by Hohmann while taking into account a generational dimension. This approach requires cross-referencing of ethnographic, temporal and spatial situations. In particular, an understanding of the spatial distribution of migrants, of occupational selection and of temporal sequences of migrant trajectories provides useful information on their modes of functioning, and on how they negotiated the Arctic urban space. The strategies developed by migrants are complex and oblige the observer to study in detail their biographical background in order to capture their historical and social dimensions. They offer new alternatives to the difficult economic and political situation found in the modern state of Azerbaijan, characterised as it is by clientelism and presidentialism.

Aude Merlin and Taline Papazian present the results of field research carried out in Armenia in June 2016. This fieldwork questions the trajectories of veterans of the Karabakh war (1991–1994) and of former combatants in the post-war Armenia situation. They explore the diverse, even divergent, trajectories of these veterans once they come back from war to civilian life: with a habitus of war acquired in the period from 1988 to 1994, some of them have been able to make use of it in building a new social, economic and political status and gaining new positions in Armenian society, while others continue to feel marginalised. Merlin and Papazian attempt to identify sociological profiles of winners and losers, and what explains the quite stark divergences in

10 *Laure Delcour, Kevork Oskanian and Derek Averre*

their post-war situations. They tackle these questions based on interviews with war veterans and former combatants that represent a varied sample of post-war trajectories, as well as on statistical data. The post-war situation itself is also part of the problematique: if it can be said to be post-war, since large-scale warfare had been halted by the 1994 cease-fire, it cannot be said to be post-conflict, as the Karabakh conflict is still very much alive and prone to reignite at any time, as the recent episode of short but intense hostilities in April 2016 has demonstrated. The authors also pay close attention to the meaning that veterans and former combatants give to their participation in the war, both in the 1990s and in retrospect.

The final chapter in the volume, by Eviya Hovhannisyan, also deals with the aftermath of the Nagorno-Karabakh conflict of 1988–1994, which forced hundreds of thousands of people to flee their homes in an environment of insecurity. Fearing for their lives, Armenians living in the Azerbaijan Soviet Socialist Republic fled the country. In turn, the vast majority of ethnic Azerbaijanis left Armenia. Some of the deported Armenians later settled in abandoned former Azerbaijani villages in Armenia. This historic event left a deep imprint on the consciousness of two societies, changing the entire pattern of the socio-cultural institutions and intra-ethnic relations in two countries. This chapter deals with the pattern of micro-level societal dynamics, introducing field research findings on the issues of the construction of refugee women's stereotyping after their forced relocation to Armenia and the deformation of this stereotype influenced by local discourses. The empirical material for the research was gathered from the Vardenis region of Armenia, which is populated by two socio-cultural groups – local Armenians and Armenian refugees from Azerbaijan – and reflects the social and cultural dichotomy of these two groups. The research aim is to understand the reasons and the patterns of the construction of the refugee women's negative image in post-conflict Armenia, and to explore the impact of these stereotypes on subsequent marital relationship with the locals and the long process of levelling of cultural otherness between the different socio-cultural groups.

The chapters in this volume reflect the complexities of a region unable to overcome legacies of conflict, and populated by recognised and de facto states that are struggling to establish viable political systems capable of sustaining economic and societal stability in the face of poverty, inequality, corruption and aggressive nationalism. The challenge of moving towards a future where democratic reform may unleash the tremendous potential of its diverse populations and provide a lasting guarantee of peace and security is considerable. By exploring in depth the interaction between state and society, and the sources and effects of local perceptions and concerns, the authors in various ways seek to interrogate the meaning of political culture, citizenship, economic dependence, social change and belief systems and thereby to generate a deeper understanding of the fundamental link between security and democracy in the context of the Caucasus. We hope that this volume contributes to developing conceptual and policy frameworks that may allow us both to grasp the nature of the changes taking place in the region and to form responses to these changes.

Note

1 Original research for this edited volume has received funding from the European Union's Seventh Framework Programme for research, technological development and demonstration under the European project CASCADE, GA No. 613354.

Bibliography

Börzel, T.A. and B. Lebanidze (2015). 'European Neighbourhood Policy at the Crossroads: Evaluating the Past to Shape the Future'. MAXCAP working paper 12, July.

Cadier, D. (2014). 'Eastern Partnership vs Eurasian Union? The EU-Russia Competition in the Shared Neighbourhood and the Ukraine Crisis'. *Global Policy*, 5 suppl. 1.

Cheterian, V. (2008). *War and Peace in the Caucasus: Ethnic Conflict and the New Geopolitics*. New York: Columbia University Press.

Christou, G. (2010). 'European Union security logics to the east: the European Neighbourhood Policy and Eastern Partnership'. *European Security*, 19(3).

Coppieters, B. (ed.) (1996). *Contested Borders in the Caucasus*. Brussels: VUBpress.

Delcour, L. and K. Wolczuk (2015). 'Spoiler of facilitator of democratization? Russia's role in Georgia and Ukraine'. *Democratization*, 22(3).

EuroEast (2012), 'FP7 research call: Security and democracy in the neighbourhood: the case of the Caucasus,' 20 December, at http://enpi-info.eu/maineast.php?id=31598&id_type=1&lang_id=450&subject=3-6.

European Commission (2015). 'Review of the European Neighbourhood Policy'. JOIN (2015) 50 final, Brussels, 18 November.

European Commission (2013). 'European Neighbourhood Policy: Working towards a Stronger Partnership', JOIN(2013) 4 final, Brussels, 20 March.

European Commission (2008). 'Eastern Partnership, Communication from the Commission to the European Parliament and the Council', *COM* 823/4, 3 December.

Flockhart, Trine (ed.) (2005). *Socializing Democratic Norms: The Role of International Organizations for the Construction of Europe*. Basingstoke and New York: Palgrave Macmillan.

Hughes, J. (2007). *Chechnya: From Nationalism to Jihad*. Philadelphia: University of Pennsylvania Press.

Jackson, S. (2008). 'Potential Difference: Internal Borderlands in Africa.' In: Pugh M., Cooper N., and Turner M. (eds) *Whose Peace? Critical Perspectives on the Political Economy of Peacebuilding*. London: Palgrave Macmillan, pp. 266–283.

Kirchner, E. and J. Sperling (2007). *EU Security Governance*. Manchester: Manchester University Press.

Large, Judith and Timothy D. Sisk (2006). *Democracy, Conflict and Human Security: Pursuing Peace in the 21st Century*. Stockholm: International Institute for Democracy and Electoral Assistance.

Lavenex, S. (2004). 'EU External Governance in "Wider Europe"'. *Journal of European Public Policy*, 11(4).

Lavenex, S. and F. Schimmelfennig (2011). 'EU democracy promotion in the neighbourhood: from leverage to governance?' *Democratization*, 18(4).

Levitsky, S. and L.A. Way (2002). 'The Rise of Competitive Authoritarianism'. *Journal of Democracy*, 13(2).

Nodia, G. and C. Stefes (2015). *Security, Democracy and Development in the Southern Caucasus and the Black Sea Region*. Bern: Peter Lang.

O'Loughlin, John, Vladimir Kolossov and Gerard Toal (2014). 'Inside the post-Soviet de facto states: a comparison of attitudes in Abkhazia, Nagorny Karabakh, South Ossetia, and Transnistria'. *Eurasian Geography and Economics*, 55(5).

Sanders, T., E. Tucker and G. Hamburg (eds) (2004). *Russian-Muslim Confrontation in the Caucasus: Alternative Visions of the Conflict between Imam Shamil and the Russians 1830–1859*. New York: Routledge Curzon.

Tolstrup, J. (2009). 'Studying a negative external actor: Russia's management of stability and instability in the "Near Abroad"'. *Democratization*, 16(5).

Youngman, M. (2016). 'Broader, vaguer, weaker: The evolving ideology of the Caucasus Emirate leadership'. *Terrorism and Political Violence*, 15, 1–23.

Zürcher, C.M. (2007). *The Post-Soviet Wars: Rebellion, Ethnic Conflict and Nationhood in the Post-Soviet Era*. New York: New York University Press.

1 The tip of the democratisation spear?

Role and importance of the Georgian Armed Forces in the context of democratisation and European integration

Marion Kipiani

Introduction

When Georgia emerged as an independent state after the Soviet Union's collapse, the country had no organised armed forces to speak of. Various warlord-led paramilitary groups and militias and a rudimentary national guard were implicated in the violent denouement of secessionist conflict in Abkhazia and South Ossetia as well as in a civil war accompanying the overthrow of Georgia's first president, Zviad Gamsakhurdia.

However, a quarter of a century later Georgian soldiers are deployed in multilateral peace support missions, from Afghanistan to the Central African Republic (CAR), as an expression of Georgia's tangible commitment to international stability and European foreign and security policy. Successive governments since the early 2000s have endorsed military professionalisation and civilian control over the armed forces, attempting to turn the defence sector into a poster child for governance reform. Georgian leaders have thus followed the example of transitional societies in Central and Eastern Europe, for whom security sector reform (SSR) played a significant role in their integration into NATO and the European Union (EU) in the 1990s.

The EU itself has increasingly emphasised the nexus between security, development and democracy in its external actions and has recently designated stabilisation as a priority theme in relations with countries in its Eastern and Southern neighbourhoods. This chapter traces the trajectory of defence reform and the involvement of the EU in good governance and support to national and human security in Georgia, also taking into account EU-Georgia cooperation in the framework of the Common Security and Defence Policy (CSDP). We will specifically examine whether there is a role for the EU, alongside NATO, to strengthen democratic oversight, transparency, and accountability of the Georgian defence sector.

It is important to point out that security sector reform (SSR) as a concept – also encountered in the literature as security governance reform or security system reform – has progressively enlarged to encompass the governance not only of core security actors such as the armed forces, police and border guards but also of security oversight and management bodies (ministries of defence

14 *Marion Kipiani*

and internal affairs, financial management bodies, public complaints commissions) as well as justice and law enforcement institutions and non-statutory security forces (Dursun-Ozkanca and Vandemoortele, 2012). Contemporary approaches to SSR also aim to integrate the notion of human security, emphasising the well-being of the population and respect for their human rights. Security is thus being increasingly treated as a public policy and governance issue, and greater public scrutiny of security policy is encouraged (Bloching, 2012; Darchiashvili, 2004; Dursun-Ozkanca and Vandemoortele, 2012).

It is beyond the scope of this chapter to examine all elements and aspects of SSR in Georgia. While being mindful that it is not easy to compartmentalise reforms in the defence sector from those in the security sector writ large, we will thus limit our analysis to the Georgian armed forces and its public management and oversight bodies such as the Ministry of Defence, the National Security Council, the relevant committees of the Georgian parliament and independent oversight mechanisms. Our focus will be the basic elements necessary to ensure democratic control of the armed forces, including the legal and constitutional mechanisms defining the relationship between the head of state, the government, the parliament and the armed forces; civilian control over the Ministry of Defence; effective parliamentary oversight; and the degree of transparency and openness of the defence sector to scrutiny by non-governmental organisations (NGOs), research institutions and the media (Lunn, 2005). This is in line with the requirements set by the European Union and NATO for the political and democratic aspects of defence reform in their partner countries (Cole, Fluri and Lunn, 2015).

The Georgian armed forces from 1990 to 2016The first decade: building state institutions of security and defence

Early attempts to form security forces in Georgia were made under its first president, Zviad Gamsakhurdia. In December 1990 the National Guard was created, followed shortly by the Ministry of Defence (MOD). At the same time, however, Georgia was beset by armed struggles within the political elite and conflict with the breakaway territories of Abkhazia and South Ossetia (Darchiashvili, 2004; Lynch, 2005; Osidze and Haindrava, 2003; Vashakmadze, 2005).

In 1995 Eduard Shevardnadze consolidated power in Georgia and disbanded the paramilitaries (Osidze and Haindrava, 2003; Vashakmadze, 2005). A new constitution was adopted, laying down the foundations of a political and security system broadly mirroring Western traditions of civil-military relations (Darchiashvili, 2004; Osidze and Haindrava, 2003; Vashakmadze, 2005). From 1998 onward Georgia cooperated with the NATO Partnership for Peace (PfP) programme the cornerstone of defence reform and initiated legislation to increase democratic oversight and reorganise the defence ministry (Pataraia, 2006; Pataraia, 2008). Importantly, the functions of the General

The tip of the democratisation spear? 15

Staff were separated from the Ministry of Defence (MOD), without, however, achieving a clear redistribution of competencies or the 'civilianisation of the ministry' (Darchiashvili, 2004; Johnson, 2004; Lortkipanidze, 2010b; Lynch, 2005; Pataraia, 2006; Simons, 2012). The U.S.-sponsored Georgia Train and Equip Program (GTEP) assisted the creation of four GAF battalions as professional military units to carry out anti-terrorist operations (Darchiashvili, 2004; Fritz, 2004; Osidze and Haindrava, 2003; Pataraia, 2006).

Nevertheless, Georgia's defence sector remained beset by an inefficient organisational structure, chronic under-funding, rampant corruption and a consequent lack of military professionalism. Due to parallel and overlapping structures, armed formations were dispersed under six different state agencies, with no precise functional borders between civilian law enforcement and the military (Darchiashvili, 2004; Darchiashvili, 2006). Procedures of the National Security Council (NSC) were ill-defined in the legislation, turning it into an instrument for the president to take control of enforcement bodies (Darchiashvili, 2006). Democratic and judicial oversight was weak; the Parliament did not react to the President's unilateral decision (formally precluded by the constitution) to use military force internally on two occasions in 1998. Criminal behaviour of security officials was rarely, if ever, punished (Pataraia, 2006).

In addition, Shevardnadze had a clear motive to avoid challenges to his hold on power from the so-called 'power ministries' (defence, internal affairs and state security), who were allegedly implicated in several assassination attempts on the president. Systematic under-funding of the security sector was a result of such considerations, coupled with the desire not to exacerbate tensions with Russia and with strict budget constraints imposed on Georgia by the International Monetary Fund (IMF) (Darchiashvili, 2006; Fritz, 2004; Lynch, 2005). At around 0.5 percent of GDP, financing of the MOD was among the lowest in the successor states of the Soviet Union, as it was regularly allocated less than what it had budgeted for its needs (Darchiashvili, 2006; Osidze and Haindrava, 2003; Pataraia, 2006). Furthermore, sequestration, whereby the actual amount received was even below those stipulated in the budget, was a regular practice: in 2000 only 56 percent of authorised funds were dispersed to the MOD (Pataraia, 2006).

Predictably, the outcome of strategic vacillation and lack of funds was not only armed forces too weak to threaten the president at home but also stalled reforms and endemic corruption. MOD officials were allegedly involved in protection rackets in private enterprises and illegal arms sales. Darchiashvili (2006, n.p.) cites the figure of 14,000 units of firearms lost during the Shevardnadze period, while an estimated 40 to 50 percent of international donor funds to the ministry were embezzled (Darchiashvili, 2004; Fritz, 2004). The ranks suffered from human rights abuses, malnutrition of soldiers and lack of access to medical services. Desertion and suicide rates among service personnel were alarmingly high, and instances of mutiny recurred. Young men attempted to dodge the draft by any means: military units were manned only

16 *Marion Kipiani*

to about 30 or 40 percent of authorised strength (Fritz, 2004; Johnson, 2004; Lynch, 2005; Osidze and Haindrava, 2003; Vashakmadze, 2005).

The situation was exacerbated by Russia's support to the breakaway territories of Abkhazia and South Ossetia. The zones of so-called frozen conflict were a haven for illicit activities, often involving local criminal elements in cahoots with Russian peacekeepers and Georgian law enforcement officers. Weapons and drugs were smuggled across the regions' *de facto* borders. The infiltration of Chechen rebels into Georgia's Pankisi Gorge led to the bombing of the area by Russia's air force. Finally, Georgia's location as a transit corridor between the hydrocarbon-rich states of Central Asia and European markets encouraged the trafficking of human beings and illegal substances (Darchiashvili, 2004; Fritz, 2004; Osidze and Haindrava, 2003).

The rise of the power structures after the Rose Revolution

When Mikheil Saakashvili came to power after the 2003 Rose Revolution, the security sector lacked a strategic vision of reform or any legitimacy in the eyes of the public whatsoever. A defence restructuring process was quickly initiated, transferring Interior Ministry troops to the MOD and thus making it the only body responsible for national defence (Fluri and Lortkipanidze, 2006; Kakachia, 2005; Sikharulidze, 2005). In early 2004, the ministry's management staff down to the level of department directors was 'civilianised' and its roles and responsibilities clearly delineated from those of the General Staff (subsequently transformed into the Joint Chiefs of Staff in 2006) (Akubardia, 2010b; Fluri and Lortkipanidze, 2006; Lortkipanidze, 2005; Pataraia, 2008; Sikharulidze, 2005). In September of the same year, a Strategic Defence Review (SDR) process was launched to evaluate armed forces capacity and develop concepts for national defence based on strategic documents (*inter alia*, a National Security Concept and military threat assessment) and realistic cost assessments (Akubardia, 2010a; Lortkipanidze, 2010b; Pataraia, 2008; Sikharulidze, 2005). In a gesture of greater transparency, selected NGOs and independent experts were also invited to participate in the process (Pataraia, 2008).

NATO integration as a priority foreign policy goal

Defence sector restructuring was spurred by the Saakashvili government's ambition to approximate to the standards of, and ultimately join, NATO (for an overview of Georgia-NATO relations see Kipiani, 2016; Kipiani 2015). The reform process was aligned with the Individual Partnership Action Plan (IPAP) that Georgia concluded with the Alliance in 2004 and the Partnership Action Plan-Defence Institution Building (PAP-DIB) launched in 2005 (Akubardia, 2010a; Kakachia, 2005; Lortkipanidze, 2010b; Pataraia, 2008). One year later, NATO initiated an Intensified Dialogue (ID), holding out the suggestion that, at the end of a process of further reform, the country might be granted a Membership Action Plan (MAP), the road map toward joining the Alliance. As NATO paid increasing attention not only to the compatibility of the military with Alliance armed forces but also the strengthening of democratic institution and the rule of law, several assistance programmes were launched for Georgia in these spheres (Pataraia, 2008; Trapans, 2005). The largest bilateral initiative remained U.S. military cooperation under the renamed Sustainment and Stability Operations Program (SSOP), which also trained the newly created GAF ground-forces headquarters to conduct command and control (C2) (Pataraia, 2008).

Another aspect of Georgia's NATO approximation was the stepped-up deployment of GAF contingents to international peacekeeping and combat operations. Georgian troops served as part of NATO's KFOR in Kosovo and alongside U.S. forces in Iraq. Their participation in these missions was seen as a way to train and equip military units as well as to make a contribution to international security (Kakachia, 2005; Pataraia, 2008; Pataraia, 2010).

The super-presidential system: lack of democratic oversight

The Georgian defence sector made huge reform progress in the years after the Rose Revolution, but some serious problems persisted while new ones were created. Chief among them was the unprecedented concentration of political power in the hands of Saakashvili. Following a raft of hastily passed constitutional amendments in early 2004, the MOD was directly subordinated to the presidency. Special legislation granted the president the right, among others, to appoint principal military commanders and directly participate in strategic military decisions. The National Security Council, appointed and chaired by the president, was not accountable to parliament even though it decided on strategic questions of foreign and security policy (Pataraia, 2008; Vashakmadze, 2014).

The restructuring of the MOD had significantly increased *civilian* control over the armed forces, whereby defence policy institutions are staffed and led by civilian personnel and subordinated to control by a civilian government. This situation has endured in Georgia since 2004, and there has been no evidence of attempts by the military to influence governance. On the other hand, *democratic* control, which should ensure 'a transparent and accountable security sector [and] the efficient use of public funds' (Born, 2015, p. 68) remained underdeveloped. The fact that parliament was not entitled to participate in the elaboration of the state budget or propose line-by-line amendments to the government's budget draft (MPs could only endorse or reject the budget in its entirety) represented a systemic weakness in democratic oversight. A detailed breakdown of budget expenditures was available only to the Group of Confidence (GC), a security-vetted group of lawmakers elected from within the parliament's Defence and Security Committee (DSC), after adoption of the budget (Lortkipanidze, 2010a; Pataraia, 2008; Vashakmadze, 2014). Between 2003 and 2008, the MOD only once discussed detailed budget figures with the GC (Pataraia, 2008, p. 62). The government also was not

18 *Marion Kipiani*

obliged to report to the legislative branch about even the largest defence procurements (Lortkipanidze, 2010a). Spiralling defence expenditures and diversion from strategic documents was the result. Presidential interventions were used to increase funding of the military during the budget year. For instance, the defence budget for 2007 was augmented from 513.3 million Georgian lari (GEL) to a total of GEL1.27 billion: an increase of 150 percent, passed without the submission of a budgetary amendment or parliamentary debate (Lortkipanidze, 2010b, p. 58).

Similarly, personnel development of the GAF did not follow strategic planning. A 2005 report by the International Security Advisory Board (ISAB) had recommended reducing the strength of the armed forces to improve long-term affordability. Instead, the GAF stood up a fourth brigade and increased the size of the reserve forces. In total, this represented a rise of 25 to 30 percent over the figures envisaged in IPAP negotiations with NATO (Pataraia, 2008, pp. 55, 58). Just prior to the August 2008 war the GAF counted 37,000 service members, as against an authorised figure of 26,000. The increase negatively impacted on military capabilities, as it led to a shortage of officers and non-commissioned officers (NCOs). According to Akubardia, nearly every brigade commander at the time lacked the training and experience to perform his duties effectively (2010a, pp. 15 et seq.).

Other inconsistencies included the structural organisation of the security sector, with some of the reforms undertaken in public agencies not reflected in the country's legislative base (Fluri and Lortkipanidze, 2006). Furthermore, the National Security Concept and Military Strategy contained mutually contradictory clauses, with some of the threats defined in the military strategy differing from those in the Concept. Security sector officials seemed to operate on the general belief that transparency would compromise their effectiveness (Cole, 2006; Pataraia, 2008), a perspective encouraged by the fact that an increasing part of defence-related information became confidential (Pataraia, 2008). This climate of limited oversight facilitated human rights violations in the GAF and ill-treatment of service members by their officers. NGOs drew attention to the fact that they were not authorised to enter military units or distribute brochures containing information on soldiers' rights. Consequently, incidents of abuse came to public attention only when the parliamentary majority changed after the October 2012 elections (United States of America State Department, 2012).

The aftermath of the August 2008 war

The August 2008 war between Georgia and Russia over the separatist region of South Ossetia brought to light the military consequences of the lack of executive accountability. In its aftermath, NATO recommended that the personnel management system of the GAF be improved, the transparency of the budget process increased and the governance of the defence sector brought into line with Alliance standards. A NATO-Georgia Council (NGC) was

The tip of the democratisation spear? 19

established in 2009, and Georgia committed to implementing Annual National Programs (ANPs) agreed with the Alliance (Akubardia, 2010a; Lortkipanidze, 2010b; Pataraia, 2010). The Georgian government also revised its strategic defence documents in view of the failure of the 2005 National Security Concept to identify threats that had ultimately materialised. However, independent experts criticised both the process of strategy development – as lacking coordination between the National Security Council, other government agencies and the legislative branch – as well as the substance of the resulting Concept, claiming it was a document for the consumption of domestic and external audiences rather than a thorough analysis of security policy (Akubardia, 2010a; Lortkipanidze, 2010b; Vashakmadze, 2014).

Meanwhile, constitutional amendments in 2009 further consolidated the role of the president in security governance. The constitution now stipulated that the president had the right to suspend or repeal the actions of state institutions if those were contrary to the constitution. In practice, this meant that the president was able directly to control the defence and security-related institutions (Akubardia, 2010b). Combined with greater leeway for the president to dismiss the parliament if it failed to pass a budget, the amendments resulted in a further weakening of parliamentary oversight since lawmakers were now even less inclined to demand strict accountability and effectiveness in the spending of state resources or the deployment of the armed forces. For instance, when the government decided to dispatch a GAF battalion to serve in the International Security Assistance Force (ISAF) in Afghanistan, there was no debate in parliament based on the cost of deployment or a risk assessment for troops (Akubardia, 2010b; Lortkipanidze, 2010a). Similarly, the main body of independent oversight of the government, the State Audit Office (SAO), apparently did not audit the MOD for several years, even though the ministry's budget constituted about 8 percent of GDP in 2007–2008 (Akubardia, 2010b, p. 32).

Despite the widespread recognition that the 2008 war had revealed major deficiencies in the combat readiness and preparation of the GAF as well as in security sector governance as such, real changes in the quality of democratic control and oversight were not immediate. They had to await the change of government that took effect in Georgia after the 2012 parliamentary elections.

Defence institutions after the 2012 change of power in Georgia

One of the major events that caused the defeat of the ruling United National Movement (UNM) party in the October 2012 parliamentary elections was the publication of video tapes showing the abuse of detainees in Georgian prisons. The leaked materials had tremendous resonance in society as just one symptom of a pervasive lack of accountability and respect for human rights in

20 *Marion Kipiani*

the government, and they ultimately contributed to a clear victory of the opposition Georgian Dream coalition at the polls.

The change of electoral majorities was accompanied by a profound shake-up of the structures of governance in Georgia due to a set of constitutional amendments passed in 2010 and timetabled to come into force after the presidential elections of 2013. These amendments transferred powers from the presidency to the government led by the prime minister. Responsibility for foreign and security policy was to be shared between the president and the government, with a clearly defined supreme role for the government. The constitution now specified that the government was 'the highest body of the executive power' and accountable to parliament only (Pataraia et al., 2014, pp. 12, 14).

More than 40 laws were drafted to bring security and defence-related state structures and processes into line with the new constitutional reality. The amendments to the law on the NSC limited the role of the Council to dealing with national defence only, thus reflecting the limitations on the powers of the president. In December 2013, amid a growing dispute about the respective roles of the president and prime minister in foreign and security policy, the government established the National Security and Crisis Management Council (NSCMC) to respond to natural disasters or emergency situations. It thus consolidated consultative functions and inter-agency cooperation under the office of the prime minister (Pataraia et al., 2014). Even though, in theory, responsibilities of the NSC and NSCMC were separate, the practical functions of the two councils regularly became a bone of contention between the president and prime minister (Civil Georgia, 2014b).

Parliamentary oversight remains weak

In general, the constitutional changes expanded the powers of the prime minister at the expense of those of the president but did not significantly strengthen the oversight and control function of the parliament. As regards security and defence, the Georgian parliament is entitled to, *inter alia*, adopt relevant laws; ratify or annul international treaties and military agreements; debate and approve the state budget; approve the country's military doctrine and the strength of the armed forces; and approve relevant presidential decrees (Pataraia et al., 2014, p. 48).

A special oversight role falls to the parliament's Defence and Security Committee but independent experts assessed the activity of the DSC since 2012 as relatively weak. Security agency officials were summoned to report to the committee only on rare occasions, and in these cases they themselves usually determined the format of hearings. This may be a sign of the close connections and informal influence over majority MPs by the executive that has also been observed in the drafting of legislative initiatives. It is note-worthy that one of the more ambitious pushes for greater transparency actually came from former Minister of Defence Irakli Alasania, who initiated the preparation of a law obliging the MOD to report every military procurement deal worth GEL 2m (currently approximately 840,000 USD) and above to the parliament (Pataraia et al., 2014, pp. 42 et seq.).

Pataraia et al. point out that the culture of debate in the Georgian parliament generally became more open after the 2012 elections, but discussion of security and defence issues was hampered by MPs and parliamentary staffers' lack of expertise and knowledge (2014, pp. 29, 42). Since 1999 the Georgian parliament actively participates in formats of international cooperation, particularly in the NATO Parliamentary Assembly (PA), which supports cooperation and capacity building between NATO and partner country parliaments in Eastern Europe. However, its research resources remain rather limited, nor does it draw extensively on the expertise of independent research organisations (Hobbs and Popa, 2015; Pataraia et al., 2014). Born notes that lack of cooperation with independent sources of expertise commonly leads to parliaments relying for information on the very institutions they are supposed to oversee, thus creating asymmetrical dependence relations between the legislature, the executive and the military (Born, 2015, p. 80 et seq.).

One of the most pernicious and significant challenges for Georgian lawmakers remains their limited access to information regarding the defence budget and their inability to propose line-by-line changes to the budgetary draft (Pataraia et al., 2014). In this situation, reports by the State Audit Office (SAO) could be a basis for greater parliamentary scrutiny of defence expenditures. There is, however, no record of an audit of the Ministry of Defence even though the SAO's strategic plan for the period 2014–2017 listed defence and security as a priority sector (Pataraia et al., 2014, p. 22 et seq.). The Georgian parliament also continues to play no role in the appointment of the leadership of the MOD and the Joint Staff (Pataraia et al., 2014) and cannot recall forces participating in international operations, even though it has to ratify such agreements at the outset. As a rule, parliament carries out no juridical or political analysis of specific missions before taking decisions on the deployment of GAF contingents: the repeated deployments of Georgian soldiers to Afghanistan were approved without much debate. Similarly, parliamentary delegations hardly ever participate in visits to the troops regularly undertaken by MOD officials and the president (Pataraia et al., 2014; Vashakmadze, 2014).

In summary, Georgia's defence sector underwent a remarkable transformation over the past 25 years. Military professionalism has significantly increased, the MOD 'civilianised' and the structures of defence institutions aligned with NATO standards. When looking deeper, however, we notice that issues of democratic oversight, transparency and accountability are still lacking in practice. These deficiencies have not been adequately addressed by constitutional and legislative changes undertaken since the change of government in 2012.

22 *Marion Kipiani*

EU assistance to Georgia

The frequently voiced criticism of the technical, as opposed to political, character of EU assistance to Georgia tends to overlook both the shifts to a more comprehensive approach in EU governance support and the increasing influence of the EU on human security in Georgia. As noted at the outset of this paper, defence sector reform is not equivalent but rather a subset of the broader notion of security sector reform. Any transformation of behaviours and attitudes in the security sector, and indeed in a country's system of governance, towards more transparency, accountability and respect for human rights will at least indirectly influence defence institutions. At the same time, unresolved territorial and ethno-political conflicts, insecurity along a country's borders and external threats to the physical integrity of the population clearly impact on public and elite perceptions, military threat assessments, national security doctrines and civil-military relations. Thus, while the EU has not directly been involved in defence sector reform in Georgia, as a political and security actor in the South Caucasus it has certainly influenced the country's defence institutions.

The Partnership and Cooperation Agreement (PCA) which entered into force in July 1999, although foreseeing the establishment of a political dialogue, was in fact focused on supporting reforms to enhance economic relations, trade and investment through financial and technical assistance (Johnson, 2004; Lynch, 2004). This was logical to the extent that the European Union was only just evolving into a political union itself and did not yet have a clear conception of its own 'actorness' in the field of foreign and security policy. Moreover, the South Caucasus was relatively crowded with international actors in security, given the NATO PfP programme, the increasing interest of the U.S. in the region and the activities of the Organization for Security and Cooperation in Europe (OSCE) in border assistance and conflict management. Before the 2004 EU enlargement, the South Caucasus seemed not to represent an immediate threat to EU security. In addition there was little demand by Georgia or the other newly independent states in the region for a reinforced EU role in the security sector (Lynch, 2004).

Two developments transformed this situation in the early 2000s. In April 2001, the European Commission (EC) disseminated a Communication on Conflict Prevention, stipulating greater attention to the security sector in EU cooperation programmes with third countries, specifically emphasising police reform and decommissioning of weapons of mass destruction. The eastern enlargement and the 2003 adoption of the European Security Strategy (ESS) provided further impetus for the EU to reconsider the potential and actual threats emanating from its periphery and the policies that should be adopted in response. The 2003 Wider Europe Communication of the EC, a foundational document for the European Neighbourhood Policy (ENP), was intended to develop cooperation formats for countries outside the EU enlargement process, which in the Western Balkans had served as a sort of EU foreign policy substitute (Lynch, 2004).

In 2003 Georgia was still but a footnote in the Wider Europe Communication. The EU had no intention to include the South Caucasus in the ENP, even though Sweden had successfully advocated the appointment of a regional EU Special Representative (EUSR) (Lynch, 2004, pp. 36, 45). Arguably, the Rose Revolution and subsequent election of President Mikheil Saakashvili and his UNM party, at the polls evaluated as largely free and fair, were the single most important developments prompting the EU to open the ENP also for Georgia, Armenia, and Azerbaijan. Suddenly, it appeared that the South Caucasus might come to resemble the EC's vision of a '"ring of friends", with whom the EU enjoys close, peaceful and co-operative relations' (Commission of the European Union, 2003, p. 4).

Georgian experts hoped that the change in the EU's approach to Georgia and the framework provided by the European Neighbourhood Policy would translate into assistance to the modernisation and reform of the country's security sector (Kakachia, 2005; Lortkipanidze, 2010a; Pataraia, 2008). But the EU did not venture into questions such as defence resource management or parliamentary oversight, either under the ENP or its enhanced iteration, the Eastern Partnership. What did grow was the EU's involvement in good governance reforms more broadly and, particularly after the August 2008 war over South Ossetia, in the conflict management processes between Georgia and the *de facto* independent regions of Abkhazia and South Ossetia. The EU became one of the co-chairs of the Geneva International Discussions (GID) held to tackle humanitarian issues and to ensure stabilisation of the security situation in the conflict-affected areas. Furthermore, it provided funds for confidence-building measures (CBMs) and for the resettlement and support of internally displaced persons (IDPs). Through its policy of 'engagement without recognition' towards Abkhazia and South Ossetia, the EU also attempted to maintain space for interaction with the disputed regions.

Cooperation under the Common Security and Defence Policy (CDSP)

The significant impact developments in Georgia had on the emergence of the EU as a foreign policy actor in the eastern neighbourhood is also visible in the implementation of the Common Security and Defence Policy (CSDP). Under CSDP, the EU can deploy civilian *missions* and military *operations* as short-term crisis management instruments targeting the security sector and/or rule of law in third countries.

EUJUST THEMIS, dispatched to Georgia in July 2004, represented multiple firsts for the European Union: it was the first CSDP mission outside Africa and the Western Balkans and the first rule-of-law mission, with objectives to promote judicial reform and assist in combating corruption. While not strictly a crisis-management intervention, THEMIS was a signal from Brussels that the EU would support President Saakashvili and his reform-oriented policies in the judicial and law enforcement sectors (Huff, 2011; Kakachia, 2005). The mission also piloted the model of embedding EU member state experts with third-country ministries and public agencies at the central government level, now a standard operating procedure for CSDP missions (Simons, 2012, pp. 281 et seq.).

Following the August 2008 war, Brussels dispatched the EU Monitoring Mission (EUMM) to provide stabilisation support along the administrative boundary lines (ABLs) between Georgia and Abkhazia/South Ossetia. As a civilian crisis response measure, the mission has been ongoing since October 2008 and has received praise for helping prevent a resumption of hostilities across the ABLs. However, the EUMM has so far been denied access to Abkhazia and South Ossetia, which severely hampers its ability to carry out its mandate of confidence-building and normalisation of relations (Simons, 2012).

Cooperation between Georgia and the EU under the CSDP has not been completely one-sided. In 2002 the European Council had already adopted a document to lay down the modalities for third countries providing contributions to EU crisis management operations, and since 2004 such cooperation has been regulated through the signing of Framework Partnership Agreements (FPAs) (Tardy, 2014). In November 2013, Georgia pledged a company-sized unit to a CSDP operation in the Central African Republic, supporting an existing African Union mission. The Georgian contribution was particularly welcome since the EU encountered difficulties in the force generation process for EUFOR RCA (Republic of Central Africa). Ultimately, out of approximately 750 authorised troops, 140 were Georgian soldiers, making the country the second largest contributor after France (Tardy, 2015, pp. 21 et seq.).

By taking part in CSDP operations – including, to date, military training missions in the Central African Republic and Mali as well as civilian missions with military elements in Libya (EUBAM Libya) and the Horn of Africa (EUCAP Nestor) – Georgia is following a pattern it had established in its approximation process to NATO. To demonstrate its commitment to the Alliance, Georgia has since 2009 contributed to NATO's ISAF and Resolute Support missions in Afghanistan, dispatching the largest non-NATO member troop contingent and foregoing any security caveats on their deployment. This has resulted in Georgian soldiers serving in some of the Afghan areas most affected by the Taliban insurgency, and in a relatively high number of casualties.

Contributions to EU crisis management were earlier made by the central and eastern European states, all of which participated in CSDP missions prior to becoming EU members. Turkey and the current candidate countries in the Western Balkans have also done so, albeit to vastly differing degrees. By providing significant support to EU military operations, Georgia is thus flagging its ambitions for Euro-Atlantic integration and showing its readiness to make a tangible commitment to the EU's foreign and security policy in areas where its national interests are not directly at stake (Tardy, 2014).

The way forward for increased cooperation on defence sector reform

The EU's assistance strategy in Georgia has thus gradually evolved from a development approach along mostly technical parameters to including advice and support on issues relating to political stability, conflict resolution and the security sector in its broad conception. There is still a perception that the EU does not fully pull its weight as a foreign policy actor in its neighbourhood, while the tragic events of the August 2008 war have clearly demonstrated the shortcomings of NATO assistance with regard to democratic control of the armed forces. So what can be done to leverage EU governance assistance in the Georgian defence sector alongside NATO, and what role can the European Union play in strengthening democratic oversight?

To answer these questions, we first need to appreciate that NATO assistance to third countries has undergone a transformation since the 1990s. Readying the post-Communist states of eastern Europe for Alliance membership required not only military professionalisation but also an overhaul of governance practices to bring defence institutions under civilian control, depoliticise them and make them accountable to democratically elected governments (Slocombe, 2007). Drawing on the experiences of the first round of NATO enlargement concluded in 1999, the Alliance developed the Membership Action Plan (MAP) as a tool to guide future candidate countries through the approximation process. The MAP also contains four non-military chapters dealing with economic and political issues, including the rule of law and a commitment to economic liberty and social justice (Lunn, 2007).

Nevertheless, the bilateral assistance rendered by NATO members to Georgia has generally focused on military capacity-building and interoperability of forces (Cole, 2006; Lynch, 2004), with some attention paid to the professionalisation of MOD staff and transparency of defence procurement. The EU has increased governance assistance in parallel to NATO's engagement with the country but the two organisations' activities have rarely overlapped. This experience is quite similar to that of new EU members states and candidate countries in central-eastern Europe and the Western Balkans, where NATO has concentrated on the reform of defence institutions and the EU on 'everything else' (Lunn, 2007, p. 7).

Yet the reform of defence institutions and civilian and democratic oversight over them are integral to ensuring the sustainable security fundamental to a country's development, highlighting the nexus between security, democratisation and prosperity. Defence institutions are a crucial, if sensitive, component of a country's governance system. In post-authoritarian societies in particular, parliaments and independent oversight bodies need to develop and defend a role in security and defence governance, safeguarding concepts of human rights, inclusiveness, accountability, and transparency. The commensurate changes in attitudes and behaviour necessitate a long-term perspective and in many cases external expertise and support (Born, 2015).

26 *Marion Kipiani*

The EU conception of security recognises multiple dependencies between development, good governance, security, conflict prevention and crisis management. This 'comprehensive' approach was predicated by the fact that the EU came of age as a security actor when the nature of the global system appeared to be shifting to a post-Westphalian understanding of the state, requiring the pooling of sovereignty to address transnational security concerns. At the same time, trends in academic thinking and policy practiced softened the hard boundaries of 'national security' to encompass many more relevant actors as well as more, including non-military, issue areas (Oskanian and Averre, 2016).

Based on the logic that external intervention can affect all areas of state governance, the European Security Strategy of 2003 established SSR as a part of broader institution building processes undertaken by the EU in third countries (Dursun-Ozkanca and Vandemoortele, 2012; Galantino, 2013). In 2005 and 2006, the Council and then the European Commission elaborated SSR concepts to provide a policy framework for EU action. The duality of the approach reflected the prerogatives of EU institutions: the Council concept focused on providing political advice, mentoring and monitoring on SSR, primarily through the CSDP toolkit. The Commission document on the other hand referred mainly to the promotion of democracy and rule of law through long-term assistance instruments (Bloching, 2012), stressing that:

> security system reform goes beyond the notion of effectiveness of individual services [...] and instead focuses on the overall functioning of the security system as part of a governance reform policy and strategy of the public sector. In other words, SSR should be seen as a holistic process, strengthening security for all citizens as well as addressing governance deficits.
>
> (Commission of the European Union, 2006, p. 3)

This approach would make SSR a cross-cutting issue for EU governance assistance and could be interpreted as another area for the transfer of European values such as democratic accountability and the protection of human rights. Indeed,

> The EU has, however, encountered difficulty in putting its vision of SSR into practice. In part this has been due to the above-mentioned duality of institutions, which is reflected in the EU's approach to its relations with and activities in third countries.

The Treaty of Lisbon explicitly aimed at a more coherent and cohesive EU foreign policy by harmonising external action through the newly created European External Action Service (EEAS), an EU proto-diplomatic service led by the High Representative for External Relations who doubles as a Vice

President of the Commission (HR/VP). The EEAS incorporated various departments of the Council and the Commission dealing with CSDP and external relations, aimed at a greater integration of EU foreign and security instruments and capabilities (Bloching, 2012; Freire, 2013; Huff, 2011). The delegations of the European Commission in third countries were transformed into EU Delegations, that is, single units included in the EEAS and representing all EU institutions in a given country. This was envisaged to allow for increased cohesiveness and impact of diverse assistance activities as well as for better coordination between the delegations and EU Special Representatives (EUSRs) dealing with specific conflict zones (Balfour, 2013; Bloching, 2012).

This institutional overhaul has undoubtedly improved coherence (Balfour, 2013; Huff, 2011; Tardy, 2015) but cooperation between relevant departments of the EEAS as well as EU Delegations and EUSRs on the ground need to be further strengthened. This is particularly relevant in the case of Georgia, where long-term assistance is provided through the European Neighbourhood Policy/Eastern Partnership, while the EU Monitoring Mission continues its activities with a CSDP mandate and an EU Special Representative for the South Caucasus and the crisis in Georgia supports conflict prevention and confidence building. These instruments have not always worked in support of one another and at times have clashed outright (Huff, 2011).

Moreover, the Lisbon Treaty neither transferred all the external relations competencies from the European Commission to the EEAS nor diminished the role of the member states (Balfour, 2013). As a result, the EU more often acts on the smallest common denominator of 28 national interests than on the basis of a truly common foreign and security policy. In terms of CSDP missions and operations, Tardy notes that:

> nothing is possible [...] without the initiative, commitment and support of member states. [...] From the decision-making process leading to the establishment of an operation to the provision of capabilities, financial resources and political support of the operation itself, the role of member states is central.
>
> (Tardy, 2015, p. 43)

Individual states are sometimes unwilling (or unable) to put forward the requisite human and financial resources to staff and equip missions and operations. They may also oppose deploying CSDP tools when they consider the respective crisis situation as either not an immediate threat and/or not vital to their national interest (Bloching, 2012; Dursun-Ozkanca and Vandemoortele, 2012; Tardy, 2015).

In the case of Georgia, some authors have posited that the EU has been reluctant to deploy its CSDP tools – such as a requested border support mission in summer 2005 – because member states wanted to avoid antagonising Russia. Huff has drawn attention to EU attempts to stress the 'nonpolitical' nature of the European Neighbourhood Policy in the South

28 *Marion Kipiani*

Caucasus, Moldova and Ukraine, thus portraying ENP assistance as less controversial than CSDP missions. Nevertheless, the events in Ukraine since 2013 have borne out her assertion that:

> this concept of the ENP as 'non-political' seems confined to Brussels, and does not necessarily reflect the reality of the EU's engagement with its Eastern neighbours. [...] Russia, meanwhile, sees both ENP and EaP [Eastern Partnership] as instruments for the EU to expand its political influence in the region.
>
> (Huff, 2011, pp. 13 et seq.)

Lingering institutional rivalries and the divergence of member states' interests have contributed to the ongoing lack of an EU strategic vision on security governance assistance. CSDP missions and operations are short-term tools to respond to and contain a crisis situation, perhaps also to create space for a political resolution. There is no clarity how longer-term security objectives such as the reform of law enforcement and defence institutions could build on these crisis-management interventions. Would they be still within the remit of CSDP or be managed through other support instruments? Current practice suggests both options are viable and even complementary, with the Lisbon Treaty providing for a broad range of activities under CSDP that are not strictly limited to acute crisis response (Bloching, 2012; Dursun-Ozkanca and Vandemoortele, 2012; Gross, 2013; Tardy, 2015; Tardy, 2016).

Arguably, the EUMM in Georgia has played a role in post-conflict stabilisation but CSDP missions in general cannot produce structural reforms or resolve conflicts. They can only be part of the 'comprehensive approach to external conflicts and crises' envisaged by the EU, and thus need to be tied in with other programmes, such as the ENP/EaP, in order to contribute to the strategic objectives of stabilisation and resiliency (Gross and Menon, 2013; Huff, 2011; Tardy, 2015). The relationship between crisis management and SSR in EU external actions remains to be defined: a comprehensive approach would require a functional integration (1) of assistance objectives (conflict prevention, peacekeeping, mediation, peace-building, governance reform, and so on), (2) among actors (between different EU institutions, with member states, and with third actors such as NATO) and (3) of means (military and civilian inputs, short-term and long-term assistance instruments) (Galantino, 2013, p. 6).

Entry points for the EU in Georgia's defence sector reform

The EU has since 2003 developed a certain capacity to conduct crisis management and security sector reform in third countries. The security-development nexus has been acknowledged, with the importance of SSR as a tool of democracy promotion and governance reform growing steadily (Dursun-Ozkanca and Vandemoortele, 2012; Tardy, 2015).

Given its political and economic nature, and the past trajectory of leaving military reform tasks to NATO in its partner countries, it is unlikely that the EU will assume a fully fledged role in military advice or Ministry of Defence reform in Georgia. However, the experience accumulated by the EU in diverse geographical contexts through its CSDP missions and operations – including police, military training, border support, observer and rule of law missions – as well as its existing wide range of assistance instruments could bring added value to the activities of other actors in defence sector reform. Extensive involvement in the Georgian governance reform process, and continued elite and popular support for closer European integration, would allow the EU to assume a coordination function among various Georgian stakeholders. In addition, such a role could also be extended to donor coordination, which the EU has already carried out in other assistance areas. Its legitimacy as a donor and its long-term and broad commitment to support Georgia could translate into a natural role for the EU in fostering greater coherence and comprehensive in the reform of a sensitive and complex governance areas such as defence (Freire, 2013; Gross, 2013; Simons, 2012).

As demonstrated above, a major problem emerging since the Rose Revolution has been the lack of democratic oversight over the sector: while Georgia has complied with international standards in 'civilianising' its defence institutions, parliamentary and independent control over these institutions has not developed commensurately. In this context, the EU could provide direct support to the Georgian parliament, where appropriate in coordination with the NATO PA. This might range from developing options for closer cooperation between the MOD, parliament and civil society, promoting the training of parliamentary staffers and strengthening of parliamentary research services, to supporting a greater role for the parliament in defence policy outside the budget approval process. The EU could also directly support independent oversight mechanisms such as the State Audit Office (SAO), raising awareness and building capacity for greater scrutiny of defence institutions (Patararaia et al., 2014; Simons, 2012; Tardy, 2016).

The defence sector is traditionally viewed as tightly tied to the protection of state sovereignty, making its reform extremely sensitive and typically characterised by a top-down, state-centric approach. However, there is a growing consensus that support to the technical capacities of the defence sector must be accompanied by helping a broad range of societal stakeholders participate in the oversight of defence institutions and policy-making. These include institutions and actors outside formal state structures, whose involvement promotes transparency and accountability as well as sustained momentum of reform (Cole, 2006; Tardy, 2016). As demonstrated above, the paradigm of human security which, contrary to the traditionally exclusive focus on national security, emphasises the security of the individual, has been integral to the emergence of the EU as a security actor. Strengthening the competencies and voice of civil society would thus represent a natural area of involvement for the EU, since it widely cooperates with NGOs in conflict prevention and CBMs as well as across

30 *Marion Kipiani*

different priority areas of reform. Future interventions could target defence-related capacity building for think tanks and research institutions, promoting civic monitoring functions and enhanced cooperation between the parliament – particularly the DSC – and civil society.

The Public Defender's Office (PDO) would also be a crucial interlocutor for the EU regarding issues of human rights and human security. In the absence of a designated military ombuds institution, the responsibilities of protecting human rights in the armed forces fall under the remit of the PDO. It is entitled to access military installations, propose legislative amendments and recommendations to government institutions, initiate criminal and constitutional proceedings, and submit an annual report on the human rights situation to parliament. In addition to safeguarding the rights of service members, the PDO also pays particular attention to the human security of the local population in conflict-affected areas. However, the decisions of the PDO are not legally binding and its reports are often ignored (Pataraia et al., 2014). Vashakmadze in particular has emphasised the importance of strengthening the PDO in terms of the effective monitoring of the security sector (2014, pp. 27 et seq.).

Apart from these cross-cutting measures, the EU could get involved in providing policy-specific advice and technical assistance. Pataraia has flagged Georgia's need to adapt its legislation to EU standards and eliminate loopholes on arms transfer control (2008, pp. 67 et seq.). The cooperation framework between Georgia and the EU makes reference to combating illegal arms transfers, and Tbilisi's ratification of the Arms Trade Treaty (ATT) as well as its increasing (albeit still modest) role as an exporter of military and dual-use goods increases the importance of a robust arms transfer regime. Vashakmadze on the other hand points to emerging issues such as cyber security and the division of responsibilities and competencies between law enforcement and the military in combating terrorism as areas where EU expertise would be required (2014, pp. 7, 16 et seq.).

Finally, the EU might draw on NATO experience to further institutionalise and improve its partnership with third countries in the framework of joint military operations under the CSDP. Currently, non-member states contributing troops are brought at a very late stage into the formal process of conceptualising and planning CSDP operations. While their participation implies a certain degree of acceptance of EU practices of peace-enforcement or peace-keeping, in practice third country contingents are largely viewed as filling gaps in force generation (Tardy, 2014). This represents a missed opportunity for the EU to build military-to-military relations with partner countries and leaves little if any space for military-to-military value transfer (for an overview from a U.S. perspective, see Blair, 2013).

Conclusion

Since Georgia gained independence in 1991 the country's defence sector has undergone an impressive reform process. At the outset of its statehood Georgia was struggling with a multiplicity of armed formations of questionable

The tip of the democratisation spear? 31

loyalty and the absence of formal defence institutions. Paramilitary groups were involved in the country's civil and ethno-political conflicts and suspected of committing egregious human rights violations. Even after hostilities ended and relative stability was maintained, the armed forces and Ministry of Defence remained bywords of corruption, crime, and bad governance - a symbol of the country's designation as a near-failed state.

Nowadays, Georgian service members receive praise for their professionalism in multilateral military operations, from their involvement in NATO missions in Afghanistan to their participation in the EU's most robust military operations such as EUFOR RCA. The Ministry of Defence, meanwhile, has frequently been cited both by domestic and international actors as one of the government institutions in the vanguard of governance reform and modernisation.

It is obvious that Georgia's ambitions to integrate into Euro-Atlantic institutions, and the commensurate external assistance, have constituted the main driver, and respectively enabler, of reform. Yet gaps remain: there have been allegations of misconduct, human rights infringement and sexual abuse by Georgian soldiers deployed in EUFOR RCA and ISAF (Kucera, 2016; Rubin and Shah, 2013). The MOD has seen its fair share of scandals over non-transparent procurement processes and exertion of political influence by the executive government (Civil Georgia, 2014a). The development of democratic and independent oversight over the defence sector has, as a whole, not kept pace with the professionalisation and modernisation of the relevant institutions. Such lack of oversight has contributed in tragic ways to the war that broke out in August 2008 between Georgia and Russia over South Ossetia.

Successive governments in Tbilisi have largely followed the example set by the Central and Eastern Europe countries that successfully reformed their security sectors and integrated into NATO and the EU. Georgia's experience, however, differs from those states in that it is unlikely to receive a membership perspective in either organization in the foreseeable future. While there are at present no competing international models of security governance that would be viable within the country's current political and institutional framework, it will be necessary to provide Georgia with new formats of cooperation and assistance in order to sustain the defence reform process and plug the gaps identified. If the EU is willing and able develop such options, its currently high legitimacy as a donor and foreign policy actor in Georgia might prove meaningful and beneficial for value transfer in defence sector governance. Simultaneously, the EU would deepen bilateral security cooperation, providing another vector to firmly anchor and align Georgia with EU foreign policy goals.

The EU disposes without doubt of attractive assets to become more involved in defence governance, even if its contribution will almost certainly not consist of large-scale military assistance or MOD reform. More likely, coordination functions and targeted advice and assistance on parliamentary and independent oversight, the respect for human rights in and by defence institutions, and on tackling emerging security challenges will lend themselves

32 Marion Kipiani

to EU input. The EU can bring to bear the expertise it has gained as an international actor in crisis management and security sector reform. The recent experience of the central and eastern European member states of carrying out defence reform can be a valuable asset for Georgia as it undergoes a similar process. Moreover, the EU can build on its track record of almost 20 years in assisting institution building in Georgia and, increasingly, in helping maintain peace and stability in the South Caucasus. This involvement has afforded it, despite all criticism and shortcomings, a legitimacy and footprint second to none among Georgia's populations and governing elites.

Despite the findings urging an increased EU role in defence sector reform, some caveats are in order. As with any governance assistance, meaningful and sustainable reform of defence institutions will depend first and foremost on the political will of Georgia's government, as well as on the commitment of its civil servants to modernisation and the consequent change in perceptions, attitudes and behaviours. How the long-term transfer of values postulated by the EU, such as democratic governance, transparency, accountability and the respect of human rights, occurs in external assistance to defence institutions is an area that has been under-researched. It merits greater attention by both practitioners and the research community in order to tease out how the defence sector, which is particularly closely linked to state sovereignty and a delicate topic for externally driven intervention, fits into established frameworks of good governance reform.

Bibliography

Akubardia, Teona. 'Security and Defence Policy Development', in Tamara Pataraia (ed.), *Democratic Control over the Georgian Armed Forces since the August 2008 War* (Geneva: Geneva Center for the Democratic Control of Armed Forces, 2010a) 5–19.

Akubardia, Teona. 'Overview of the Legislation Facilitating the Civil Democratic Oversight of Armed Forces in Georgia', in Tamara Pataraia (ed.), *Democratic Control over the Georgian Armed Forces since the August 2008 War* (Geneva: Geneva Center for the Democratic Control of Armed Forces, 2010b) 20–38.

Balfour, Rosa. 'Institutions', in Eva Gross and Anand Menon (eds), *'CSDP Between Internal Constraints and External Challenges'*, EU-ISS Report No. 17, October 2013 (Paris: EU Institute for Security Studies, 2013) 45–50.

Blair, Dennis C. *Military Engagement: Influencing Armed Forces to Support Democratic Transition* (Washington, D.C.: Brookings Institution Press, 2013).

Bloching, Sebastian. *Security Sector Reform Missions under CSDP: Addressing Current Needs* (Brussels: Geneva Center for the Democratic Control of Armed Forces and International Security Information Service Europe, 2012).

Born, Hans. 'The Role of Parliaments', in Eden Cole, Philipp H. Fluri and Simon Lunn (eds), *Oversight and Guidance: Parliaments and Security Sector Governance* (Geneva: Geneva Center for the Democratic Control of Armed Forces, 2015) 64–84.

Civil Georgia 'Officials from MoD, General Staff Arrested', 28 October 2014, accessed 15 November 2014, www.civil.ge/eng/article.php?id=27751.

Civil Georgia.'President Tries to Put Sidelined NSC Back in Spotlight', 19 August 2014, accessed 14 October 2014, http://civil.ge/eng/article.php?id=27591.

Cole, Eden. 'The Status of Current Security Sector Governance in the CIS and its Relevance to Parliamentarians', in Katrin Kinzelbach and Eden Cole (eds), *Democratising Security in Transition States. Findings, Recommendations and Resources from the UNDP/ DCAF Roundtable for CIS Parliamentarians Prague, October 2005* (Bratislava: United Nations Development Program, 2006) 16–37.

Cole, Eden and Philipp H. Fluri. 'Georgia after the "Rose Revolution"' in Philipp H. Fluri and Eden Cole (eds), *From Revolution to Reform. Georgia's Struggle with Democratic Institution Building and Security Sector Reform* (Vienna and Geneva: PfP-Consortium of Defence Academies and Security Studies Institutes, 2005) 7–24.

Cole, Eden, Philipp H. Fluri and Simon Lunn. 'Introduction' in Eden Cole, Philipp H. Fluri and Simon Lunn (eds), *Oversight and Guidance: Parliaments and Security Sector Governance* (Geneva: Geneva Center for the Democratic Control of Armed Forces, 2015) 9–11.

Commission of the European Union. 'Communication from the Commission to the Council and the European Parliament. Wider Wider Europe – Neighbourhood: A New Framework for Relations with our Eastern and Southern Neighbours', 11 March 2003, accessed 7 November 2016, https://eeas.europa.eu/enp/pdf/pdf/com03_104_en.pdf.

Commission of the European Union. 'Communication from the Commission to the Council and the European Parliament. A Concept for European Community Support for Security Sector Reform', Brussels, 24 May 2006, accessed 10 November 2016, http://eur-lex.europa.eu/LexUriServ/LexUriServ.do?uri=COM:2006:0253:FIN:EN:PDF.

Commission of the European Union. 'Communication from the Commission to the Council and the European Parliament. Wider Wider Europe — Neighbourhood: A New Framework for Relations with our Eastern and Southern Neighbours', 11 March 2003, accessed 7 November 2016, https://eeas.europa.eu/enp/pdf/pdf/com03_104_en.pdf.

Darchiashvili, David. 'Georgian Security Sector Reform: Achievements and Failures' in Anja Ebnöther and Gustav E. Gustenau (eds), *Security Sector Governance in Southern Caucasus. Challenges and Visions* (Vienna and Geneva: PfP Consortium of Defence Academies and Security Studies Institutes, 2004) 84–114.

Darchiashvili, David. 'Georgian Security – Challenged from Within and Without', in Philipp H. Fluri and David Darchiashvili (eds), *After Shevardnadze. Georgian Security Sector Governance after the Rose Revolution* (Geneva: Geneva Centre for the Democratic Control of Armed Forces, 2006).

Dursun-Ozkanca, Oya and Antoine Vandemoortele. 'The European Union and Security Sector Reform: Current Practices and Challenges of Implementation', *European Security*, 21:2, April 2012, 139–160.

Fluri, Philipp H. and Shorena Lortkipanidze. 'Georgian Security Sector Governance after the Rose Revolution', in Philipp H. Fluri and David Darchiashvili (eds), *After Shevardnadze. Georgian Security Sector Governance after the Rose Revolution* (Geneva: Geneva Centre for the Democratic Control of Armed Forces, 2006).

Freire, Maria Raquel. 'On decision-making, capabilities and the local dimension in EU operations', in Walter Feichtinger, Maria Raquel Freire and Maria Grazia Galantino (eds), *Achievements | Failures | Perspectives. EU's Role in Multilateral Crisis Management. Findings and Conclusion* (Vienna: Federal Ministry of Defence and Sports, 2013) 15–21.

34 *Marion Kipiani*

Fritz, Antje. 'Status Report on Security Sector Governance in Georgia', in Anja Ebnöther and Gustav E. Gustenau (eds), *Security Sector Governance in Southern Caucasus. Challenges and Visions* (Vienna and Geneva: PfP Consortium of Defence Academies and Security Studies Institutes, 2004) 116–164.

Galantino, Maria Grazia. 'On the comprehensiveness and legitimacy of CSDP', in Walter Feichtinger, Maria Raquel Freire and Maria Grazia Galantino (eds), *Achievements | Failures | Perspectives. EU's Role in Multilateral Crisis Management. Findings and Conclusion* (Vienna: Federal Ministry of Defence and Sports, 2013) 5–14.

Gross, Eva. 'Missions', in Eva Gross and Anand Menon (eds), *CSDP Between Internal Constraints and External Challenges*, EU-ISS Report No. 17, October 2013 (Paris: EU Institute for Security Studies, 2013) 38–44.

Gross, Eva and Anand Menon. 'European Defence: An Inventory for the December Summit', Eva Gross and Anand Menon (eds), *CSDP Between Internal Constraints and External Challenges*, EU-ISS Report No. 17, October 2013 (Paris: EU Institute for Security Studies, 2013) 5–10.

Hobbs, David and Ruxandra Popa. 'The Role of the NATO Parliamentary Assembly', in Eden Cole, Philipp H. Fluri and Simon Lunn (eds), *Oversight and Guidance: Parliaments and Security Sector Governance* (Geneva: Geneva Center for the Democratic Control of Armed Forces, 2015) 85–110.

Huff, Ariella. 'The role of EU defence policy in the Eastern neighbourhood', EU-ISS Occasional Paper 91, May 2011 (Paris: European Union Institute for Security Studies, 2011).

Johnson, Gary. 'Security Sector Reform in the Southern Caucasus', in Anja Ebnöther and Gustav E. Gustenau (eds), *Security Sector Governance in Southern Caucasus. Challenges and Visions* (Vienna and Geneva: PfP Consortium of Defence Academies and Security Studies Institutes, 2004) 48–56.

Kakachia, Kornely. 'Problems of Post-Conflict Public Security Management in Georgia', in Philipp H. Fluri and Eden Cole (eds), *From Revolution to Reform. Georgia's Struggle with Democratic Institution Building and Security Sector Reform* (Vienna and Geneva: PfP-Consortium of Defence Academies and Security Studies Institutes, 2005) 95–115.

Kipiani, Marion. 'NATO and Georgia: The Ever Closer Partnership', Analysis Paper, BİLGESAM – Center for Strategic Studies, 2 February 2016, accessed 15 November 2016, www.bilgesam.org/en//incele/2313/-nato-and-georgia–the-ever-clo ser-partnership/

Kipiani, Marion. 'Georgia's Road to NATO: Everything but Membership?' in Studium Europy Wschodniej (eds), *Warsaw East European Review Yearbook 2015* (Warsaw: University of Warsaw, 2015).

Kucera, Joshua. 'Georgian Soldiers Accused In African Child Sex Crime Investigation', *EurasiaNet*, 30 January 2016, accessed 15 November 2016, www.eurasianet. org/node/77091.

Lortkipianidze, Shorena. 'Parliamentary Oversight of the Security Sector: Mechanisms and Practice', in Tamara Pataraia (ed.), *Democratic Control over the Georgian Armed Forces since the August 2008 War* (Geneva: Geneva Center for the Democratic Control of Armed Forces, 2010a) 39–51.

Lortkipianidze, Shorena. 'Decision-Making in Georgia's Defence Sector', in Tamara Pataraia (ed.), *Democratic Control over the Georgian Armed Forces since the August 2008 War* (Geneva: Geneva Center for the Democratic Control of Armed Forces, 2010b) 51–63.

Lortkipanidze, Shorena. 'The Georgian Security Sector: Initiatives and Activities', in Philipp H. Fluri and Eden Cole (eds), *From Revolution to Reform. Georgia's Struggle with Democratic Institution Building and Security Sector Reform* (Vienna and Geneva: PfP-Consortium of Defence Academies and Security Studies Institutes, 2005) 233–248.

Lunn, Simon. 'Introduction', in Philipp H. Fluri and Simon Lunn (eds), *NATO, EU and the Challenge of Defence and Security Sector Reform* (Geneva: Geneva Center for the Democratic Control of Armed Forces, 2007) 5–8.

Lunn, Simon. 'Parliamentary and Executive Oversight of the Defence Sphere' in Philipp H. Fluri and Eden Cole (eds), *Defence Institution Building. 2005 Partnership Action Plan on Institution Building Regional Conference* (Vienna: Bureau for Security Policy at the Austrian Ministry of Defence; National Defence Academy, 2005).

Lynch, Dov. 'Security Sector Governance in the Southern Caucasus – Towards an EU Strategy', in Anja Ebnöther and Gustav E. Gustenau (eds), *Security Sector Governance in Southern Caucasus. Challenges and Visions* (Vienna and Geneva: PfP Consortium of Defence Academies and Security Studies Institutes, 2004) 34–47.

Lynch, Dov. 'Georgia: An Emerging Governance. Problems and Prospects', in Philipp H. Fluri and Eden Cole (eds), *From Revolution to Reform. Georgia's Struggle with Democratic Institution Building and Security Sector Reform* (Vienna and Geneva: PfP-Consortium of Defence Academies and Security Studies Institutes, 2005) 249–268.

Osidze, Archil and Ivlian Haindrava. 'Civil-Military and Interagency Cooperation in the Security Sector Reform', in Philipp H. Fluri and Velizar Shalamanov (eds), *The Way Ahead in Security Sector Reform* (Sofia: Geneva Center for the Democratic Control of Armed Forces and George C. Marshall Association - Bulgaria, 2003) 192–212.

Oskanian, Kevork and Derek Averre. 'Security and Democracy in the Security and Democracy in the Caucasus', CASCADE Working Paper, Work Package 2 (Birmingham: University of Birmingham, 2016).

Pataraia, Tamara. 'Civilians in National Security Structures and Civil-Military Relations in Georgia', in Philipp H. Fluri and David Darchiashvili (eds), *After Shevardnadze. Georgian Security Sector Governance after the Rose Revolution* (Geneva: Geneva Centre for the Democratic Control of Armed Forces, 2006).

Pataraia, Tamara. 'Defence Institution Building in Georgia', in Philipp H. Fluri and Viorel Cibutaru (eds), *Defence Institution Building: Country Profiles and Needs Assessments for Armenia, Azerbaidjan, Georgia and Moldova. Background Materials* (Geneva: Geneva Centre for the Democratic Control of Armed Forces, 2008) 49–73.

Pataraia, Tamara. 'Introduction', in Tamara Pataraia (ed.), *Democratic Control over the Georgian Armed Forces since the August 2008 War* (Geneva: Geneva Center for the Democratic Control of Armed Forces, 2010) 1–4.

Pataraia, Tamara et al. *Evaluation of Parliamentary Powers Related to Oversight of the Defence Sector in Georgia* (Geneva and Tbilisi: Geneva Center for the Democratic Control of Armed Forces, 2014).

Rubin, Alissa J. and Taimoor Shah. 'Taliban Attack Kills 7 Georgian Soldiers in Afghanistan', *The New York Times*, 7 June 2013, accessed 2 December 2016, www.nytimes.com/2013/06/08/world/asia/taliban-attack-base-guarded-by-georgians-in-afghanistan.html

Sikharulidze, Kakha. Presentation at the PAP-DIB launching event and seminar in Tbilisi, Georgia (25–29 April 2005) in Philipp H. Fluri and Eden Cole (eds),

36 *Marion Kipiani*

Defence Institution Building. 2005 Partnership Action Plan on Institution Building Regional Conference (Vienna: Bureau for Security Policy at the Austrian Ministry of Defence; National Defence Academy, 2005).

Simons, Greg. 'Security Sector Reform and Georgia: the European Union's challenge in the Southern Caucasus', *European Security*, 21:2, April 2012, 272–293.

Slocombe, Walter B. 'NATO, EU and the Challenge of Defence and Security Sector Reform', in Philipp H. Fluri and Simon Lunn (eds), *NATO, EU and the Challenge of Defence and Security Sector Reform* (Geneva: Geneva Center for the Democratic Control of Armed Forces, 2007) 9–16.

Tardy, Thierry. 'Tackling the challenges of SSR', EU-ISS Issue Brief 14/2016, April 2016 (Paris: European Union Institute for Security Studies, 2016).

Tardy, Thierry. 'CSDP in action. What contribution to international security?' EU-ISS Chaillot Paper No. 134, May 2015 (Paris: European Union Institute for Security Studies, 2015).

Tardy, Thierry. 'CSDP: getting third states on board', EU-ISS Issue Brief 6/2014, March 2014 (Paris: European Union Institute for Security Studies, 2014).

Trapans, Jans Arveds. 'Georgia, the Black Sea and the Approaching West', in Philipp H. Fluri and Eden Cole (eds), *From Revolution to Reform. Georgia's Struggle with Democratic Institution Building and Security Sector Reform* (Vienna and Geneva: PfP-Consortium of Defence Academies and Security Studies Institutes, 2005) 293–311.

United States of America State Department. 'Georgia 2012 Human Rights Report', accessed 15 November 2016, www.state.gov/documents/organization/204499.pdf.

Vashakmadze, Mindia. *The Legal Framework of Security Sector Governance in Georgia* (Geneva and Tbilisi: Geneva Center for the Democratic Control of Armed Forces, 2014).

Vashakmadze, Mindia. 'Democracy and Security. The Legal Framework of Security Sector Governance', in Philipp H. Fluri and Eden Cole (eds), *From Revolution to Reform. Georgia's Struggle with Democratic Institution Building and Security Sector Reform* (Vienna and Geneva: PfP-Consortium of Defence Academies and Security Studies Institutes, 2005) 29–50.

2 Russian governance of the North Caucasus

Dilemmas of force and inclusion

Julie Wilhelmsen

Introduction

While Vladimir Putin's Russia struggles to strike a balance between security and freedom within the Russian polity, nowhere is the problem as acute as in the eastern parts of the North Caucasus. This chapter reviews Russia's approach to the republics in that region since Putin came to power, and asks what the potential for mobilisation against Russian rule in the North Caucasus amounts to. The current decrease in violence in the region is often taken as a sign of 'success' in curbing the insurgency. I argue that the heavy focus on repression and exclusion in Russian policies may well backfire and create conditions for a new mobilisation against Russian dominance.

The analysis is guided by the assumption that, to achieve efficient governance, the state needs to cater for a broad set of needs in the population. Not only does it have to provide security and welfare, but it also has to keep open bottom-up channels for a voice in the system, and articulate an inclusive state identity. The two latter needs are particularly important in establishing effective governance over populations in formerly colonised, ethnically and religiously diverse areas like the North Caucasus. Informed commentators argue that the social contract in Russia primarily hinges on economic efficiency and does not concern political questions (Makarkin 2011: 1471). This chapter suggests that this is too narrow a focus if we want to understand the potential for mobilisation and opposition against the state in the North Caucasus.

Starting with the second post-Soviet war in Chechnya from 1999 onward, Russian governance in the North Caucasus has relied heavily on the maintenance of security. Even if conscious efforts have been made to complement this approach with socioeconomic development, inclusive articulations of identity in official rhetoric and opportunities for North Caucasian populations to have a say in the political system have dwindled. This chapter reviews developments in Russian policies in the eastern part of North Caucasus since the coming to power of Vladimir Putin. I begin by mapping the policy of force in the region and suggest that Russian counter-terrorist efforts often amount to the physical repression of broad sections of the population. I then move on to discuss Moscow's socioeconomic policies in the region. In the

38 *Julie Wilhelmsen*

third section I look at opportunities for political representation and participation of regional elites, in particular their part in policymaking in their own republics. Finally, the politics of identity are discussed; I suggest that the subjection of key groups in the North Caucasus to exclusionary state policies has triggered a new emergence of distinctive religious and ethnic identities. At the same time the Russian leadership has begun to articulate a less inclusive Russian state identity. This situation creates fertile ground for alternative political entrepreneurs who claim to offer security from state repression, alternative socio-economic services, and differing visions of where the North Caucasian populations belong.

The policy of force

Since the start of the second Chechen war, the use of force has been a core instrument in Russian efforts to govern the North Caucasus. The war institutionalised violent state practices as the prime instrument to curb dissent and control Chechnya's population. It also made agents that administer violence, both Russian and Chechen, the key interlocutors in Moscow's relations with Chechnya (Gilligan 2010, Wilhelmsen 2017). Akhmed Kadyrov's rule over the territory formed a continuation of this type of rule. Today, Russian governance in Chechnya, carried on by Kadyrov's son Ramzan, takes the form of imperial indirect rule through a middleman (in the ideal-typical sense), relying even more heavily on practices of brute force than the Russian government (Wilhelmsen 2018). Indeed, as Memorial (2016: 29) notes, abductions, unlawful detentions and forced disappearances continue to be widespread and systematic in the republic. Moreover, this middleman operates through the use of force against the population in Chechnya – and, in fact, beyond – with near total impunity (Wilhelmsen 2018).

Chechnya is a special case in the North Caucasus; when the insurgency subsided in Chechnya, it re-emerged in the neighbouring republics, Ingushetia, Kabardino-Balkaria, Karachai-Cherkessia and Dagestan (O'Loughlin, Holland and Witmer 2011). While the federal counterterrorist operation in Chechnya officially ended in 2009, more limited versions of this operation soon emerged in these other republics. The re-organisation of the North Caucasus Federal Military District into the Southern Federal Military District in October 2010, aimed at strengthening the counterterrorist campaign in the wider region, was another concrete manifestation of this development. The heavy-handed imposition of force by Russian servicemen spread to Chechnya's neighbouring republics. As documented by Toft and Zhukov (2012 and 2015) the counterinsurgency strategy in this region over the past ten years has relied heavily on repression, focusing on the selective but widespread liquidation of insurgents. This practice has been particularly pervasive in Dagestan, often as part of counterterrorist operations involving police, military, security, civil defence and emergency ministry forces. But it is also manifest in calmer republics such as

Kabardino-Balkaria. Government forces usually kill rebels instead of negotiating their surrender, and arrests of suspected militants are rare (Regnum 2016a).

Still, what Memorial (2016: 5) refers to as a 'new direction' in Russian counterinsurgency in the North Caucasus developed from 2009 to 2012. These policies involved dialogue with various sectors of society and religious communities, law abidance during counter terrorist operations and reintegration of armed insurgents (Parfitt 2011). They were pursued in Dagestan under the leadership of Magomed salam Magomedov (2010–2013) and in Ingushetia under Yunus-bek-Yevkurov (2008–present), but not in Chechnya. The 'new direction' was short lived, however: in Dagestan it ended in 2012. While it had been supported by the Dagestani elite and was conducive to the cultural traditions and social fabric of Dagestan, it was opposed by the state security agencies; it was also undermined by the armed insurgents (Aliyev 2013).

According to *Caucasian Knot*, the most reliable available source of data, casualty numbers for the eastern republics of the North Caucasus dropped significantly from 2012 onward following the decapitation of the insurgent leadership. This trend continued into 2016, corresponding with a decrease in the level of insurgent activity.[1] However, this does not necessarily indicate that Russian governance in the region has relied less on the threat or use of force in these past few years. Federal policies are still driven by the Russian government's counterterrorist efforts in the region; in the official Russian definition 'counterterrorism operations are special operations intended to suppress a terrorist attack, secure civilians, neutralise terrorists and minimise the effects of the attack' (Ministry of Defence of the Russian Federation).[2] The renewed emphasis on the terrorist threat in official discourse in connection with the crisis in Syria has renewed the focus on counterterrorism in the North Caucasus as well. Indeed, despite the exodus of fighters from the North Caucasus to Syria in the past couple of years, and a reduction in the immediate threat, the preoccupation with 'preventive' counterterrorist activities in the region has only increased with the rise of Islamic State, the Russian military engagement in Syria, and the growing fear that radicalised fighters there could return to the North Caucasus (Stepanova 2015).

From 2013 onward there has been a continuous pattern of reprisals and repressions, targeted in particular against Salafi communities – in Chechnya, merely manifesting Salafi views is severely punished. In Dagestan, 'cleansing' operations in villages and towns, involving gross violations of the law and of the rights of local inhabitants, were carried out in 2013 and 2014, with some lasting over two months and affecting entire village populations (Memorial 2016: 40–44). While the Dagestani authorities seemed to be aware of the devastating effects such policies have on the delicate social structure and balance between different religious and ethnic communities in the republic, a return to the policies of dialogue and reparation from 2010 to 2012 has not transpired.

40 *Julie Wilhelmsen*

When what looked like religious sectarian conflict between officially sanctioned Sufi on one side and Salafi communities on the other escalated in Dagestan in 2015–2016, the republican authorities intensified repression of the latter, including the detention and arrests of worshippers, the dismissal of Salafi Imams and the forceful closure of mosques by security personnel, at times even through arson. The introduction of so-called 'preventative' practices targeting large sections of the Dagestani population, including watch-lists of thousands of people who are considered potential extremists or terrorists and are frequently checked and detained by the police or security services, was a new trend. Police officers interviewed by Memorial stated that they lack the personnel to carry out the required practices of control and repression of these Salafi communities in connection with the new campaign (Memorial 2016: 47, see also Economist 2016).

Given the key social and political role Islam plays in the eastern part of the North Caucasus, a particularly problematic development is the attempt by the authorities to employ 'traditional' Sufi Islam and its official structures as tools to subdue Salafism and the insurgency. The attempt to shut down the Salafi mosque on Kotrova Street in Makhachkala, Dagestan in November 2014 is illustrative. While police forces were brought in to carry out the raid, up to 200 Sufi adherents acting on behalf of the Spiritual Administration of the Muslims of Dagestan were mobilised to appear at the Mosque after it had been emptied. Moreover, the Sufi Imam who was appointed to take over the Mosque alleged that he was pressured to do so by the security forces and the Dagestani authorities, who otherwise threatened to close down the Mosque altogether (Memorial 2016: 47–48). Such practices of using official religious structures as a cover to repress Salafists have a long precedent in the neighbouring republic of Chechnya. Under the Kadyrovs, Sufism has been amplified, projected and instrumentalised both ideologically and practically to overcome radical Salafi influence (Wilhelmsen 2018, Falkowski 2016).

Recently, Ramzan Kadyrov has also tried to spread and enhance the use of Sufism as a counter-force against Salafism to the neighbouring republics. In February 2016, a meeting of Sufi brotherhoods from Chechnya, Dagestan and Ingushetia took place in Grozny, where Kadyrov announced that he would fight Salafism across the Caucasus. A *fatwa* was issued, representing Salafists as dangerous separatists and only recognising followers of the Sufi *tariqat* as true Muslims (*Caucasian Knot* 2016b, 30 September). Kadyrov's initiative has been widely criticised by Muslim leaders elsewhere in Russia, but could affect developments in the tiny neighbouring republic of Ingushetia especially negatively. Despite contributing to the general anti-Salafi campaign in the North Caucasus in connection with the Sochi Olympics, the republic's head, Yunus-Bek Yevkurov, has in the past few years strived to reconcile sectarian interests within Ingushetia, reportedly preventing official clergy from seizing the most important Salafi mosque in Nasyr-Kort, Nazran. The Ingush authorities have not made general watch-lists of Salafis, and the latter are in general not harassed. Accordingly, Yevkurov's policy toward Salafis and returning insurgents has been considered the region's most moderate (ICG 2016: 23). This Ingush 'model' is coming under pressure with Kadyrov's growing influence in the region, however (Le Huérot 2016).

Thus, not only in Chechnya, but also in Dagestan and to some degree Ingushetia, Kabardino-Balkaria and Karachai-Cherkessia, the use or threat of force is becoming more widespread as the government increases its efforts to fight off extremists and terrorists. Government policies also seem to be turning more intrusive into the social, cultural and religious life of the republics, in addition to touching ever-larger segments of the population. This development is likely driven by the dominance of actors that administer violence in the Russian governance apparatus. Here, Ramzan Kadyrov's key role and growing influence are important, as is the influence of agencies such as the Russian investigative committee, the Ministry of Internal Affairs and the Federal Security Service. The recent anti-Salafi campaign in Dagestan, for example, is not primarily a result of sectarian conflict, and was not initiated by the Sufi Imams in the Council of Muftis. It was, rather, instigated by the authorities and the security forces. Such initiatives are primarily driven by increasing counterterrorist efforts in the face of the rising influence of Islamic State (Regnum 2016b, Memorial 2016: 48).

On the wider regional level, we have observed a similar trend towards the increasing influence of security actors. Preparations for the Sochi Olympics in 2014 included a broad set of security measures (Coaffee 2015). On the leadership level the substitution of the business-oriented Aleksandr Khloponin with Interior Ministry General Sergei Melikov, formerly the region's anti-terrorist chief in his role as head of the North Caucasus Federal District in 2014, was symptomatic of this development (*Eurasia Daily Monitor* 2014, 16 May). In July 2016 Melikov was replaced by Vice Admiral Oleg Belaventsev, Presidential Envoy to Crimea from 2014, closely allied with Defence Minister Sergei Shoigu, signalling what kind of policy tools were viewed as most adequate in Moscow's rule of this region. Even the new Federal Agency for Nationalities Affairs (established in March 2015), potentially of major importance for Moscow's governance of the North Caucasus, is headed by a security service veteran, Igor Barinov. The use of security actors as middlemen and agenda-setters in Russian governance in the North Caucasus is also evident in government support for the Cossacks and their militarised self-defence groups in Kabardino-Balkaria, as well as in other republics (North Caucasus Weekly 2016, Goble 2016).

These developments raise several questions about the social contract between the Russian state and the population in the region. Firstly, do the policies of force pursued by the Russian government there actually decrease the threat from militant Salafi Islam? Many (such as two foremost experts on developments in the North Caucasus, Irina Starodubrovskaya and Akhmed Yarlikapov) argue that it does not, pointing to the fact that the current counterterrorist practices merely contribute to violent radicalisation and an increase in the ranks of the insurgency (Falkowski 2016 Memorial 2016). If

42 *Julie Wilhelmsen*

this is the case, the Russian state will be even less capable of delivering on the very basic aspect of the social contract: providing the population with security. Secondly, a very high cost – in terms of repression and violence – has been inflicted upon the population, far beyond the armed insurgents themselves. With the indiscriminate treatment of all Salafis as potential terrorists or bandits, the entire Salafi community (including its non-violent members) has become alienated from the Russian state. The fact that more than 5,000 Salafi believers took to the streets to protest against the forceful shutdown of the Makhachkala mosque on Kotrova Street, as discussed above, testifies not only to the inefficiency of force as a tool of governance in this region, but also to a growing local insistence on preserving cultural and religious identity and autonomy, a challenge we will discuss in the final section of this chapter. Moreover, the process of alienation from Russian rule probably goes beyond the Salafi communities: the more widespread the use of arbitrary practices of force in this region, touching ever wider circles of the civilian population, the more this population, like the Chechens during the Second Chechen War, will feel rejected by the Russian state and cultivate alternative forms of governance.

The policy of economic development

In line with the idea that the Russian social contract primarily hinges on socio-economic matters, the daunting socio-economic challenges in the region have worried Russian policy makers, not least because they are deemed to create fertile ground for terrorism. On its pages on 'Combating terrorism', the official website of the Ministry of Defence of the Russian Federation (2016) notes that 'in general, terrorism is a response to the continuous foot dragging in resolving burning social issues'. The republics in the eastern North Caucasus are the most underdeveloped of Russia's federal subjects, with the highest unemployment rates and the lowest quality of life; crime and corruption levels are also the highest in Russia. Accordingly, Russian policies there have repeatedly included economic development strategies or simply large-scale allocation of economic resources to the region from the federal budget.

Direct allocation of economic resources to the Kadyrov leadership was a key part of the 'normalisation' policies after the Chechen war (Wilhelmsen 2017). From 2004 onward, what looked like a more conscious development strategy for the entire region was embarked upon. Dmitry Kozak was appointed as the Presidential Representative to the Southern Federal District, with the special task of improving social and economic conditions in the region, in particular directed at the creation of new jobs. These policies were followed up during Dmitry Medvedev's presidency: in line with his modernisation approach, Medvedev (2009) announced that Russian policies would be aimed at alleviating the 'root causes of violence' in the region. Subsequently, the politician and businessman Aleksandr Khloponin was appointed head of the new Northern Caucasus Federal District, in 2010. A 'Strategy for the Socioeconomic Development of the North Caucasus Federal District Until 2025' was adopted that same year, with the aim of making the republics in the North Caucasus 'self-sufficient' through business development and major investment projects guaranteed by the state, particularly in the tourist and agricultural sectors (see Holland 2015).

However, the strategy was not based on firm knowledge about local conditions and set unrealistic goals; it produced meagre results in terms of economic development as a result (Starodubrovskaya and Kazenin 2014). The replacement of Khloponin by General Melikov in 2014 symbolised a shift away from the policy of economic modernisation, towards re-emphasising security policy in the region (*Caucasian Knot* 2014, 13 May).[3] Still, being acutely aware of the potential danger of growing social and economic grievances, the Russian government has continued to invest generously in the region's economies and social services through large-scale state programmes in recent years. Ironically, from 2014 onwards, the Western sanctions regime and the ensuing embargo of Western products and goods also seem to have facilitated a certain development in the agricultural sector in the region (in Kabardino-Balkaria for example).

Nevertheless, the net result of Moscow's economic policies in the region is a dangerous reliance on economic subsidies from the federal centre, which, for example, accounted for 85 percent of Chechnya's and 48 percent of Kabardino-Balkaria's budget in 2015. Such reliance is not a problem when oil prices are high and the economy is growing, making the re-allocation of funds to poorer regions possible. But it can represent a serious challenge to Moscow's rule over the region in a time of economic crisis – like the one in effect since 2014 – if Moscow decides to cut down on economic transfers to the North Caucasus republics. Such decreases would make it difficult for the republican authorities to continue carrying out even their present low level day-to-day economic and social responsibilities towards the population. While the economic situation is not all that matters for the residents of this region, social-scientific surveys conducted in the North Caucasus identified it as a primary concern of the residents (Dannreuther 2014). Combined with increasing use of force and repression, this development could exacerbate their perception that Moscow's rule does not provide for their basic needs.

This view is reinforced by the way in which resources and funds are allocated. While Putin did initiate a so-called anti-corruption and -clanship campaign in 2013 – resulting in the arrest of numerous officials in Dagestan and Kabardino-Balkaria –federal funds have for years been allocated to the regional leadership without corruption being dealt with at all. In fact, the mismanagement of budget funds is deemed to be the largest source of corruption in the region (ICG report 2015); while tolerance of such corruption linked to resource allocation has been a key way for Moscow to secure the loyalty of the regional elite, it may have the opposite effect for the population at large. Nowhere is the result of this practice, in terms of economic inequality between the regional leadership and its population, as glaring as in

44 *Julie Wilhelmsen*

Chechnya (Wilhelmsen 2018). For the North Caucasian population, which the Russian leadership ultimately aims to govern, this pattern of corruption and unequal economic distribution creates a sense of exclusion and alienation, not only from the regional elite but also from the Russian state. Moscow's economic policies in the region do not seem to enhance the federal authorities' ability to deliver on the most crucial aspect of the social contract in the Russian context: economic efficiency and development for the population.

The policy of political participation

The North Caucasus is a very complex region, not only in terms of ethnicity and religion, but also in terms of elites and types of political participation and representation. Elites in this region are closed groups, prefer to remain in the shadows, are highly traditional and replenish their ties through ethnicisation, authoritarianism and kinship (Salgiriev 2016); meanwhile, the study of political participation, representation and recruitment at this 'local' level remains crucial to understanding developments in the region. This account will focus on the extent to which North Caucasians are represented and have a say at the official regional political level, over questions concerning the way they organise their lives. We are interested in whether developments in this field can alleviate the 'deficiencies' of the Russian state in terming of provide security and socio-economic development to the people of this region. There might not be a strong political participatory component to the social contract for most Russians; but it is reasonable to assume that there is one for the peoples of the North Caucasus because of their distinct ways of organising religious and social life. This was already evident during Soviet times, when the first protests against Soviet rule emerged in the North Caucasus and were underpinned by *ethnic* rather than *socio-economic* concerns (Kozlov 2002).

Looking at participation and representation in today's North Caucasus, Chechnya again emerges as a special case. While the Kadyrovs are Chechens, the strictly authoritarian system which has been erected around them contradicts the traditionally egalitarian and clan-based nature of Chechen society, undermining social institutions where power was negotiated and decisions made in a less top-down fashion (Bullough 2010 and 2015). We have few means to assess systematically what goes on today, but it is unlikely that any Chechen outside of the Kadyrov clan has any influence over how his republic should be governed. As expressed by Ramzan Kadyrov during a televised meeting with Chechen officials in 2011 'I'm the boss…and no one else but me, understand?' (Yaffa 2016). Federal policies on Chechnya are, for their part, shaped through the personal contractual relations between the Russian president and the leader of the Chechen republic (Wilhelmsen 2018). Kadyrov's militias can act with total impunity in the Federation beyond Chechnya, to the frustration of the Russian law enforcement agencies (Moscow Times 2013). Kadyrov can also secure continued generous funding for his republic simply by complaining publicly at a time when budgets are being cut across the board. In return, Kadyrov keeps Chechnya under control and secures the continued legitimacy of the Putin regime. For example, the presidential party, United Russia, received 96.29 percent of the votes in Chechnya during the September 2016 parliamentary elections (RIA Novosti 2016). This speaks of the mutual and personal dependence between Putin and Kadyrov, and shows how policies on Chechnya are decided within this relationship.

The dominance of Kadyrov in the governance of neighbouring republics at the expense of their leaderships is an emerging trend. We have already mentioned Kadyrov's recent attempt, at the meeting of Sufi brotherhoods in Grozny, to define and decide religious affairs in the wider North Caucasus. Moreover, during the past five years, Kadyrov has on several occasions carried out policing functions in neighbouring republics; the Kadyrov regime has 'tried to claim a role for itself in shaping the direction and implementation of regional counterterrorist operations across the rest of the North Caucasus' (Snetkov 2014: 177). While Kadyrov might be perceived in Moscow as a useful tool to control the eastern parts of North Caucasus, the expansion of his influence serves to disenfranchise the leaderships of the neighbouring republics. It also triggers animosity and potential conflict on the popular level: the Chechens are already viewed with great scepticism by many of their neighbouring peoples, who are eager to preserve their own distinctive ways and protect their autonomy.[4]

Kadyrov's increasing influence is a particularly disturbing development because it is complemented by federal policies directed at curbing regional representation and power in the neighbouring republics. In line with Putin's ambition of erecting a 'power vertical' in Russia, and following the terrorist attack in Beslan in 2004, a new system of selecting governors was introduced. It substituted the direct elections of governors and presidents in the regional units with their temporary appointment by the Kremlin, subject to confirmation by regional legislatures. In practice, this has meant that the Kremlin chooses the governors. To begin with, the Kremlin continued to select regional representatives as governors/presidents in the North Caucasus republics, and in some cases incumbent heads were simply re-appointed. This centralisation of government skewed the regional policy agenda towards the Kremlin's: Sokolov (2016) argues that the regional governments were co-opted into the federal cause of fighting the war on terrorism and extremism during these years. This implied a loss of autonomy, which was compensated for by high subsidies and the opportunity to suppress internal political opponents in favour of one's own supporters. Moreover, although the system afforded part of the regional elite a key role in governing the republics in line with the Kremlin's agenda, it served to deny political representation and participation to the population at large.[5]

In the past few years, this system has seemed to be moving in a direction which gives even the regional elite less of a say in the politics and governance of their region. Again, the 2014 appointment of Sergei Melikov as head of the

46 *Julie Wilhelmsen*

North Caucasus Federal District is illustrative. Together with the establishment of the North Caucasus Development Ministry that same year, the appointment granted the layer of federal administration *above* the republics more weight. Moreover, although Melikov is a Tabasaran, an ethnic group indigenous to North Caucasus, he is first and foremost a General in the Federal Interior Ministry, with close ties to the core group of *siloviki* in Moscow. The new head of the North Caucasus Federal District, Oleg Belaventsev (appointed July 2016), has the same close affiliation to the centre. In this gradual transfer of official power and representation towards the centre and away from the region, the appointing, by Moscow, of people from outside the republics as governors has proved most significant. In 2013, Ramazan Abdulatipov, a Moscow-based politician, was appointed to lead Dagestan, and Yurii Kokov, a security services officer, was appointed as head of Kabardino-Balkaria. The reasoning behind this shift seems to be that these people are detached from the region's intricate tensions, conflicts and corruption, while forming an integral part of the Moscow elite (Dzutsati 2016).

In addition to this development, Sokolov (2016) observes that the pressure on governors to stay loyal to Moscow's agenda is increasing. There are many ways to interpret the overwhelming support (compared to what was observed in other federal subjects) for the presidential party – United Russia – in the eastern North Caucasus republics during the September 2016 parliamentary elections.[6] Nevertheless, it seems reasonable to suggest that the results testify to a willingness of current regional elites to give Moscow what it demands. Moreover, Moscow has not only abandoned the strategy of aligning itself with established local elites, but is even moving to dismantle their regional empires without giving anything in return (Sokolov 2016). This trajectory of decreasing regional representation and participation in the North Caucasus' structures of governance is bound to create resistance to central rule. Although this pertains to all the republics in the region, Dagestan, which has a long tradition of community-based decision-making and direct democracy (Ware and Kisriev 2010, Souleimanov 2011), is particularly vulnerable to the decreasing political space afforded local institutions and elites.

The policy of identification and belonging

While security, economic development and political participation are key factors in creating loyalty and deference to the state, the latter's ability to project an inclusive identity that encompasses the various social groups on its territory is also a significant and underrated factor, particularly in a multi-ethnic and multi-confessional polity such as Russia. In Russian scholarly debates, social problems and state terror/repression are given as the primary reasons for radical mobilisation.[7] Such expert explanations omit the wider societal developments that have been taking place within the Russian Federation in recent years, resulting in deep identity divides between North Caucasians and Russians, widespread distrust in the

Russian government among much of the North Caucasus' youth, and the view that Islam, rather than the current Russian model, is the ideal model for society (Vatchagaev 2016).

In Soviet times, communist ideology, despite all its faults, resulted in the projection of an inclusive state identity. Regardless of religious or national origin, anyone could become part of socialist society and a citizen of the Soviet state. This overarching ideological construct disappeared when the Soviet Union started to unravel; on the regional level, lingering nationalisms and religious identities reappeared to fill the void. During the 1990s, few new ideas were launched by the rulers in Moscow on what kind of state the Russian Federation *was* and who the people belonging to this state *were*. [8] While this clearly was an inadequate strategy for nation-building, it meant that the ethnically and religiously distinct North Caucasians were not explicitly excluded from the new Russian state by the country's leadership. As I will outline below, this has changed over the past 15 years because certain groups – and in particular the North Caucasians – have been subjected to exclusionary practices by the Russian authorities, while these authorities have simultaneously begun to articulate a less inclusive Russian national identity.

During the Second Chechen War – labelled a counterterrorist campaign – the Russian leadership took care to use the word 'terrorist' rather than 'Chechen' or 'Muslim' to identify Russia's enemy (Wilhelmsen 2017, chapter 5); this was not always the case among deputies in the Federal Assembly, nor in expert and media language, however (Wilhelmsen 2017, chapters 7–9). Moreover, the constant cohabitation of the words 'terrorist' and 'Chechen' in public discourse during the war served to constitute and merge these social groups into one category of danger and otherness. The net effect of the campaign against Chechnya was the social exclusion of Chechnya from Russia and Chechens from Russian society. This exclusion was not only manifested in words, but also through the massive violence employed during the war, as well as other exclusionary practices against Chechens in Russian society (Wilhelmsen 2017, chapters 10–12). One should not underestimate the radical estrangement of the Chechens from Russia as a result: although public opinion polls are not available, Chechnya today bears all the marks of a society insisting on its distinctive identity in opposition to the norms of Russian society. While Ramzan Kadyrov dictates the use of headscarves and traditional codes of conduct to Chechen people, these people would most probably be easily mobilised in defence of their distinct identity against Russian rule, if so called upon.[9]

Building on this logic, the spread of counterterrorist campaigns and the intensified use of force outlined in the second section of this chapter is likely to be fostering a similar feeling of social exclusion from Russia among other groups in the eastern parts of the North Caucasus (Vatchagaev 2016). Such exclusion engenders social cohesion within the threatened group, and an insistence on preserving the distinctiveness of the group's identity. This problematique is particularly acute for groups with a primarily Salafi or Muslim

48   *Julie Wilhelmsen*

identity; but it is also a social logic that seems to be at work in relations between Russian authorities and secular activist groups in the region. One example is the relation between the authorities and Circassian activists. While the Russian authorities sought to legitimise repressive security measures before the Sochi Olympics with reference to the protection of the people from terrorism, it was perceived as a policy of exclusion by the social groups who were subjected to it. Circassian activists endured heavy harassment in early 2014 (Eurasia Daily Monitor 2014, 8 January). A year on, responses to exclusionary practices manifested themselves in the accentuation of a distinct Circassian identity, and a clearer rejection of Russian rule through the acti-vists' increasingly tough rhetoric on the Russian authorities (Eurasia Daily Monitor 2015, 5 January).

These processes of exclusion on the regional level are enhanced by recent developments in the articulation of Russian identity by the Russian leader-ship. During the past 15 years, that leadership has consciously tried to for-mulate a history that binds the Tsarist, Soviet and contemporary eras into a coherent narrative. They were also initially careful to project Russia as a multi- ethnic and multi-confessional state (Hale 2016, Laruelle 2016). At the same time, there has been a movement in the Russian population towards embracing a more ethnic Russian national identity, visible in the emergence of right-wing nationalist groups like the Russian Civil Union, the Russian Public Movement, the Russian Platform and the New Force party, in public opinion polls and indeed during the first mass demonstrations against the Putin regime in autumn 2011.[10] To some extent this insistence on a more Russian identity among Russians themselves is a result of the mobilisation during the 'anti-terrorist campaigns' in Chechnya, produced in juxtaposition to North Caucasian identity (Wilhelmsen 2017): the numbers show a rise in xenopho-bia directed against North Caucasians among the Russian population fol-lowing the Second Chechen War.[11] The centrality of North Caucasians as a significant Other in the new Russian nationalist movement was also demon-strated in the 2011 campaign to 'Stop feeding the Caucasus' (RT 2011). As was noted by several analysts, the North Caucasus and the North Caucasians were increasingly construed as 'foreign' to Russia in nationalist milieus, and there were demands for apartheid-like policies, or for separating the North Caucasus from Russia (Markedonov 2013, Petrov 2013b).

In efforts to offset what seemed like an emerging protest movement headed by Russian nationalists, the Russian leadership moved to adopt a more ethnic state identity (Hale 2016). In January 2012, Putin wrote that 'the Russian people are state-forming [*gosudarstvoobrazuyushchy*] by the very fact of Rus-sia's existence. The great mission of [ethnic] Russians is to unite and bind civilisation' (*Nezavisimaya Gazeta*, 23 January). With the annexation of Crimea, the accentuation of Russianness as constitutive of Russia's state identity became even more explicit in official rhetoric (see, for example, Putin 2014). Judging by official statements in the past couple of years, the Russian leadership is retreating to a less ethno-nationalist state identity more fitting

Russian governance of the North Caucasus 49

for a multi-ethnic and multi-confessional state such as the Russian Federation (Pain 2016: 72, Laruelle 2016); but the Russian public might still continue to pressure and challenge its leadership to articulate a more exclusionary identity, and the leadership may have to respond.[12] This dilemma was amply illustrated during one of the Russian President's recent annual call-in shows, where Putin (2016) confirmed his support for Ramzan Kadyrov's rule over Chechnya. But at the same time, his representation of the Chechens/Caucasians had to conform to representations among the Russian audience:

> One needs to understand what sort of people they are... Considering the fact that we are talking about the Caucasus where people are hot-headed, the very involvement of these people in a governing job at a high political level is not an easy thing.

Thus, the social differentiation and exclusion of North Caucasians in the Russian Federation is clearly expressed in words at the official, as well as at the popular levels. But it also materialises in concrete policies that make North Caucasian lives more dispensable than those of other Russians. As Pavel Felgenhauer (2016) recently commented on the news that the Chechen *Vostok* and *Zapad* Battalions will be sent to Syria as the only Russian forces to take part in ground operations, 'the majority of Russians do not really consider Chechnya or the Chechens as truly Russian, so potential Chechen casualties in Syria will not cause unwanted alarm or tension among the general population'. Current trends in Russian policies of identification and belonging might undermine the basis for loyalty and deference to the Russian state among the populations of the North Caucasus, but here, once again, the Chechens might turn out to be a special case.

Conclusion

Since Putin came to power, Russian policies in the eastern part of the North Caucasus have been dominated by the use of force. While this has particularly been the case in the treatment of the Chechen population, it has in recent years also affected the populations of Chechnya's neighbouring republics. In their efforts to protect Russia from terrorism and extremism, the Russian authorities have subjected ever larger sections of the civilian inhabitants in the wider region to such policies. This situation is perhaps inevitable where the insurgency is deeply intertwined with the local population, and where Islamism has increased its social reach, but it is also the result of the growing influence of security actors in the federal apparatus of governance in the North Caucasus. The counterterrorist campaigns in the North Caucasus over the past 18 years may have increased security for Russia and the Russians, but for large parts of the local population, these campaigns have resulted in insecurity. It is unlikely that a state can subject part of the population to this

50 *Julie Wilhelmsen*

type of physical exclusion over a long period without triggering a quest for other sources of security.

This situation becomes particularly acute because of its reinforcement by a growing identity divide between Russians and North Caucasians. The latter are increasingly viewed as foreign to Russia: as we have seen, there are even voices in favour of excluding North Caucasus from the Russian territorial state. This new rejection of the region even impinges on official articulations of identity, threatening to fracture the state-wide and inclusive national identity that the Russian leadership has sought to construct. The North Caucasians seem to be prone to a similar rejection of the Russians. There is hardly a Russian left in Chechnya, and we see the same kind of exodus taking place in the other republics of the eastern part of North Caucasus (Petrov 2013a, Markedonov 2016). Moreover, as an alternative identity and source of social community, Islam will continue to have enormous traction among groups of Muslim heritage. This process of revival is not going to stop any time soon. For those who have a strong ethnic identity – such as the Circassians – the tendency to retreat into and strengthen that smaller, ethnic social unit will increase if exclusionary state practices and narratives persist.

A policy of economic inclusion and development has been consciously pursued by the Russian leadership in the North Caucasus, in an effort to curb extremism and terrorism and thereby make the widespread use of force superfluous in the longer run. But even this potential instrument of inclusion as a counterbalance to the policies of force is becoming dysfunctional. Not only have these populations long been excluded from their share in economic development due to corruption and clientelism at the elite level, but economic crisis and growing discontent in the Russian elite with the flow of money away from the federal budget, directly into the North Caucasian republics' could result in a sharp decline in these flows.

Finally, the recent move by the Russian government towards decreasing North Caucasian representation and participation in regional politics, in a challenge to established regional elites, is bound to create resistance and shift the balance between *force* and *inclusion* in favour of the former. Giving the North Caucasians a say in how to deal with the substantial security and economic challenges ahead could have functioned as a safety valve: regional elites would have had to carry responsibility for a coming crisis, they would have a stake in continuing Moscow's rule, and thus less opportunity and interest in leading resistance against it. While Derluguian (2005) identified a lack of leadership as an obstacle to revolution in the North Caucasus, precisely because incumbent elites enjoyed Moscow's support, this obstacle is about to be removed. Moreover, while representation at the highest federal level might not be so important for the population of a region that is becoming increasingly distinct from Russia in cultural, religious and social terms, *regional* representation and the possibility of having a say over the organisation of life within the republics has become all the more important. The lack of such representation and participation adds to the feeling of alienation from the Russian state among the North Caucasian populations; and, worryingly, it makes them easier targets for any future mobilisation against Russian rule by disgruntled regional elites.

Notes

1 For a recent compilation of casualty numbers based on *Caucasian Knot* see Klimenko and Melvin (2016). *Caucasian Knot* can be accessed at www.eng.kavkaz-uzel. eu/.

2 As summarised by Stepanova (2005), Russia's anti-terrorist policies and measures have been shaped by four principles since the 2002 Nord-Ost theatre hostage crisis: make no concessions to terrorists; destroy them or bring them to justice; isolate and apply pressure on the actors (both state and non-state) which sponsor or support terrorism; and bolster the anti-terrorist capabilities of your partners.

3 A North Caucasus Development Ministry was set up in 2014 to follow up the implementation of economic policies in the region. However, the recent multiplication of administrative bodies there decreases rather than increase the government's ability to stimulate economic development (Starodubrovskaya and Kazenin 2014).

4 While the Dagestanis supported the Chechens during the First Chechen War, they did not during the Second War, as evidenced in the treatment of the Chechen Akkintsy in Dagestan in 1999 (see for example *Nezavisimaya Gazeta* 17 and 29 September 1999). Repeated Chechen law enforcement actions on Ingush territory in recent years have given rise to hostile exchanges between Chechnya and Ingushetia at the government level (Vatchagaev 2012).

5 It should be noted that there is a lot of variation between the republics in the eastern part of the North Caucasus. While in Kabardino- Balkaria power is highly centralised, democratic institutions are weak and censorship of the press widespread, Karachai-Cherkessia is more democratic and the population there enjoys more freedom of expression (Gunya 2016).

6 Chechnya 96.29 percent, Dagestan 88.90 percent, Ingushetia 72.41 percent, Kabardino-Balkaria 77.71 percent, Karachai-Cherkessia 81.67 percent. Only Tatarstan (85.27 percent) Kemerovo (77.33 percent) Mordovia (84.36 percent) and Tuva (82.61 percent) have similar numbers (RIA Novosti 2016).

7 For example, recent seminars and roundtables organised by the Institute for African Studies at the Russian Academy of Sciences (Kavkazsky Uzel 2016) and *Memorial*/*Novaya Gazeta* (Vatchagaev 2016).

8 See Kolstø (2016) on how the Russian Federation is far less multicultural that the Tsarist Empire and the Soviet Union and how the turn to ethno-nationalism in official Russian rhetoric came only after the turn of the century.

9 Impressions from interaction during seminars with Chechen students from the State University in Grozny in connection with the project 'Dialogue and learning across the Russian/North Caucasian Divide' 2012–2015.

10 For a thorough account of the new Russian nationalism see Kolstø and Blakkisrud (2016).

11 For a collection of statistics that illustrate the sharp divide between Chechens/ North Caucasians and Russians, see the 2013 report by the Valdai Club, available at http://vid-1.rian.ru/ig/valdai/Russian_Identity_2013_rus.pdf.

12 As Hale (2016) notes, Russia is ruled through 'patronal presidentialism', which means that although president Putin is constitutionally strong and also wields power through extensive networks of personal acquaintances, he is still dependent on popular support and is highly sensitive to public opinion.

52 *Julie Wilhelmsen*

Bibliography

Aliyev, H. (2013). 'Dagestan's Commission for Rehabilitation of Rebel Fighters: A Failed Experiment?' *The Central Asia-Caucasus Analyst*, 20 February, available at www.cacianalyst.org/publications/analytical-articles/item/12650-dagestans-commission-for-rehabilitation-of-rebel-fighters-a-failed-experiment?.html.

Bullough, O. (2010). *Let Our Fame Be Great*. London: Penguin Books.

Bullough, O. (2016). 'Putin's closest ally – and his biggest liability'. *The Guardian*, 23 September.

Caucasian Knot (2014). 'Kremlin's reshuffle in the North Caucasus shows force trend in policies, experts say'. 13 May, available at /www.eng.kavkaz-uzel.eu/articles/28117.

Caucasian Knot (2016a). 'Kremlin refuses to reduce subsidies to Chechnya'. 5 December, available at www.eng.kavkaz-uzel.eu/articles/37739/

Caucasian Knot (2016b). 'Russian Council of Muftis suggests holding all-Russian discussion of Grozny fatwa'. 30 September, available at www.eng.kavkaz-uzel.eu/articles/37062/.

Coaffee, J. (2015). 'The Uneven Geographies of the Olympic Carceral: From Exceptionalism to Normalisation'. *The Geographical Journal*, 181(3), 199–211.

Dannreuther, R. (2014). 'Shifting dynamics of the insurgency and counter-insurgency in the North Caucasus'. *Ethnopolitics*, 13(4), 377–395.

Derlugian, G. (2005). 'The Coming Revolutions in the North Caucasus'. PONARS Policy Memo, No. 378, available at www.ponarseurasia.org/sites/default/files/policy-memos-pdf/pm_0378.pdf.

Dzutsati, V. (2016). 'Moscow's desire to micro-manage the North Caucasus causing multiple inefficiencies'. *North Caucasus Weekly*, 17(5), available at https://jamestown.org/program/moscows-desire-to-micro-manage-the-north-caucasus-causing-multiple-inefficiencies/.

The Economist (2016). 'Salafis mustered'. 7 May, available at www.economist.com/news/europe/21698111-police-shut-dagestans-salafi-mosques-believers-head-fight-islamic.

Eurasia Daily Monitor (2014a). 'Appointment of General Melikov to Replace Khloponin Points to Kremlin Bid to Subdue Dagestani Insurgency'. 11(92), available at: https://jamestown.org/program/appointment-of-general-melikov-to-replace-khloponin-points-to-kremlin-bid-to-subdue-dagestani-insurgency-2/#sthash.ybNXL3E2.dpuf.

Eurasia Daily Monitor (2014b). 'On the eve of Sochi Russian authorities step up harassment of Circassian civil activists'. 11(3), available at https://jamestown.org/program/on-eve-of-sochi-russian-authorities-step-up-harassment-of-circassian-civil-activists-2/.

Eurasia Daily Monitor (2015). 'Circassian activists toughen rhetoric on Russian authorities'. 12(2), available at https://jamestown.org/program/circassian-activists-toughen-rhetoric-regarding-putin-regime-2/.

Falkowski, M. (2016). 'Russia's "Middle East": the escalation of religious conflicts in the Northern Caucasus'. *OSW Commentary*, No. 207, available at www.css.ethz.ch/content/specialinterest/gess/cis/center-for-securities-studies/en/services/digital-library/publications/publication.html/196730.

Felgenhauer, P. (2016). 'Chechen Special Battalions Sent to Syria as Reinforcements'. *Eurasia Daily Monitor*, 13(193), available at http://us11.campaign-archive1.com/?u=28b6673fcc2022a1dd557acae&id=a7ed5c04fb&e=000deac4aa.

Russian governance of the North Caucasus 53

Gilligan, E. (2010). *Terror in Chechnya. Russia and the Tragedy of Civilians in War.* Princeton, NJ: Princeton University Press.

Goble, P. (2016). 'Moscow's Use of Cossacks Leading North Caucasians to Think about Forming "Savage Divisions", Rights Activist Warns'. *Window on Eurasia – New Series,* 25 June, available at http://windowoneurasia2.blogspot.no/2016/06/moscows-use-of-cossacks-leading-north.html.

Gunya, A. (2016). 'From democracy to disorder: comparing governing strategies in the North Caucasus'. Feature article, Policy Documentation Centre.

Hale, H. E. (2016). 'How nationalism and machine politics mix in Russia'. In P. Kolstø and H. Blakkisrud, eds, *The New Russian Nationalism.* Edinburgh: Edinburgh University Press.

Holland, E.C. (2015). 'Economic Development and subsidies in the North Caucasus'. *Problems of Post-Communism,* 63(1), 50–61.

ICG report. (2015). 'North Caucasus: The challenges of Integration: Economic and Social Imperatives'. Europe Report No. 237, 31–34.

ICG report. (2016). 'The North Caucasus Insurgency and Syria: An Exported Jihad?'. Europe Report No. 238, available at www.refworld.org/docid/56eab9f84.html.

Kavkazsky, Uzel. (2016). 'Eksperty: neustroennye v zhizni molodye lyudi bolee drugikh podversheny verbovke IG'. 28 June, available at www.kavkaz-uzel.eu/articles/284854/?mc_cid=62741081e8&mc_eid=000deac4aa.

Klimenko, E. and N. Melvin. (2016). 'Decreasing violence in the North Caucasus: is an end to the regional conflict in sight?'. 15 June, available at www.sipri.org/commentary/blog/2016/decreasing-violence-north-caucasus-end-regional-conflict-sight.

Kolstø, P. (2016). 'The Ethnification of Russian nationalism'. In P. Kolstø and H. Blakkisrud, eds, *The New Russian Nationalism.* Edinburgh: Edinburgh University Press

Kolstø, P. and H. Blakkisrud (eds) (2016). *The New Russian Nationalism: Imperialism, Ethnicity, Authoritarianism, 2000–2015.* Edinburgh: Edinburgh University Press.

Kozlov, V. A. (2002). *Mass Uprisings in the USSR: Protest and Rebellion in the Post-Stalin Years.* Armonk, NY: M.E. Sharpe.

Laruelle, M. (2016). 'Russia as an anti-liberal European civilization'. In P. Kolstø and H. Blakkisrud, eds, *The New Russian Nationalism.* Edinburgh: Edinburgh University Press

Le Huérot, A. (2016). 'An Ingushetia "Counter Model" of bringing peace at home? The commission of reintegration of former fighters into civilian life'. Paper presented at Cascade conference, 'The Democracy-Security Nexus in and around the Caucasus', Brussels, 20–21 October.

Magomed-Rasul, I. and Kimitaka, M. (2014). 'Contextualized violence: politics and terror in Dagestan'. *Nationalities Papers,* 42(2), 286–306.

Makarkin, A. (2011). 'The Russian social contract and regime legitimacy'. *International Affairs,* 87(6), 1459–1475.

Malashenko, A. (2009). 'A rollback is in full swing in the Russian Caucasus, and it's not even clear what century it's going back to'. *The New Times,* 6 July.

Markedonov, S. (2013). 'The North Caucasus: the value and costs for Russia'. *Russia in Global Affairs,* 27 December, available at http://eng.globalaffairs.ru/number/The-North-Caucasus-The-Value-and-Costs-for-Russia-16287.

Medvedev, D. (2009). Speech at expanded format Security Council meeting, available at http://en.kremlin.ru/events/president/transcripts/4383.

Memorial (2016). 'Counter-terrorism in the North Caucasus: a human rights perspective. 2014–first half of 2016'. Report by the Memorial Human Rights Centre,

54   *Julie Wilhelmsen*

available at http://memohrc.org/sites/all/themes/memo/templates/pdf.php?pdf=/sites/default/files/doklad_severnyy_kavkaz_-_angl.pdf.

Moscow Times (2013). 'FSB Officers Go on Strike After Release of Chechen Cops'. Report. 25 March, available at www.themoscowtimes.com/news/article/fsb-officers-go-on-strike-after-release-of-chechen-cops-report-says/477488.html.

Nezavisimaya Gazeta (1999a). 'Potok bezhentsev narastayet'. 29 September.

Nezavisimaya Gazeta (1999b). 'Voina posle voiny'. 17 September.

North Caucasus Weekly (2016). 'Terek Cossacks claim special rights in Kabardino-Balkaria'. 17(3), available at http://us11.campaign-archive1.com/?u=28b6673fcc2022a1dd557acae&id=24a7ba9d8a&e=000deac4aa.

O'Loughlin, J. and F .D. W. Witmer (2011). 'The Localized Geographies of Violence in the North Caucasus of Russia, 1999–2007'. *Annals of the Association of American Geographers*, 101(933126806), 178–201.

O'Loughlin, J., E. C. Holland and F. D. W. Witmer. (2013) 'The Changing Geography of Violence in Russia's North Caucasus, 1999–2011: Regional Trends and Local Dynamics in Dagestan, Ingushtia, and Kabardino-Balkaria'. *Eurasian Geography and Economics*, 52(5), 596–630.

Open Russia (2015). 'The Family', available at www.youtube.com/watch?v=krXLTNNeNZs.

Pain, E. (2016). 'The imperial syndrome and its influence on Russian nationalism'. In P. Kolstø and H. Blakkisrud, eds, *The New Russian Nationalism*. Edinburgh: Edinburgh University Press.

Parfitt, T. (2011). 'Jihadist rehabilitation in the North Caucasus', available at http://pulitzercenter.org/articles/makhachkala-dagestan-muslim-boyeviki-insurgency-jihad.

Petrov, N. (2013a). 'Failed North Caucasus Policy'. *The Moscow Times*, 22 July, available at https://themoscowtimes.com/articles/failed-north-caucasus-policy-26015.

Petrov, N. (2013b). 'Russia minus Caucasus. Carnegie Endowment for Peace'. 16 July, available at http://carnegie.ru/commentary/?fa=52409.

Putin, V. V. (2014). Address by President of the Russian Federation. 18 March, available in English version at http://eng.kremlin.ru/news/6889.

Putin, V. V. (2016). In April 2016 Q&A with the Russian population referred in 'Kadyrov Tries To Parry Putin Criticism, Calls Crosshairs Video "A Joke"', available at www.rferl.mobi/a/russia-kadyrov-putin-criticism-crosshairs-video/27676887.html.

Regnum (2016a). 'V Kabardino-Balkarii obnaruzhili laboratoriyu po izgotovleniyu bomb'. 15 June, available at https://regnum.ru/news/accidents/2144827.html.

Regnum. (2016b). 'Vrio glavy Dagestana: Dzhamaatu nado brat v svoi ruki navedenie poryadka v sele Gimri'. 8 August, available at https://regnum.ru/news/kavkaz/1692893.html.

RIA Novosti. (2016). 'Vybory v Gosdumu 2016'. 23 September, available at https://ria.ru/infografika/20160918/1476912507.html.

Russia Today. (2011). 'Nationalists demand Moscow stop feeding the Caucasus'. 29 September, available at www.rt.com/politics/moscow-stop-feeding-caucasus-651/.

Salgiriev, A. (2016). 'The Northern Caucasus: Tribal clan structure of the political elites as a factor of political tension'. *Central Asia and the Caucasus*, 17(1), 31.

Snetkov, A. (2014). *Russia's Security Policy under Putin: A Critical Perspective.* Abingdon and New York: Routledge.

Sokolov, D. (2016). 'Can the North Caucasus adapt to political change?' 25 January, available at www.opendemocracy.net/RBK.

Starodubrovskaya, I. and K. E. Kazenin (2014). 'Administering or governing, that is the question'. *Russian Economic Developments*, No. 6, 44–46.

Souleimanov, E. A. (2011). 'The Republic of Dagestan: The Epicenter of Islamist Insurgency in Russia's North Caucasus'. Portuguese Institute of International Relations and Security: IPRIS Occasional Paper.

Stepanova, E. (2005). 'Russia's approach to the fight against terrorism'. In J. Hedenskog, V. Konnander, B. Nygren, I. Oldberg and C. Pursiainen, eds, *Russia as a Great Power: Dimensions of Security under Putin*. London: Routledge-Curzon, 301–322.

Stepanova, E. (2015). 'North Caucasus – a Wall against or a Bridge for IS?' International Security // Analysis, Russian International Affairs Council, available at http://russiancouncil.ru/en/inner/?id_4=6269#top-content.

Toft, M. D. and Y. M. Zhukov (2012). 'Denial and Punishment in the North Caucasus: Evaluating the Effectiveness of Coercive Counter-Insurgency'. *Journal of Peace Research*, 49, 785–800, available at http://jpr.sagepub.com/content/49/6/785.short.

Toft, M. D. and Y. M. Zhukov (2015). 'Islamists and Nationalists: Rebel Motivation and Counterinsurgency in Russia's North Caucasus'. *American Political Science Review*, 109(2), 222–238.

Vatchagaev, M. (2012). 'Relations Between Leaders of Chechnya and Ingushetia Deteriorate'. *Eurasia Daily Monitor*, 21 September, available at https://jamestown.org/program/relations-between-leaders-of-chechnya-and-ingushetia-deteriorate/#.

Vatchagaev, M. (2016). 'Russian Observers Fail to Understand What Is Radicalizing North Caucasian Youth'. *Eurasia Daily Monitor*, 1 July, available at https://jamestown.org/program/russian-observers-fail-to-understand-what-is-radicalizing-north-caucasian-youth/.

Ware, R. B. and E. Kisriev (2010). *Dagestan: Russian Hegemony and Islamic Resistance in the North Caucasus*. Armonk, NY and London: M.E. Sharpe

Wilhelmsen, J. (2017). *Russia's Securitization of Chechnya*. Abingdon and New York: Routledge.

Wilhelmsen, J. (2018). 'Colonized children'. In K. Haugevik and I. B. Neumann, eds, *Kinship in International Relations*. Ann Arbor, MI: University of Michigan Press.

Yaffa, J. (2016). 'Report from Grozny: Putin's Dragon'. *The New Yorker*, 8 and 15 February, available at www.newyorker.com/magazine/2016/02/08/putins-dragon.

3 Overcoming the status quo in the unrecognised states of the South Caucasus
Internal and external limitations

Roxana Andrei

Introduction

Critics have maintained that the international response to the conflicts in the South Caucasus has been limited in terms of understanding the complex dynamics of the region. Much of the literature has focused on the limitations of Europeanisation as an instrument of conflict resolution, with democratisation seen as a key ingredient of peacebuilding aimed at overcoming the status quo in the unrecognised states. The emphasis on the international level of interaction has deprived the region's internal actors of agency, in other words, of their ability to make their own choices and instrumentalise democracy and dependency for their own goals in relation with their patron states and the international community. The unrecognised states of the South Caucasus have been largely depicted as criminalised, pariah entities, highly dependent on the financial and military support of their patron states.

However, both external and internal forces are important in understanding the dynamics in the secessionist regions of the South Caucasus. While not dismissing the importance of the external dimension, this chapter will also explore the internal factors contributing to maintaining the status quo in the Caucasus conflicts. I shall explore the link between external and internal influences and argue that the entities are not mere puppets dependent on their external patrons but are actors exercising their own agency, albeit limited, adjusting strategically to the fluid interplay between democracy and dependency in seeking recognition and at the same time safeguarding the status quo. This is not to claim that the unrecognised states of the South Caucasus are completely independent in making their own political choices or to disregard their various degrees of economic, security and political dependence on their patron states; it is to highlight the fact that they are not solely passive recipients and followers at all times, but that they manifest genuine political preferences as reflected in the electoral choices, that they negotiate their position vis-à-vis the patron state and instrumentalise democratisation in relation with the Western community.

Peacebuilding and democratisation in the unrecognised states of the South Caucasus: external limitations

The end of the Cold War and of the bipolar system brought with it the decentralisation and fragmentation of peacekeeping, which became multidimensional and multilevel, incorporating a larger spectrum of actions, from humanitarian aid to democratisation, market liberalisation, development and state-building. It followed the 'liberal peace' agenda as the prevailing normative framework in building a 'liberal peacebuilding' model, reflected mainly in UN, EU and NATO-led operations; contemporary peace operations have thus mirrored the normative priorities of the Global North (Wiharta et al., 2012), focusing on fast-track democratisation, marketisation and promotion of human rights. The EU's engagement in conflict transformation processes in the unrecognised states of the former Soviet Union has been mainly dominated by the principle of exporting the liberal peace model to both the parent states and the secessionist regions.

In the 1990s, the EU showed little interest in the breakaway entities of the South Caucasus and hesitated to engage directly in conflict management in the region, being more concerned with the wars in the Balkans (Baev, 1997; Whitman and Wolff, 2010; Simão, 2012; Pashayeva, 2015; Relitz, 2016; Shelest, 2016). The EU played a rather peripheral role, with the OSCE being the main responsible actor dealing with the conflicts of the South Caucasus (Whitman and Wolff, 2010; Pashayeva, 2015; Paul, 2015; Shelest, 2016), allowing Russia to play the role of a security guarantor for the secessionist regions (Baev, 1997).

The EU's change of approach and increased motivation to engage with the South Caucasus in the 2000s stemmed partly from its interest in the natural gas and oil resources of the region (Baev, 1997; Whitman and Wolff, 2010; Simão, 2012; O'Loughlin et al., 2014; Paul, 2015), which provided a potential alternative to Russia in terms of sources of supply. Thus, Azerbaijan gained in importance in European strategic calculations as a supplier through the Southern Corridor pipelines projects. At the same time, securing the transiting routes passing through Georgia also became a key motivating element in the EU's promotion of stability in both the parent state and in the secessionist entities of Abkhazia and South Ossetia. Nevertheless, the South Caucasus was not made a priority by the EU, which faced more pressing challenges in its immediate neighbourhood, such as the tensions in the Balkans, the rise of transnational terrorism, the destabilisation in the Middle East and, more recently, the conflict in Eastern Ukraine. The EU's transition towards adopting conflict prevention as a key objective of its external relations policy also led to geographical and functional overlaps with the OSCE in the field of conflict prevention, mainly with respect to the tools used, including diplomacy, civilian crisis management, promotion of democracy and human rights (Stewart, 2008).

58 *Roxana Andrei*

Furthermore, the EU has avoided directly tackling conflict resolution in the unrecognised states and adopted a rather power-based, top-down approach to mediation, which disengaged the local societies from the peace process and also reinforced questions regarding its impartiality and enhanced feelings of distrust and suspicion (Popescu, 2007; Hoch, 2011; Simão, 2012; Relitz, 2016). The European Neighbourhood Policy (ENP) and, from 2009, the Eastern Partnership (EaP) have been the main mechanisms employed by Brussels to promote democratisation and conflict resolution in the South Caucasus. Nevertheless, the approach proved to be limited, in the absence of accession prospects (Kirova, 2012; Simão, 2012; Paul, 2015) and in its failure to engage with the unrecognised states of the region. In Abkhazia, for example, the EU based its peacebuilding process on the ENP, which excludes unrecognised states from the negotiation process. An action plan has been developed only for Georgia, which is supposed to approve any projects designed for Abkhazia. By excluding one of the parties to the conflict, the EU has widened the gap between Georgia and Abkhazia instead of narrowing it (Hoch, 2011:79; Relitz, 2016). Moreover, NGOs in Abkhazia who decide to apply for these funds are met with distrust in their own society, being accused of disloyalty (Relitz, 2016). In turn, the OSCE did not invite representatives of Nagorno-Karabakh to the negotiating table, due to its legitimacy being contested by Azerbaijan, which prefers to negotiate directly with Armenia (De Waal, 2010; Minasyan, 2017).

The EU's reliance on long-term objectives such as democratisation and human rights and its focus on mainly confidence-building, technical assistance and trade privileges (Kirova, 2012; Relitz, 2016; Tarkhan Mouravi, 2016) has meant that it has failed to engage with the crucial short-term issues of conflict resolution (Whitman and Wolff, 2010; Simão, 2012). Its approach has thus had a limited impact (Popescu, 2007; Whitman and Wolff, 2010; Hoch, 2011; Kirova, 2012; Simão, 2012; Shelest, 2016), proving to be unconvincing both for the local elites, which were not offered the prospect of recognition, and for the population in the unrecognised states, suspicious of the provision of Western funding to the parent state's authorities.

As a result, the EU – while more engaged as a security actor after 2008 and providing more funding for post-conflict reconstruction – could not rival either Russia's multilevel support, investment and influence over the breakaway regions, or its role in the conflict resolution process (Whitman and Wolff, 2010; Kirova, 2012; Pashayeva, 2015; Relitz, 2016). Brussels acted as a mediator within the framework of the Geneva peace forum, designed to deal with Georgia's territorial conflicts, and for the first time assumed the role of a key security actor in the region. However, the success of the process is debatable, since Russia implemented the peace agreement only partially and managed to consolidate its position in Abkhazia and South Ossetia after granting them recognition in 2008; the Geneva peace forum itself has been seen as contributing to maintaining the status quo in the region (Paul, 2015:81) and to maximising Russia's role in the conflict resolution process (Pashayeva,

Overcoming the status quo in the Caucasus 59

2015). The Ukraine crisis put further strain on the EU's success as a mediator in the conflicts of the former Soviet space (Shelest, 2016), revealing a security deficit in the EaP (Paul, 2015).

In turn, the OSCE has been leading the Minsk peace process in Nagorno-Karabakh since 1992. The subsequent failure of the Minsk Group to broker a peace settlement between the parties prompted Russia to take the initiative and mediate a ceasefire between Armenia, Azerbaijan and Nagorno-Karabakh in 1994, formalised in the Bishkek Protocol, consequently leading to accusations of 'hijacking the negotiations' (Kolstø, 2006:12). Nevertheless, the conflict in Nagorno-Karabakh has not been a 'frozen' one; sporadic clashes have taken place along its borders, culminating in the eruption of the highest level of violence since the 1994 ceasefire, in April 2016. Various assumptions may be made about the re-escalation of conflict, including the very high oil and natural gas revenues recorded by Azerbaijan in the last two decades and their investment in military expenditure; the more recent economic stagnation in Azerbaijan, caused by the constant drop in the world oil prices and in the country's oil exports; and the polarisation of the regional scene in the context of the previous year's tensions between Russia and Turkey, with Russia traditionally supporting Armenia and Turkey backing Azerbaijan. In addition, domestic factors contributed to a resurgence of the conflict, such as the elites' attempt to regain popular support through a military victory, in the context of an internal economic crisis and their search for prestige and status recognition at regional level. All the same, the Minsk Process has been seen as 'consist[ing] of a conference which was only occasionally convened, a group which never meets as a group and a co-chairmanship functioning under a barely known mandate, all named after a city where the mediators never met' (De Waal, 2010:162).

As a basis for building peace in the South Caucasus, the principles of territorial integrity and self-determination have been instrumentalised in different ways by the three main external actors: the EU, the OSCE and Russia. Differing normative approaches have led to the breakaway regions, as well as their patron states, adjusting to a fluid situation. While the EU focused on the territorial integrity of Georgia through the ENP and the EaP, limiting the participation of Abkhazia and South Ossetia in any negotiations (Whitman and Wolff, 2010; Simão, 2012), Russia has been privileging the principle of self-determination over territorial integrity in support of its protégés (Allison, 2008), leading to tensions with the parent states, with the 2008 conflict with Georgia as the most notable result. The OSCE's generic response to conflict has been based on the implementation of the human dimension principles in the form of preventive measures, complemented by the principles of respect for territorial integrity and the right to self-determination after the emergence of conflict. However, as so often happens, these two principles collided with each other and proved hard to reconcile (Mychajlyszyn, 2001). In the case of Nagorno-Karabakh, the entity's claim to self-determination clashed with the need to secure the territorial integrity of Azerbaijan. The OSCE, like the EU,

60 *Roxana Andrei*

tends to reject secession leading to independence, especially when it is exercised through violence and without mutual consent, and leans towards favouring the principle of territorial integrity; this support for the principle of territorial integrity has caused the secessionist forces in Nagorno-Karabakh to reject all the OSCE's proposals, and the conflict thus remains as yet unsettled (Mychajlyszyn, 2001).

The post-Cold War peacekeeping model in the unrecognised states of the former Soviet Union has witnessed the emergence of new state and intergovernmental actors assuming the mandate and the role of peacekeepers. However, the target states' own agency should not be omitted. As shown above, their mistrust in some of the regional actors acting as peacekeepers, fearing that they might interfere in the process and pursue their own agenda (Kolstø, 2006), makes the parties to the conflict often reluctant to endorse the peacekeeping efforts and more inclined towards maintaining the status quo (Pashayeva, 2015) and the stability it affords.

New peacekeeping actors gained momentum in the context of a crisis of legitimacy in the global governance structures and of the blurring of boundaries between contemporary peacekeeping and international interventions. However, the emerging powers, such as Russia, still prefer to follow the mainstream normative behaviour within established international institutions and to subscribe to, rather than oppose, dominant global norms (Wiharta et al., 2012). Thus, the international recognition of Kosovo's independent status was instrumentalised by Russia as a legal, normative argument to claim international legitimacy for its actions in supporting similar recognition for South Ossetia and Abkhazia (Karagiannis, 2014).

Russia's unilateral interventions in the secessionist conflicts of the Caucasus and its search for full control over the peacekeeping operations in the region (Hoch et al., 2014) may be regarded as a matter of perception and articulation of its own interests. Historical experience plays an important role in shaping states' international behaviour (Becker et al., 2015); Russia perceives itself as a regional power, while considering the post-Soviet space its traditional sphere of influence, and has utilised the conflicts in the South Caucasus as means to counter the expansion of the Western influence in the region, seen as a direct threat to its interests (Hoch et al., 2014; Fischer, 2016). It has been interested in maximising its power, security, and military and economic capabilities, at the same time aiming to gain recognition by the West as a great power, in accordance with its self-perception going back to Tsarist and Soviet times (Kropatcheva, 2012). Material motivations were complemented by nonmaterial aspirations for recognition of its lost status and prestige and acceptance by the Western counterparts.

In the 1990s Russia, as a new regional peacekeeper, mainly undertook missions in its 'near abroad' focused on stabilisation rather than on peacebuilding (Fischer, 2016), an approach which enabled the establishment of a long-term military presence 'to "police" protracted conflicts' (Wiharta et al., 2012:18). Thus, it employed a combination of peacekeeping and unilateral

Overcoming the status quo in the Caucasus 61

military interventions (Lynch, 2000), and played the role of the patron state (in Abkhazia and South Ossetia) or supported patron states other than itself during their periods of acute weakness (e.g. Armenia in Nagorno-Karabakh – Broers, 2013). Its military presence has been seen as contributing to prolonging the conflicts and the status quo by deepening the divisions between the secessionist regions and the parent states, by enhancing distrust and feelings of insecurity and by entrenching the separatist character of these entities by patrolling their borders (Lynch, 2002). The unrecognised states of the South Caucasus are considered to be 'net importers of security' (Blakkisrud and Kolstø, 2012:290), relying on their patron states for military support, which in return entrenches the maintenance of the status quo. As financial support from Russia compensated for inferior military capabilities compared to their parent state, Abkhazia and South Ossetia found themselves under the umbrella of Russian military protection following their recognition in 2008, under the form of the Joint Peacekeeping Forces in South Ossetia and of the CIS peacekeepers in Abkhazia (Blakkisrud and Kolstø, 2012). In Nagorno-Karabakh, the military assistance of Russia has been of a more indirect nature, through the weapons provided to the Armenian army, whose forces are integrated with those of Nagorno-Karabakh.

In the past two decades, peace operations have frequently been used in order to support the political, institutional and social transformations necessary to overcome protracted conflicts and prevent their re-emergence (Wiharta et al., 2012). To this end, international organisations have played several roles vis-à-vis the unrecognised states: they have denied their recognition, acted as a collective external patron or have engaged in negotiations and peacekeeping; although they favoured a peaceful settlement of the conflicts, they attained the opposite effect by contributing partly to the prolonged existence of the unrecognised states (Kolstø, 2006). In this sense, the Minsk process in Nagorno-Karabakh, the Geneva forum for the territorial conflicts in Georgia and the overall hesitant involvement of the international community perpetuated the status quo (Von Steinsdorff and Fruhstorfer, 2012) and failed to prevent reigniting the violence (Pashayeva, 2015). In addition, the peripheral presence of the democratic external actors in the unrecognised states of the South Caucasus facilitated the emergence of Russia as a more assertive regional actor, taking the lead in peacekeeping and post-conflict reconstruction. This, combined with its military interventions, reflected Russia's preference for maintaining the status quo and its leverage on the states of the region, and for prioritising security over democracy building.

Nevertheless, interpreting Russia's support solely in terms of instruments of control takes away agency from the unrecognised states, and deprives them of any power of choice and decision-making. The following sections will assess their coping mechanisms and examine instances of their exercising their own agency and making their own political choices. While the room for manoeuvre for these entities is limited, the fact that they do follow their own agenda – whether this leads to *more* or *less* independence from the patron

62 *Roxana Andrei*

states – should be taken into account. This is not to claim that the unrecognised states of the South Caucasus are completely independent in making their own political choices or to disregard their various degrees of economic, security and political dependence on their patron states; it is to highlight the fact that they are not solely passive recipients and followers at all times, but that they manifest genuine political preferences as reflected in the electoral choices, negotiate their position vis-à-vis the patron state and instrumentalise democratisation in relation with the Western community.

From external to internal coping mechanisms for state survival: limitations on independence and democratisation

In the absence of sustained engagement and support from the international community, the unrecognised states were left with few alternatives to ensure their survival; they had to find coping mechanisms to generate support, both at local and at international level, including reliance on shadow economies, funding from the diaspora and support from their patron states. However, the actors providing such support have little interest in the democratisation of the unrecognised states.

The unrecognised states have been associated with the negative image of high regional insecurity, and have, by extension, been seen as a source of security threats at the international level (Von Steinsdorff, 2012) – such as illegal trafficking in weapons, drugs, oil and other commodities and money laundering – reinforcing the perception in the international community of them as highly criminalised territories or pariah entities (Berg and Mölder, 2012; Ó Beacháin et al., 2016). This interpretation has led, however, to ignoring other factors than ethnicity and criminality that are at play in the complex dynamics of the region, as well as to a lack of engagement with the elites of the secessionist states (Caspersen, 2008). This was further reinforced by economic sanctions (Hoch, 2011) and the banning of any forms of financial assistance that could have supported their democratisation (Caspersen, 2011; Kopeček et al., 2016). The international community failed to convince the unrecognised states to abandon the idea of independence in exchange for foreign investment during the reconstruction phase, as the entities – able to survive with the financial support of their external patrons – prioritised political over economic goals (Hoch, 2011).

At the domestic level, in the absence of the formal institutions responsible for regulating economic life during conflicts, the unrecognised states had to develop coping mechanisms that would secure their survival. As a consequence, business relationships have been confined to an already established circle of relatives or members of the same ethnic or confessional group, leading to the development of kinship- or clan-based networks (Glinkina and Rosenberg, 2003; Aliyev, 2015; Prelz Oltramonti, 2015; Kopeček, 2016). These networks have become entrenched in the societies of the unrecognised states and have favoured clientelism and corruption, thus impeding democratisation and maintaining the status quo (Lynch, 2002; Aliyev, 2015). These clientelistic networks have become key elements of shadow economies that in some ways benefited parent and patron states as well, contributing to the status quo (Caspersen, 2009). The shadow economies in post-Soviet conflict zones of the Caucasus can be traced back to the Communist period, when a parallel economy flourished, compensating for the scarcity and the deficiencies of the state-controlled planned economy. Together with the flourishing tourism on the Black Sea coasts of Abkhazia and Ajaria and the production of exotic agricultural products (citrus fruits, tea, tobacco), the Georgian parallel economy ensured a higher standard of living and access to the black market goods, otherwise restricted to the other Soviet citizens (Cheterian, 2008).

The shadow economies in the former Soviet Caucasus are thus often organised around ethnic and religious networks, and the ethnification of power structures has been adopted by most of the parties involved in the conflicts of the region. It has been further argued that the empty space left by the dissolution of state authority and power has been filled by private criminal groups, likewise often organised around some form of identity (ethnic, religious, tribal), which engage in a competition for resources (Newman, 2004; Kaldor, 2001, 2013). The distinction between state and private security actors has been blurred (Broers, 2015), articulating common interests around the revenues generated from the lack of taxation, smuggling of high-priced commodities, absence of legal controls and restrictions on trade relations. The criminalised economy has been a key source of revenue, generating profit for the local elites while also benefitting significant parts of the population (Whitman and Wolff, 2010).

On the one hand, international actors such as the EU lack the means to address and counter these groups, while on the other hand they must engage these elites – criminalised or not – in any attempts at conflict settlement (Whitman and Wolff, 2010; Caspersen, 2011). The fact that the shadow economies have been benefitting both the local elites and the population, allied to the absence of support from democratic international actors, offered little incentive for combating the local parallel economies and for supporting conflict resolution efforts that would put an end to them (Broers, 2015). In the absence of recognition, no international conventions can be applied and no monitoring from international organisations can be put into practice (Kolstø, 2006). Thus, it has been argued that 'state weakness is of obvious benefit to the unrecognized regimes. Business can be carried on with neighbouring states without paying production taxes or tariffs' (King, 2001:536).

In addition to domestic coping mechanisms, the unrecognised states of the South Caucasus seek to rely on external support that would guarantee their survival. In the absence of funding opportunities and resources from the sections of the international community interested in promoting democratisation, they have been pushed to depend on the financial support of other external actors which, as indicated above, may well not support democracy-

64 *Roxana Andrei*

building, whether sovereign states or non-state actors such as their diasporas (Blakkisrud and Kolstø, 2012; Broers, 2013; Caspersen, 2015). The role of the Armenian diaspora in Nagorno-Karabakh (Broers, 2013) has proved to be essential for ensuring the enclave's only connection to the outside world, in addition to important funding for its survival. The Armenia diaspora has proved to be influential not only in Nagorno-Karabakh, but also in the international community, exercising its impact in France, USA and Russia (Minasyan, 2017). The Abkhaz diaspora in Turkey and the Middle East has played a key role in inclining the ethnic balance of the region in favour of the Abkhaz ethnic group (Berg and Mölder, 2012; Ó Beacháin et al., 2016), while the Ossetian and the Abkhaz diasporas in the Russian Federation have acted as social links with Russia and instruments of its soft power in the unrecognised states (Gerrits and Bader, 2016).

Among the external providers of support criticised for increasing the dependency of the unrecognised states, for not supporting their democratisation and for prolonging the status quo, the patron states play a central role. Russia in particular has been disparaged as a non-democratic player and an enabler of the status quo, acting as patron state for Abkhazia and South Ossetia and as supporter of a weak patron state, Armenia, in the case of Nagorno-Karabakh (Broers, 2013). If in the 1990s, in the context of its own internal fragility and weakness, Russia did not provide official support for the separatists of the South Caucasus fearing a contagion effect on its own troubled North Caucasus (Hoch et al., 2014), after the beginning of the 2000s it chose a more assertive role and became actively engaged in the protracted conflicts of the region and in the domestic politics of the unrecognised entities (Hoch et al., 2014; Karagiannis, 2014; Ó Beacháin et al., 2016).

As a consequence, Russian policy in the unrecognised states of the former Soviet Union has been multilevel, centred around more lines of support and direct involvement in the domestic and regional dynamics of the entities. Russia has opted for both soft and hard power mechanisms when engaging with the breakaway regions of the South Caucasus. As such, it has acted as a security guarantor (Baev, 1997; Kirova, 2012), peacekeeper and economic provider for the entities, offering consistent financial support to the secessionist regimes combined with economic sanctions imposed on the parent states (King, 2001; Caspersen, 2011; Fischer, 2016). At the same time, it has been using soft power tools, by delivering educational support in the form of textbooks or scholarship opportunities in Russia for students from Abkhazia and South Ossetia (Kirova, 2012; Fischer, 2016; Gerrits and Bader, 2016). Granting Russian citizenship and free movement facilities to the inhabitants of the unrecognised states (King, 2001; Fischer, 2016) was yet another way of gaining popular support in the breakaway regions (Kirova, 2012; Gerrits and Bader, 2016); citizenship triggered the right to receive pensions, salaries for state officials and social benefits for Abkhaz and South Ossetian residents facing severe economic and social deprivations (Hoch et al., 2014; Kopeček et al., 2016). Russia's 'passportisation policy' (Fischer, 2016:20) has been justified by Moscow as a form of humanitarian assistance, granting these residents, otherwise isolated, an opportunity for mobility (Kirova, 2012; Hoch et al., 2014). But it also provided grounds for justifying its intervention in South Ossetia as support for Russian citizens abroad (Allison, 2008; Karagiannis, 2014), bolstering its claim to have a legitimate interest in the entities (Petro, 2008; Gerrits and Bader, 2016; Ó Beacháin et al., 2016).

The survival and stability of the unrecognised states, it is thus argued, are closely linked to external support (Hoch et al., 2014; Broers, 2015). Some consider, however, that dependence on external support makes the unrecognised states vulnerable (Caspersen, 2015), even when that support comes from democratic international organisations (Lynch, 2002). Opinions on the domestic dynamics in the unrecognised states seem to converge on the assumption that dependence on external support reduces the role and the control of the elites, transforming them into mere puppets of external actors (Hoch, 2011) and passive beneficiaries of external financial and security aid, which, in return, impacts on the successful prospects for building legitimacy and democracy (Broers, 2014; Frear, 2014).

Democratisation and dependency: strategic adjustments by the unrecognised states towards recognition and the status quo

I would argue, however, that democratisation and dependency constitute a fluid environment faced by the unrecognised states of the South Caucasus. The environment varies across entities, as well as within the same entity at different moments in time. Moreover, the breakaway regions instrumentalise democratisation and dependency according to the goals they prioritise or to their perceptions of various security threats, adjusting strategically as the situations demand.

For the unrecognised states, democracy and regime performance seem to come second to independence and sovereignty; they thus display a preference for strong presidential regimes (Berg and Mölder, 2012; Blakkisrud and Kolstø, 2012; Kopeček, 2016; Ó Beacháin et al., 2016; Tarkhan Mouravi, 2016) and the stability they associate with them. They instrumentalise democracy in a rather pragmatic manner, embracing democratic ideals and practices at least at a rhetorical and symbolic level (Blakkisrud and Kolstø, 2012; Broers, 2015) in an attempt to emulate the model of the Western partners (Broers, 2013) and convince them that they share similar democratic values and have the ability to establish rightful authorities (Berg and Mölder, 2012) which in the end would entitle them to international recognition (Caspersen, 2011; Bakke et al., 2014). The strategies adopted by the unrecognised states in order to comply with Western norm and move closer to recognition are nevertheless fluid and have shifted across time due to the fact that recognition is itself a 'moving target' (Broers, 2014:146), as the discourses, norms and standards of the international community have also kept changing. At the same time, the breakaway regions have also tried to emulate the Russian

66 Roxana Andrei

model of a political system by establishing similar political parties, institutions and legislation (Fischer, 2016; Gerrits and Bader, 2016), thus opting for a convenient 'hybridity' of Western models of governance with local forms (Caspersen, 2015).

As highlighted in the previous sections, it has been considered that the refusal of the international community to recognise the newly emerged entities in the South Caucasus after the break-up of the Soviet Union has led to the isolation of the separatist regions, which were left with no alternative other than to rely on their patron states (Kirova, 2012; Gerrits and Bader, 2016), thus jeopardising their decision-making independence (Kopeček et al., 2016) and chances for democratisation. This is said to have been rather the result of the resistance of the sovereign states to engage with the unrecognised states, and to have contributed to extending the status quo (Berg and Toomla, 2009), which was also perpetuated by unproductive and prolonged peace negotiations (Kolstø, 2006).

However, legal recognition does not have to be the only option available in the negotiations with the unrecognised states; maintaining the status quo may involve different forms of normalisation without recognition (Berg and Toomla, 2009) or engagement without recognition (Cooley and Mitchell, 2010), based on a certain level of acceptance of the entities and backed-up by a comprehensive set of economic, security, confidence-building and societal measures to support normalisation (Lynch, 2004; Cooley and Mitchell, 2010). Moreover, non-recognition and democratisation are not mutually exclusive; unrecognised entities may choose to pursue democracy-building as a strategy to be accepted as part of the international democratic community and to be finally granted recognition (Broers, 2014; Kanol, 2015; Kopeček, 2016; Kopeček et al., 2016). Therefore, not only does non-recognition not impede democratisation (Caspersen, 2011), but it can also act as a catalyst to it (Voller, 2015).

With their efforts to prove their compliance with Western norms and standards of democracy, in the mid-2000s Abkhazia and Nagorno-Karabakh reached their highest peak in terms of political pluralism, institution-building and democratic progress (Hoch, 2011; Broers, 2014). Although the democratisation efforts have been impeded by their own internal limitations, as well as by the pariah status attributed to them by the international community (Caspersen, 2008; Berg and Mölder, 2012; Relitz, 2016), the lack of international recognition does not seem to have impacted on their level of democratic development, as the unrecognised states do not appear to score less on democracy than the parent states, their patrons or other recognised states in the post-Soviet space (Caspersen, 2011; Blakkisrud and Kolstø, 2012; Kanol, 2015; Gerrits and Bader, 2016; Ó Beacháin et al., 2016). Moreover, the status quo in itself, by being accepted by all parties, can be considered democratic, despite obvious dysfunctionalities and the persistent problems it poses (Berg and Mölder, 2012).

Despite their efforts, the democratising endeavours of the unrecognised states of the South Caucasus in the first two decades of their existence received no acknowledgement or reward from the international community in terms of engaging with them or granting recognition. Both the elites and the populations of these entities were consequently deprived of incentives to continue to adhere to international standards and to emphasise democratisation as a priority objective (Simão, 2012; Paul, 2015; Kopeček et al., 2016; Ó Beacháin et al., 2016). Democracy became a 'peripheral goal' (Tarkhan Mouravi, 2016:702) and the local elites chose to focus on countering external threats which appeared more pressing than state- and institution-building; in the words of Voller (2015:616), 'security and defence trump democratisation'. Democratisation has thus been a fluid process and it has been strategically instrumentalised and adjusted to by the local elites, according to their priorities and to the local and international context.

Furthermore, regardless of the effort to emulate the model of Western democratic practices and institutions, some of the unrecognised states display a 'symbolic or virtual democracy' (Broers, 2015:16) or a 'façade democracy' (Voller, 2015:613). They imitate the formal aspects of democratic institutions (Tarkhan Mouravi, 2016), holding procedural and regular parliamentary and presidential elections and allowing space for the electoral opposition, but without that opposition being capable of transferring power from the ruling elites (Simão, 2012; Kanol, 2015). As a result, 'hybrid regimes' emerge, combining democratic and authoritarian features and Western and local models of governance (Caspersen, 2015; Kopeček, 2016; Tarkhan Mouravi, 2016).

The recognition of Abkhazia and South Ossetia by Russia in 2008 impacted significantly on the democratisation of and security dynamics in the unrecognised entities, in particular in Abkhazia. In the years prior to the Russian recognition, Abkhazia displayed the highest level of pluralist, competitive and consensus-based politics among the unrecognised states of the region (Broers, 2015), in what has been considered a clear example of democratisation (Kopeček et al., 2016). At the same time, it offered the appearance of a genuine drive for independence (Whitman and Wolff, 2010; Kirova, 2012), culminating in the defeat of the Moscow-supported candidate, Raul Khajimba, in the 2004 presidential elections (Hoch et al. 2014). The 2011 presidential elections were once more held in a competitive environment, demonstrating the accumulation of democratic experience (Kopeček et al., 2016:94). Moreover, a more pluralistic civil society and media had developed as well (Caspersen, 2011). However, Abkhazia's recognition by Russia in 2008 attracted an unprecedented level of funding from Moscow, which led to an eight-fold increase of its budget in 2012 compared to 2006 (Broers, 2015; Egorova and Babin, 2015). Another consequence of Russian recognition was that links with Georgia decreased, while internal conflict over resources, corruption and ethnocratic politics aimed at excluding the Georgian electorate intensified (Broers, 2015), leading to a model of 'exclusive democracy' (Kopeček et al., 2016:98).

Abkhazia's drive for independence in the first two decades of its existence was genuine. However, the lack of engagement of and support from the

68   *Roxana Andrei*

Western community caused frustrations and left the separatist region with no alternative to seeking a closer relationship with Russia (Kirova, 2012; Gerrits and Bader, 2016). Furthermore, the entities of the South Caucasus perceived the attitude of the international community as reflecting double standards (Pashayeva, 2015); Abkhazia did not benefit from the same status as Kosovo, despite its democratisation efforts (Kopeček et al., 2016).

An increased dependency on the patron state seems to have been reflected in the democratisation level of Abkhazia, which regressed in the 2014 presidential vote when Khadjimba, again the Russian-backed candidate, was finally elected president in what are considered to have been undemocratic elections (Kopeček et al., 2016; Ó Beacháin, 2016). Nevertheless, the direct impact of economic dependence on Russia on the political choices in the breakaway regions of Abkhazia and South Ossetia is hard to pin down given the peaceful transfer of power in the previous elections in Abkhazia and even in the more dependent South Ossetia in 2011 (O'Loughlin et al., 2014; Gerrits and Bader, 2016; Ó Beacháin et al., 2016). Although these elections expressed the population's drive for independence and for limiting Russia's influence (Kirova, 2012; Kopeček et al., 2016), in the end the Moscow-backed candidates managed to impose themselves by having the election results cancelled or the winners arrested (Hoch et al., 2014; Kanol, 2015).

South Ossetia's budget is almost entirely covered by Russian aid, to the tune of 98.7 percent in 2010 (Blakkisrud and Kolstø, 2012; Hoch et al., 2014; Broers, 2015). Unlike Abkhazia, South Ossetia does not show an obvious drive for independence, lacking geographical access to the outside world as well as significant natural resources, remaining dependent on the rents generated by the patron state (Broers, 2015; Gerrits and Bader, 2016). It has thus been argued that, given its almost total dependency on its patron, South Ossetia is indeed a 'puppet state' (Hoch et al., 2014:66) or a 'military protectorate' of Russia (Allison, 2008:63), being unable to function as a viable state without Russian patronage and with no perspectives of real independence (German, 2016). Nevertheless, although by far the most dependent entity on its patron state, South Ossetia manifested its own political preference by voting against the Kremlin-backed candidate, Leonid Tibilov, in the April 2017 presidential elections. The winner, Anatoly Bibilov is also an advocate of closer ties and a prospective integration into the Russian Federation, however it seems that the electorate discarded his opponent's overwhelming focus and perceived dependence on Moscow (Kelekhsayeva and Kucera, 2017).

The signing of the 2015 strategic partnership treaties between Russia and Abkhazia and South Ossetia legitimised the Russian military presence in the two territories and the shared management of their borders by creating a joint defence and security space between the patron state and the breakaway regions (Caspersen, 2015; Ó Beacháin et al., 2016). The agreement has been called a 'de facto annexation' (Gerrits and Bader, 2016:302), reflecting Russia's intention of a long-term military presence. In its turn, Russia portrayed

Overcoming the status quo in the Caucasus 69

the military presence and interventions as part of its peacekeeping mission, denying its role as a direct party to the conflict (Allison, 2008). Nevertheless, the conditions of the treaties as proposed by Russia with respect to the involvement in the local power structures and the harmonisation of external policies were perceived by some political groups in Abkhazia as a threat to its sovereignty; the local elites engaged in negotiating the terms of the treaties and managed to pass through their own comments which were included in the final version (Bagdasaryan and Petrova, 2017), based on mutual respect for sovereignty and territorial integrity (German, 2016). Although South Ossetia, seeking closer relations with Moscow and being overwhelmingly dependent at economic level on Russian support (German, 2016), obtained less concessions than Abkhazia, it is notable that both entities negotiated and received considerable acceptance of their own terms in the final form of the treaties, managing to reject provisions which both argued that would have reduced their independence (Ambrosio and Lange, 2016. The process highlights the difference not only in political objectives between the two entities, but also in their level of state-building, while not dismissing their financial, economic and military dependence on Moscow.

Nagorno-Karabakh's economy is the most diverse in terms of resource extraction, relying on the intra-state loans received from Armenia, although less in the last years (Caspersen, 2011) and on the funding support provided by the Armenian diaspora (Blakkisrud and Kolstø, 2012; Broers, 2015), but also on increasing domestic resource extraction through tax collection (Broers, 2015). Financial subsidies from Armenia and the constant flow of external support reduces their accountability towards the population (Broers, 2015), which may impede the democratisation process; the rentier behaviour triggers high levels of corruption, development of clientelistic networks of patronage and lower economic growth (Renner, 2002; Di John, 2010; Almaz, 2015). Rents prove to be sufficient for the fiscal needs of the state, which will thus impose very low taxation levels, reducing the bargaining power of society and making the government less accountable and less inclined to be democratic (Renner, 2002; Di John, 2010; Almaz, 2015). Nevertheless, Nagorno-Karabakh displays not mere dependence on the patron, but rather a relationship of interdependence. Political influence works both ways (Kanol, 2015), as the Nagorno-Karabakh elites have had a major presence in Armenian politics (Simão, 2012; Kopeček, 2016), even providing Armenia's two latest heads of state. Moreover, embracing democracy has been on the political agenda along with self-determination in Nagorno-Karabakh, with the local elections being considered free and fair by the international community observers, while reform-oriented parties are in favour of decreasing the interdependence with the patron state, Armenia (Caspersen, 2011).

The degree of engagement and dependence varies considerably between Abkhazia and South Ossetia. While South Ossetia adopted the Russian political model and welcomed its military and financial support with the hope of unification (Whitman and Wolff, 2010; Kirova, 2012; Fischer, 2016; German,

2016), Abkhazia displayed a genuine drive for independence and will to limit Russia's influence (Caspersen, 2009; Blakkisrud and Kolstø, 2012; Broers, 2013; 2015; German, 2016). Russia itself resisted South Ossetia's will for unification as it would have meant losing leverage over Georgia (Fischer, 2016), as well as risking a potential spill-over of destabilisation into its North Caucasus (Whitman and Wolff, 2010). Russia's approach to the protracted conflicts and unrecognised states of the South Caucasus is oriented towards maintaining an advantageous status quo serving its own interests. South Ossetia displays the highest level of dependency to Russian aid, given its lack of natural resources, high level of corruption, geographical isolation, a shrinking population, war damage to its infrastructure and the continuation of its status as a periphery (Broers, 2015; Fischer, 2016). Abkhazia, on the other hand, showed a clear will to limit Russian influence, benefitting from a strategic and economically beneficial location on the Black Sea, a drive for individual sovereignty caused by a high level of national cohesion and identity, a higher degree of pluralism and diversity of political and societal actors (Broers, 2015; Egorova and Babin, 2015; Fischer, 2016). The dependency and orientation towards the external patron is, however, a fluid process, which suffers fluctuations according to differing historical conditions. If before Russian recognition in 2008 Abkhazia was relying solely on smuggling with Russia and Turkey, afterwards it became a major beneficiary of Russian aid, benefitting from approximately 600 million Euros between 2008 and 2013 (Relitz, 2016), even if in 2015 it received only a small part of the agreed Russian financial support, probably as a consequence of the economic recession in Russia and of Russia's attempt to put political pressures on Abkhazia (Fischer, 2016). At the lower end of the dependency spectrum, Nagorno-Karabakh is indirectly dependent on Russia, through the economic and military support provided by Moscow to Armenia, its patron (Fischer, 2016).

The unrecognised states of the South Caucasus, in particular Abkhazia and South Ossetia, are thus considered to be militarily, politically and economically dependent on their patron state in the absence of a viable alternative (Kirova, 2012; Gerrits and Bader, 2016; Kopeček et al., 2016; Ó Beacháin et al., 2016), while Nagorno-Karabakh has become a de facto province of Armenia, with integrated politics and budgets (Caspersen, 2011). Nevertheless, the degree of dependency differs between the three unrecognised states according to their economic capacities, civil society institutions and approaches towards the Western community (Pashayeva, 2015; Fischer, 2016), but also according to the different entities' political choices at specific historical conjunctures. As a consequence of these differences, the EU's 'one-size-fits-all' approach towards the region, disregarding the differences across and within the three entities, has proved to be of limited value, failing to produce results (Paul, 2015).

The unrecognised states of the region are not mere puppets and passive recipients of their patron state or of the international community, lacking their own capacities and decision-making ability (Caspersen, 2009; Tolstrup,

2009; Von Steinsdorff, 2012; Ambrosio and Lange, 2015; Prelz Oltramonti, 2015). They have an agenda of their own sometimes contradicting that of the external patron (Caspersen, 2009), and some have displayed a genuine drive for independence and a rejection of their external patron at certain times, as it happened in Abkhazia (Caspersen, 2009; Blakkisrud and Kolstø, 2012; Broers, 2013; 2015; Fischer, 2016). At other times, dependency is translated into political interdependence with the patron state, as in the case of Nagorno-Karabakh and Armenia. This shows the fluidity and cyclical character of the nature of relations between the unrecognised entities and the patron states, the parent states and the wider international community, which also impacts on domestic trends regarding sovereignty, legitimacy and democratisation. They engage adaptive strategies both at the domestic and international level by utilising democratisation and dependency according to the perceived immediate threats to their survival: 'the image of a willing puppet should perhaps be replaced with that of a coerced puppet' (Caspersen, 2008:50).

Part of their self-driven strategy is the choice for maintaining the status quo for as long as it plays to their advantage. Lacking viable alternatives of external support and sometimes of internal resource extraction, as highlighted earlier, the separatist entities choose coping mechanisms that allow their survival and a minimum of independence, based on shadow economies, support from the diaspora, or the financial and security guarantees of a patron state. To this end they opt for maintaining the status quo (Pashayeva, 2015), justified by the benefits it generates (Lynch, 2002; Whitman and Wolff, 2010). And, as a consequence, their willingness to negotiate agreements that would alter it is limited (Whitman and Wolff, 2010). The patron states encourage the preservation of the status quo as they derive their own benefits from it. Armenia, being the de facto winner of the conflict in Nagorno-Karabakh, has no interest in a new negotiated agreement that would alter its territorial conquest (Minasyan, 2017). Russia itself does not seek a permanent resolution of the conflicts in Abkhazia and South Ossetia, since this would mean losing its leverage on the states of the region (Baev, 1997; Lynch, 2002).

In addition, the parent states might themselves face economic difficulties and political instability (Kolstø, 2006; Ó Beacháin et al., 2016), which discourages the separatist entities to return to within the borders of the parent state. However, if this argument may be true for Georgia, Azerbaijan has on the contrary witnessed considerable economic growth in the past decades, but it still failed to offer an attractive alternative to Nagorno-Karabakh. In the latter case the nation-building process that takes place inside the unrecognised states, as well as ethnic homogenisation, played a more important role in the region's decision to maintain the status quo.

Moreover, time plays a role in entrenching and sedimenting this status quo. With the passing years the practical and psychological barriers to reintegration into the parent state become stronger, and the post-conflict institutional and economic arrangements become increasingly embedded (Blakkisrud and Kolstø, 2012:282). At the same time, the recognition of Kosovo's

72 Roxana Andrei

independence by the international community might contribute to a 'hardening of positions' (Caspersen, 2008:12), with the unrecognised states being more hopeful about achieving independence themselves and thus less willing to compromise.

Furthermore, the present stability is seen as close enough to peace, whereby the parties seem reluctant to disturb the equilibrium. Societies are displaying fatigue with war and suspicion about the efficiency and impartiality of the peacekeepers, both regional ones – like Russia – or international ones – like the OSCE and the EU. Thus 'the products of the wars of the Soviet succession are not frozen conflicts but are, rather, relatively successful examples of making states by making war', with the territorial separatists of the early 1990s becoming 'the state builders of the early 2000s' (King, 2001:525).

Conclusions

The democratic external actors have played a rather peripheral role vis-à-vis the unrecognised states of the South Caucasus, although they have favoured a peaceful settlement of the conflicts. They have often been considered to have contributed to the prolongation of the conflicts instead of resolving them, perpetuating the status quo. In return, this has facilitated the emergence of more assertive regional actors, namely Russia, which has taken the lead in peacekeeping and post-conflict reconstruction and undertaken military interventions. Russia's preference for maintaining the status quo and its leverage on the states of the region reflects its prioritisation of security over democracy-building.

In addition to these external limitations, internal factors further contribute to maintaining the status quo. In the absence of sustained engagement and support from the international community, the unrecognised states have been left with few alternatives to ensure their survival and have had to find coping mechanisms of support, both at the local and international level: reliance on kinship-based shadow economies, funding from the diaspora, and support from their patron states, none of which facilitate the democratisation of the unrecognised states.

As a consequence, it has been largely argued that these entities are the victims and pawns of both their patron states and of the hesitant international community, heavily dependent on external support and guidance. Nevertheless, the secessionist states of the South Caucasus are not mere puppets or passive recipients, lacking their own capacity and will; albeit with a limited space of manoeuvre and displaying various degrees of economic and security dependence to their patron states, they have however an agenda of their own and use their agency to varying extents, with some of them manifesting a genuine drive for independence and an assertive attitude towards the external patron as circumstances dictate. Relations between the unrecognised states and the patron states, the parent states and the wider international community are of a fluid and cyclical character, impacting on domestic trends in terms of sovereignty, legitimacy and democratisation. The degree of democracy and dependency varies across the separatist states, as well as within each entity at various moments in time. They engage in adaptive strategies at the domestic as well as the international level, instrumentalising democratisation and dependency according to the perceived immediate threats to their survival and the goals they prioritise, employing mechanisms that both invite recognition and safeguard the status quo.

As a consequence, the dynamics within and across the unrecognised states of the South Caucasus need a more flexible and comprehensive approach. Status quo is not only enhanced by the response of the international community, but it is also a local choice and, by being shared by the wider society, it embeds a democratic character in itself. The separatist entities make their own political choices within the available limits and exercise agency with respect to democracy, dependency to external support and maintaining the status quo. Therefore, the local preferences and actions should be brought forward when engaging with the unrecognised states of the South Caucasus. External support and action is expected to engage the local societies, while not excluding the entities' elites from the post-conflict transformation and democratisation processes. Legal non-recognition is not to equal exclusion and isolation, as the unrecognised states have proved their durability and moved beyond the role of mere puppets and dependents to external support. By exercising their own agency, to the extent available to them, they impact on the domestic political processes, but also on the regional conflict-cooperation dynamics in the South Caucasus and on the actions and preferences of other regional actors.

Bibliography

Aliyev, Huseyn (2015). 'Informal networks as sources of human (in)security in the South Caucasus', *Global Change, Peace & Security*, 27:2, 191–206.

Allison, Roy (2008). 'Russia resurgent? Moscow's campaign to "coerce Georgia to peace"', *International Affairs*, 84:6, 1145–1171.

Almaz, Alper (2015). 'Testing the Rentier State Theory: The Case of Azerbaijan', *Journal of Global Analysis*, 5:1–2, 60–66.

Ambrosio, Thomas and Lange, William A. (2016). 'The architecture of annexation? Russia's bilateral agreements with South Ossetia and Abkhazia', *Nationalities Papers*, 44:5, 673–693.

Bagdasaryan, Susanna and Petrova, Svetlana (2017). 'The Republic of Abkhazia as an Unrecognized State', *Russian Law Journal*, V:1, 98–118.

Baev, Pavel K. (1997). 'Conflict management in the former Soviet South: the dead-end of Russian interventions', *European Security*, 6:4, 111–129.

Bakke, Kristin M., O'Loughlin, John, Toal, Gerard and Ward, Michael D. (2014). 'Convincing State-Builders? Disaggregating Internal Legitimacy in Abkhazia', *International Studies Quarterly*, 58, 591–607.

Becker, Michael E., Cohen, Matthew S., Kushi, Sidita and McManus, Ian P. (2015). 'Reviving the Russian empire: the Crimean intervention through a neoclassical realist lens', *European Security*, 1:17.

74　*Roxana Andrei*

Berg, Eiki and Mölder, Martin (2012). 'Who is entitled to "earn sovereignty"? Legitimacy and regime support in Abkhazia and Nagorno-Karabakh', *Nations and Nationalism*, 18:3, 527–545.

Berg, Eiki and Toomla, Raul (2009). 'Forms of Normalisation in the Quest for De Facto Statehood', *The International Spectator*, 44:4, 27–45.

Blakkisrud, Helge and Kolstø, Pål (2012). 'Dynamics of de facto statehood: the South Caucasian de facto states between secession and sovereignty', *Southeast European and Black Sea Studies*, 12:2.

Broers, Laurence (2013). 'Recognising politics in unrecognised states: 20 years of enquiry into the de facto states of the South Caucasus', *Caucasus Survey*, 1:1, 59–74.

Broers, Laurence (2014). 'Mirrors to the World: The Claims to Legitimacy and International Recognition of De Facto States in the South Caucasus', *Brown Journal of World Affairs*, XX:II, 145–157.

Broers, Laurence (2015). 'Resourcing de facto jurisdictions: A theoretical perspective on cases in the South Caucasus', *Caucasus Survey*, 3:3, 269–290.

Caspersen, Nina (2008). 'From Kosovo to Karabakh: International Responses to De Facto States', *Südosteuropa*, 56:1, xx.

Caspersen, Nina (2009). 'Playing the Recognition Game: External Actors and De Facto States', *The International Spectator*, 44:4, 47–60.

Caspersen, Nina (2011). 'Democracy, nationalism and (lack of) sovereignty: the complex dynamics of democratisation in unrecognised states', *Nations and Nationalism*, 17:2, 337–356.

Caspersen, Nina (2015). 'Degrees of legitimacy: ensuring internal and external support in the absence of recognition', *Geoforum*, 66, 184–192.

Cheterian, Vicken (2008). *War and Peace in the Caucasus: Russia's Troubled Frontier.* London: Hurst and Company.

Cooley, Alexander and Mitchell, Lincoln A. (2010). 'Engagement without Recognition: A New Strategy toward Abkhazia and Eurasia's Unrecognized States', *The Washington Quarterly*, 33:4, 59–73.

De Waal, Thomas (2010). 'Remaking the Nagorno-Karabakh Peace Process', *Survival*, 52:4, 159–176.

Di John, Jonathan (2010). 'The "Resource Curse": Theory and Evidence (ARI)', *Real Instituto Elcano*, 172, 1–7.

Egorova, Elizaveta and Babin, Ivan (2015). 'Eurasian Economic Union and the Difficulties of Integration: The Case of South Ossetia and Abkhazia', *The Quarterly Journal*, XIV:2, 87–97.

Fischer, Sabine (2016). 'Russian Policy in the Unresolved Conflicts', *in* Fischer, Sabine (ed.), *Not Frozen! The Unresolved Conflicts over Transnistria, Abkhazia, South Ossetia and Nagorno-Karabakh in Light of the Crisis over Ukraine.* Berlin: German Institute for International and Security Affairs.

Frear, Thomas (2014). 'The foreign policy options of a small unrecognised state: the case of Abkhazia', *Caucasus Survey*, 1:2, 83–107.

German, Tracey (2016). 'Russia and South Ossetia: conferring statehood or creeping annexation?', *Southeast European and Black Sea Studies*, 16:1, 155–167.

Gerrits, Andre W. M. and Bader, Max (2016). 'Russian patronage over Abkhazia and South Ossetia: implications for conflict resolution', *East European Politics*, 32:3, 297–313.

Glinkina, Svetlana P. and Rosenberg, Dorothy J. (2003). 'The Socioeconomic Roots of Conflict in the Caucasus', *Journal of International Development*, 15, 513–524.

Hoch, Tomáš (2011). 'EU Strategy towards Post-Soviet De Facto States', *Contemporary European Studies*, 2, 69–83.

Hoch, Tomaš, Souleimanov, Emil and Baranec, Tomaš (2014). 'Russia's role in the official peace process in South Ossetia', *Bulletin of Geography. Socio–economic Series*, 23, 53–71.

Kaldor, Mary (2001). *New and Old Wars*. Stanford: Stanford University Press.

Kaldor, Mary (2013). 'In Defence of New Wars', *Stability*, 2(1), 1–16.

Kanol, Direnç (2015). 'Tutelary Democracy in Unrecognized States', *EUL Journal of Social Sciences*, VI:I, 62–70.

Karagiannis, Emmanuel (2014). 'The Russian Interventions in South Ossetia and Crimea Compared: Military Performance, Legitimacy and Goals', *Contemporary Security Policy*, 35:3, 400–420.

Kelekhsayeva, Irina and Kucera, Joshua (2017). 'South Ossetia: Voters Opt Against the Kremlin Favorite', *Eurasianet*. Available at: http://www.eurasianet.org/node/83221. Last accessed: 19/05/2017.

King, Charles (2001) 'The Benefits of Ethnic War: Understanding Eurasia's Unrecognized States', *World Politics*, 53(4): 524–552.

Kirova, Iskra (2012). *Public Diplomacy and Conflict Resolution: Russia, Georgia and the EU in Abkhazia and South Ossetia*. Los Angeles: Figueroa Press.

Kolstø, Pål (2006). 'The Sustainability and Future of Unrecognized Quasi-States', *Journal of Peace Research*, 43:6, 723–740.

Kopeček, Vincenc (2016). 'Political institutions in the post-Soviet de facto states in comparison: Abkhazia and Nagorno-Karabakh', Czech Science Foundation under Grant 15–09249S, *De Facto States in Northern Eurasia in the Context of Russian Foreign Policy*. Available at: www.researchgate.net/profile/Vincenc_Kopecek/publication/310605579_Political_institutions_in_the_post-_Soviet_de_facto_states_in_comparison_Abkhazia_and_Nagorno-Karabakh/links/5833347b08ae102f07367f93.pdf. Last accessed: 09/12/2016.

Kopeček, Vincenc, Hoch, Tomaš and Baar, Vladimir (2016). 'De Facto States and Democracy: The Case of Abkhazia', *Bulletin of Geography. Socio–economic Series*, 32, 85–104.

Kropatcheva, Elena (2012). 'Russian foreign policy in the realm of European security through the lens of neoclassical realism', *Journal of Eurasian Studies*, 3, 30–40.

Lynch, Dov (2000). *Russian Peacekeeping Strategies in the CIS. The Cases of Moldova, Georgia and Tajikistan*. Basingstoke and London: Macmillan Press Ltd.

Lynch, Dov (2002). 'Separatist States and Post-Soviet Conflicts', *International Affairs*, 78:4, 831–848.

Lynch, Dov (2004). *Engaging Eurasia's Separatist States: Unresolved Conflicts and De Facto States*. Washington, D.C.: United States Institute of Peace Press.

Minasyan, Sergey (2017). 'The Nagorno-Karabakh conflict in the context of South Caucasus regional security issues: an Armenian perspective', *Nationalities Papers*, 45:1, 131–139.

Mychajlyszyn, Natalie (2001). 'The OSCE and Regional Conflicts in the Former Soviet Union', *Regional & Federal Studies*, 11:3, 194–219.

Newman, Edward (2004). 'The "New Wars" Debate: A Historical Perspective is Needed', *Security Dialogue*, 35:2, 173–185.

Ó Beacháin, Donnacha (2016). 'Elections and Nation-Building in Abkhazia', *in* Isaacs, Rico and Polese, Abel (eds), *Nation-Building and Identity in the Post-Soviet Space: New Tools and Approaches*. New York: Routledge.

Ó Beacháin, Donnacha, Comai, Giorgio and Tsurtsumia-Zurabashvili, Ann (2016). 'The secret lives of unrecognised states: internal dynamics, external relations, and counter-recognition strategies', *Small Wars & Insurgencies*, 27:3, 440–466.

O'Loughlin, John, Kolossov, Vladimir and Toal, Gerard (2014). 'Inside the post-Soviet de facto states: a comparison of attitudes in Abkhazia, Nagorny Karabakh, South Ossetia, and Transnistria', *Eurasian Geography and Economics*, 55:5, 423–456.

Pashayeva, Gulshan (2015). 'Security challenges and conflict resolution efforts in the South Caucasus', *in* European Policy Centre, *The South Caucasus: Between Integration and Fragmentation*. Available at: www.epc.eu/pub_details.php?cat_id=1&pub_id=5598. Last accessed: 09/12/2016.

Paul, Amanda (2015). 'The EU and the South Caucasus – time for a stocktake', *in* European Policy Centre, *The South Caucasus: Between Integration and Fragmentation*. Available at: www.epc.eu/pub_details.php?cat_id=1&pub_id=5598. Last accessed: 09/12/2016.

Petro, Nicolai N. (2008). 'Legal Case for Russian Intervention in Georgia', *Fordham International Law Journal*, 32:5, 1524–1549.

Popescu, Nicu (2007). 'Europe's Unrecognised Neighbours: The EU in Abkhazia and South Ossetia', CEPS Working Documents, No. 260. Available at http://ssrn.com/abstract=1338024. Last accessed: 15/10/2016.

Prelz Oltramonti, Giulia (2015). 'The political economy of a de facto state: the importance of local stakeholders in the case of Abkhazia', *Caucasus Survey*, 3:3, 291–308.

Relitz, Sebastian (2016). 'De facto States in the European Neighbourhood: Between Russian Domination and European (dis)Engagement. The Case of Abkhazia', EURINT Proceedings. Available at: http://cse.uaic.ro/eurint/proceedings/index_htm_files/EURINT2016EURINT2016_REL.pdf. Last accessed: 18/05/2017.

Renner, Michael (2002). 'The Anatomy of Resource Wars', World Watch Paper No. 162. Washington, D.C.: World Watch Institute.

Simão, Licínia (2012). 'The problematic role of EU democracy promotion in Armenia, Azerbaijan and Nagorno-Karabakh', *Communist and Post-Communist Studies*, 45, 193–200.

Shelest, Hanna (2016). 'The Prospects of the European Union Mediation and Peacekeeping in the Eastern Partnership', *CES Working Papers*, VIII:3, 473–487.

Stewart, E. J. (2008). 'Restoring EU-OSCE Cooperation for Pan-European Conflict Prevention', *Contemporary Security Policy*, 29:2, 266–284.

Tarkhan Mouravi, George (2016). 'External Political Actors and Influences in the South Caucasus', *Sociology and Anthropology*, 4:8, 698–709.

Tolstrup, Jakob (2009). 'Studying a negative external actor: Russia's management of stability and instability in the 'Near Abroad''', *Democratization*, 16:5, 922–944.

Voller, Yaniv (2015). 'Contested sovereignty as an opportunity: understanding democratic transitions in unrecognized states', *Democratization*, 22:4, 610–630.

Von Steinsdorff, Silvia (2012). 'Incomplete state building – incomplete democracy? How to interpret internal political development in the post-Soviet de facto states. Conclusion', *Communist and Post-Communist Studies*, 45, 201–206.

Von Steinsdorff, Silvia and Fruhstorfer, Anna (2012). 'Post-Soviet de facto states in search of internal and external legitimacy. Introduction', *Communist and Post-Communist Studies*, 45, 117–121.

Whitman, Richard G. and Wolff, Stefan (2010). 'The EU as a conflict manager? The case of Georgia and its implications', *International Affairs*, 86:1, 87–107.

Wiharta, Sharon, Melvin, Neil and Avezov, Xenia (2012). 'The New Geopolitics of Peace Operations: Mapping the Emerging Landscape', *SIPRI*. Available at www.sipri.org/research/conflict/pko/other_publ/NGP-Policy-Report.pdf. Last accessed: 15/10/2016.

4 Transformation policies and local modernisation initiatives in the North Caucasus[1]

V.A. Kolosov, O.I. Vendina, A.A. Gritsenko, M.V. Zotova, O.B. Glezer, A.A. Panin, A.B. Sebentsov and V.N. Streletskii

Introduction

The North Caucasus is characterised by ethnopolitical and territorial conflict, economic crisis, social turbulence, and growing Islamic influence. Processes that are under way in the North Caucasian republics are described in terms of both "modernisation" and "demodernisation".[2] Practically all regional elites emphasise the uniqueness of "their" republics, but the federal authorities, on the contrary, strive to depart from the asymmetry of relations, seeing the solution to the problem in a wider use of unified and politically neutral approaches to development.

This chapter is focused on the analysis of processes that adapt the undertaken reforms to regional specifics, and on the symbiosis of the results of self-organisation of the population and federal and regional innovations. A number of stories related to administrative policy in the North Caucasus follow a brief analysis of the demographic situation in the region, which is viewed as a challenge, simultaneously creating opportunities for development and amplifying social instability. The chapter also maps successful private-enterprise economic projects in the North Caucasus Federal District (NCFD) and Stavropol krai. It focuses on the causes that hinder the expansion and viability of modernisation processes in North Caucasus society and emphasises their noneconomic nature. It shows that the universal mechanisms of socioeconomic development (federal subsidies and direct investments in infrastructure and public services, public-private partnerships in large projects, the creation of new well-paid jobs, and so on) are insufficient to solve local problems. Tailor-made strategies are required, involving not only investments and institutions but also measures of indirect influence resting on shared values. In conclusion, the paper provides recommendations that (in the authors' opinion) could help overcome the gap between the economic and sociocultural modernisation of society, thereby facilitating the development of the North Caucasus.

The demographic situation: crucial transformations

The asynchrony and intensity of demographic changes in the NCFD republics and Stavropol krai contributed to the escalation of interregional contradictions. *First*, economic development and the region's labour market clearly did not match the NCFD's demographic potential. For the North Caucasus republics, characterised by high birth rates and young age structures, this became a source of instability and "negative selection" in the population as a result of the outflow of the most educated and professionally trained youth to other regions of the country and abroad. At the same time, young people found a way out by turning to radical forms of Islam.[3]

Second, intensive migration processes, which favour population restructuring and replacement, have led to change not only in ethnic composition but also in habitual economic patterns. The mass migration of the Russian population from the republics of the North Caucasus resulted in the outflow of competences, the simplification of the economic structure, and personnel problems. The inflow of immigrants from Dagestan into the steppes of Stavropol krai contributed to the spread of distant-pasture cattle raising there, putting competitive pressure on other forms of farming and leading to the degradation of grazing areas and hayfields.[4] The region provides many examples of economic conflicts associated with the changing population mix.

Third, the ethno-cultural diversity of the population on the plains increased significantly, primarily in large cities and their suburbs. This is true not only in Stavropol krai, where the share of Russians decreased, but also in the republics, where the natural habitats of indigenous peoples in the lowlands became blurred, and urbanisation led to the challenges of multiculturalism. Socio-demographic processes acquired ethno-political aspects, which, in turn, began to be used as arguments in the struggle for limited economic resources, primarily land, and access to investments.

Thus, as a crucial driving force of deep political, social, and economic transformations, demographic processes reinforced the demand for a regional policy that would account for the specifics and internal diversity of the region. Combined with the post-socialist industrial crisis, rapid urbanisation, particularly in the eastern part of the region, and the massive inflow of villagers into the cities provoked, on the one hand, a tendency towards counter-modernisation, especially in the 1990s. On the other hand, it brought former rural inhabitants in contact with contemporary social institutions, creating intricate mosaics of the modern and the traditional.

Islamic vs. socioeconomic modernisation

In the post-Soviet years, all religious confessions represented in the NCFD went through a renaissance. Today, for the overwhelming majority of the region's Russian population, their confessional affiliation is almost as important as it is for peoples who profess Islam. The principal difference lies in the fact that only an insignificant minority of Orthodox believers observe the main religious precepts: taking the sacrament, confession, and regularly praying in church. The situation looks different among the Islamic population. Although in the Soviet period most of the autochthonous population of the North Caucasus departed from religious practice, Islam remained culturally important: the "Islamic" and "popular" were inseparable. In Kabardino-Balkaria and Karachay-Cherkessia, people brought up in the Islamic tradition continued to observe Muslim customs and rites without perceiving them as religious, while in Dagestan and Checheno-Ingushetia Muslim communities continued to function informally in Soviet years as well.[5, 6] After the USSR collapsed, Islam started to be seen as a major cultural component of a reviving society.[7] While Orthodoxy sought to "return to tradition," Islam showed the road to the future, associated with a rearrangement of society based on Islamic principles. The Russian lexicon expanded to include new concepts such as *fundamentalism*, *Salafism*, and *Wahhabism*. In a context of religious revival, neither the population of the North Caucasus nor their spiritual advisers seemed ready for the critical assessment of their ideas superimposed by Islamic authorities from Arabic countries—carriers of the "pure" faith, free from ethnocultural juxtapositions and Soviet influences.

The growing influence of Islamic precepts and preachers on the life of the North Caucasian population provokes sharp discussion in the scientific community. Some point to the danger that comes from religious radicalism; others highlight Islam's integrating potential; still others stress dissent in the Islamic *ummah* and preachers; and yet others emphasise the discrepancy between the declared degree of people's religiosity and their actual religious conduct.[8] In fact, the *Hajj* is an indicator of success; and in rural communities, religious precepts are perceived as part of tradition. People prefer to define themselves simply as a "believer" and not as "faithful", i.e. strictly following religious prescriptions.[9] In Karachay-Cherkessia, there are 90 percent of the former; in Kabardino-Balkaria, 66 percent; in Ingushetia, 79 percent; and in Dagestan, 64 percent. Chechnya stands out against this background; Islam plays the role of official religion there, but even in Chechnya, one-third of the population does not observe the required precepts.

The main concern is that the most active growth in adherents of the "new" Islam involves young people. In fact, this reflects a gap between the generations. While the older generation regarded religious rites as popular customs, their "children," on the contrary, tend to see traditional rites as religious rituals.

The Islamic "renaissance" in the North Caucasus has thus brought to light the correlation between religious and ethnic identities. Each of them stands for a system of values, supported by external authoritative forces, deeply incorporated into the internal social structures of North Caucasus society. One of these is the state, responsible for the economy, security, and social well-being; another is religious institutions, concerned with the spiritual state of society. Each of these forces obeys its own legal system and provides society with its own model of development. Although the end goals are clearly defined in each case—full integration into the Islamic world, or into Russia's political and economic system—the boundaries of social preferences are blurred. It is practically impossible for many inhabitants of the republics of the North Caucasus to make an unambiguous choice in favour of a secular or a religious society.[10] However, the presence of "two pillars" does not foster stability. The self-determination of ethnic groups, unlike that of religious ones, is closely related to the institutions of the secular state, supposedly an important agent of modernisation in the region, recognizing the pluralism of North Caucasus society as its major characteristic. Several generations have grown up with this idea. As a result, in spite of widespread respect for religion, the ideas of a theocratic (Islamic) state, "Muslim brotherhood", or even an increased role of Islam in the economy, education, and management encounter opposition in the NCFD republics. As the foundation of the value system of the secular state, ethnocultural pluralism makes not only the state but also the prospects for local development dependent on ethno-political relations and sentiments in society. Therefore, it is important to understand how people evaluate their prospects in life.

The North Caucasus: a traditional or contemporary society?

Unlike regions with a predominantly Russian population (such as the Stavropol krai), where social order is established through norms and values, in the republics of the North Caucasus, traditions, customs and family ties act as sociocultural regulators. This distinction is the source of North Caucasian traditionalism and a marked trend in its archaisation.[11] However, school education, the system of social security, new living standards, fashion, television, technological innovations, and Soviet bureaucratic practices have remained; the norms of common law, while still relevant, were pushed aside by national legislation. Urbanisation played a large role, as it favoured individualism and the appearance of people who do not follow religious precepts. The stratum of the secular intelligentsia grew considerably. It is also impossible to overlook the role of migrations, education, and work in other Russian regions and abroad, as well as constant contacts with other cultural realms. The traditions themselves have evolved: many things that are seen today as a legacy of the past are just as much a response to a changing context. Therefore, the traditionalism of the North Caucasus should be analysed within the context of a society aware of the depth of the modernisation challenge and the uncertainty of its future. In order to confirm or invalidate this thesis, it is important to understand the interplay of traditional and contemporary ideas in the behaviour of people, and whether the nature of that interplay is chaotic, as is typical of archaisation, or meets the requirements of development and modernisation.

To this end, a series of in-depth interviews and group discussions were conducted in 2015 in the Republic of Dagestan. It is the largest republic in terms of population and economic potential, and includes all the characteristics of the North Caucasus, comprising the largest urban agglomeration of the region (Makhachkala) and isolated peripheral districts, high mountains still populated by about 30 percent of its inhabitants, and densely populated plains, with foci of modernisation and impoverished agricultural areas. In multi-ethnic Dagestan, contradictions between the groups that have traditionally lived on the plains and in the mountains are particularly sharp.

One of the interviews took place in Kusumkent, a poor village, far removed from large urban centres, abandoned by its younger population; another discussion was held in the village of Tuybe, part of the Makhachkala agglomeration. Two focus groups were conducted in Makhachkala: one with "recent" and the other with "native-born" Makhachkala citizens, including the intelligentsia. The totality of the above sets of respondents cannot, of course, be considered a representative sample of the Dagestani population, but all these people, one way or another, are involved in modernisation processes. This enables us to generalise their statements and compare them with some important parameters of contemporary and traditional societies.

Family and society

In all the *loci* that we chose, respondents stressed the paramount importance of family and family ties as institutions that largely affect human fate, social mobility, and potential careers. As a rule, a person could name several generations of ancestors. The number of relatives in one generation could reach 500; however, no more than 15–20 people can be categorised as "close" relatives. The family is responsible not only for an individual's relationship with the past but also for her/his integration into society. Family and social status are interchangeable.

Nevertheless, closeness is determined not only by the degree of relationship but also by interpersonal relations. Altruism and mutual aid have been displaced by mercantilism and clientelism. In lowland cities and villages, where people of various origins live, ancestral differences blend. Urbanisation contributes to the reduction of the number of children and family size: having one child is not a violation of the norm. In contacts with the external world, the common Dagestani identity is important for all. People feel a sense of community, that they are part of a big state entrusted with the obligation to care for everyone.

The sense of belonging to society through the mediation of family and kindred ties manifests itself explicitly when assessing the republic's prospects for development. Local communities actively participate in discussions on projects and investments, periodically blocking actions of the authorities and lobbying in favour of local or ethnic group interests. Pluralism, which is based on ethnic diversity and group solidarity, does not allow for a single ruling clan to emerge and encourages the promotion of meritocratic principles in appointing public figures.

Mobility

At first sight, Dagestani society appears to have limited mobility. People who live in the republic rarely change their places of residence and seldom travel. Interviewees point to their involvement in family and kindred relations as the key factors behind their limited mobility.

On the other hand, natives of Dagestan live practically in all regions of Russia and abroad. Sociological studies show that half of the population of the North Caucasus republics have relatives living outside of their territories. For Dagestan, this share is 60 percent.[12] The republic and its diaspora maintain close contact; both parts of society—the "settled" and the "mobile"—act in common, ensuring the existence of a single community, its reproduction and renewal. This requires the mastering of numerous contemporary practices: the Internet, mobile communications, banking services, air travel, and others, which considerably change people's attitudes. Thus, in Kusumkent, even elderly people spoke about the importance of access to the Internet. Thanks to contacts with relatives, the village does not look like a place stuck in the past. The inhabitants of Makhachkala do not differ from those of Kusumkent in their habit of using new technologies in accessing information, but, rather, in their preference for bank loans over personal loans from relatives. This drastically differs from traditional forms of financial support, where the "sponsor" is the clan, obliged to prevent its members from falling into distress.

Education

No one questions the worth and necessity of education. It is mentioned as a priority, equal for one's respect to elders and responsibility. Higher education is acknowledged as compulsory for young men and very desirable for young women. Education is seen as a capital investment that increases the worthiness of a fiancée in the eyes of the fiancé's family. A diploma also endows a woman with greater independence in selecting her husband. Young men are free to choose their profession. For women, the socially approved choice is narrowed down to subjects such as medicine and pedagogy. Knowledge gained counts immensely in preparation for motherhood. Despite the growing interest in religion, a secular education is preferred. The main source of acquiring knowledge is school, then family, the "street," the Internet, and, finally, the mosque: *"The mosque is not for knowledge but for the right spiritual attitude."* Muslim clothing, as a rule, is not worn in school, although there are exceptions. In Kusumkent, this is a question of familial religiosity; in Tyube and Makhachkala, it is rather presented as a matter of fashion.

Success

The question of who counts as a successful person aimed at comparing the answers of Dagestan's citizens with the value scale of modernity. Connecting success with material wealth would favour the values of "survival" in

84   *V.A. Kolosov et al.*

traditional society, and a relationship with personal self-realisation would favour the values of "self-expression" and modernity. The answers obtained were ambiguous. During the group discussions, no one spoke about the importance of wealth, although demonstrative wealth is what perhaps surprises one the most in the Caucasus; neither did anyone claim that money is of no interest. Also, no one ever mentioned personal self-realisation, although a concern for children "*being able to feel competitive*" and having "*the opportunity to unlock their potential*" was cited among the motivations for migrating to Moscow and St. Petersburg. At the same time, everyone noted that connections and networks remained the main keys to success. These could originate from the clan, neighbours, communities, friends or colleagues, and rely on either pragmatic motives and material transfers, or on the call of duty and responsibility. The same people complained that "*a young person without connections will never find a job*," and stated that "*the right specialist can be hired without any connections.*" Respondents stressed that connections are not only opportunities that people use but also obligations that they bear. A man without connections was seen as a "loser."

Success in life is seen as being achieved through the appointment to a prestigious position, one which guarantees material well-being, social recognition, and authority among relatives. For instance, ideally high positions should be occupied by professionally trained specialists, who have achieved success thanks to personal qualities and efforts. Army service is also seen as a road to success. If, during the final years of the Soviet Union, people paid to avoid military service, now they pay to be drafted, because conscription from the North Caucasus regions is limited, and, without the experience of military service, it is impossible to become a law enforcement officer. In the eyes of society, personal social status is crucial, and its visual manifestation is the construction of a private home, a process which can last for decades. Women who make their living independently in other regions of Russia also channel their efforts into building a house, and leave their children with their mothers and grandmothers.

Customs and traditions

Eric Hobsbawm stressed the difference between customs and traditions, believing that the former evolve with changing life conditions, while the latter, on the contrary, represent fixed practices.[13] The stories of our respondents illustrate this thesis, with weddings providing the most vivid example. The essence of this rite lies in fostering the connectedness of society. Weddings bring the whole family together and help keep track of its composition. This is a holiday for all, the rich and the poor, the young and the old, the members of a family and clan; it is a fair of fiancés and fiancées, a place to draw agreements and solicit approval from the older members of the *tukkhum*, as well as a parade of children. The number of guests at a wedding varies greatly and is an indicator of a family's capabilities and influence.

Wedding "technologies" have modernised in the post-Soviet years. Before, weddings, either rural or urban, were celebrated in gardens; now they are performed in specialised ceremonial complexes, which offer catering, music, decorations, and so on. A two-day wedding ritual, held separately in the fiancée's and fiancé's homes, is often considered above a common holiday, limited to one day. In times past, everything necessary for a wedding was provided by the celebrators themselves; now, this is done by specialised firms. Such innovations reflect the imitation and not the observance of traditions; at the same time, several genuinely novel and stable practices have emerged.

First, the institution of patriarchal collectivism "by birth" has been supplemented by a contemporary collectivism "by workplace." The extension of the custom of "calling all to the wedding" to staff members has been combined with corporate ethics, which assume selective communication. Young people can also invite their friends from outside the family circle.

Second, all the respondents mentioned the increased popularity of alcohol-free weddings and the ambiguity of this tradition, which undermines intergenerational links and makes the observance of ancestral experiences impossible.

Third, money has become a routine wedding gift. Before, cash gifts to the newlyweds reflected the closeness of relations within a family; today this is the preferred and least burdensome form of gift. This shift entails a blurring of boundaries within family relations and a transition from the mutual exchanges typical of traditional society, to material and monetary exchanges, which helps cover wedding-related expenses.

Future

The idea that *"Dagestan's future is in its past,"* which would be expected to find support if people had been backward-looking, was interpreted in very different ways during the focus groups. For some, it meant a return to the experience of one's ancestors; for others, a nostalgia for Brezhnev's times; for others still, it stood as a reminder of the republic's economic deterioration since the end of the Soviet period. The idea of *"innovative breakthroughs"* met no support. The majority agreed that quick reforms, which might have come from Moscow, were undesirable. The development model implemented by Chechnya was also assessed without enthusiasm, despite a positive evaluation of changes in the neighbouring republic. The reason for rejecting the Chechen scenario does not lie in the fact that foul means are used there (the *order* set by Ramzan Kadyrov appears attractive because it appears stable and free from endless struggles between political clans), but in the pluralism and multiethnicity of Dagestani society. For "new" Muslims, Arab theocracies provide the model. For those who seek jobs or education in a spiritually kindred environment, it is secular Turkey; for those who strive for modern life, it is Western Europe and North America. No one opposed Dagestan's presence within Russia: the Dagestani people's visions of the future were linked to the Russian Federation.

86 *V.A. Kolosov et al.*

The survey has shown that the real life of people in Dagestan is a continuous chain of transitions from traditional forms of behaviour to modern ones and the convergence, not interexclusion, of worldviews. This has been interpreted elsewhere as implying a *disorientation of traditional society*, resulting in human social reactions becoming chaotic. Yet this interpretation raises doubts, because the importance of development, as a process implying personal efforts, growth in social mobility and well-being, is acknowledged by respondents. The definition of Dagestani society as "*transitional*" is equally dubious: the past (also seen as the future) takes pride of place, thereby guaranteeing the reproduction of a common identity, at the level of either the ethnic group or the republic of Dagestan. In fact, the model presented by categories of "new" Islam competes with images of the Western world. A return to the bosom of religion after a long period of state atheism is attractive to many, since it helps mark the succession of the past and the future. At the same time, absolute claims that undermine the authority of elders, and the depreciation of local customs are rejected.

Unsolved economic problems: what is the way out?

The land issue

The North Caucasus suffers from a combination of land scarcity and agrarian overpopulation. Besides, land here not only has economic but also symbolic value. The concepts of *ancestral lands* and *traditional land use rights* did not lose here their legislative meaning and were reactivated after the liquidation of the *kolkhoz–sovkhoz* system. Different groups of interests—from local authorities and businesses to ethnic and rural communities (*jamias*)—included in the process of redistribution of land resources developed various strategies for resolving the land issue.

A share privatisation was conducted in Stavropol krai and, partially, the North Caucasus republics; however, a fully fledged institution of land ownership and land market have not formed here. Land shares that existed on paper were not allotted on the ground, as everywhere in Russia. The incompleteness of privatisation led to a decrease in the value of "paper shares", their mass accumulation by former and acting officials and property redistribution. In many cases, former *kolkhozes* were transformed into new enterprises and local inhabitants, former share owners, became hired employees. As a result, several large vertically integrated agribusiness holding companies appeared, which specialised in the production of grain and flour and invested considerable funds into local agriculture's modernisation, infrastructure and diversification of sales channels. At the same time, they created some successful smaller farms usually specialised in cattle raising and horticulture.[14]

However, this scenario was implemented only in fertile areas where the situation in agriculture has been relatively favourable since the Soviet era. The

Transformation and local modernisation 87

rest of the territory survived economic degradation. The undervalued "paper" shares depreciated their worth as financial instruments to pledge loans for small business development and as necessary land improvements to maintain land fertility. The absence of a fully fledged land market led to the formation of a share market, where the right to acquire a rent for land use was offered for sale. A "share rent" was formed, which became a way of turning paper rights into cash. This land-use system provoked a progressive depletion of farmlands. An especially alarming situation occurred in the plains of Dagestan (Nogai district) on the border on Stavropol krai, where irrigable lands were being desertified and salinised as a result of the degradation of the irrigation ditch system.

The authorities are aware of this acute problem. Since 2009, Russia has been introducing an automated farmland accounting and control system, which is being trialled in Krasnodar krai. It is assumed that similar work on inventorying and monitoring the land fund will be conducted in Stavropol krai.

In the mountainous republics of the North Caucasus, the situation developed differently. Here, an administrative veto on land privatisation was introduced practically at once on plain and foothill territories. This was caused by both interethnic contradictions (each people claimed its own ethnic lands), and economic factors. The seasonal nature of distant-pasture cattle raising required the availability of winter pastures in the mountains and valleys. In Soviet times, *kolkhozes* in the mountains received their *kutan*[15] lands in the valleys, and kolkhozes in the valleys acquired hayfields and pastures in the mountains. The dissolution of *kolkhozes* provoked a sharp conflict of interests. The maps of winter and summer pastures assigned to *kolkhozes* became the basis for claiming rights of collective and private ownership.

The moratorium imposed on land privatisation and land transfers to the category of republican property froze the conflict of interests but led to the emergence of "sovereigns" represented by administrations with the pre-emptive right to redistribute land resources. Ex-managers of collective farms usually affiliated with the authorities became long-term land tenants. Parts of these lands are operated by new agribusinesses that rely on republican and federal support programmes. The remaining lands are subleased to local farmers under less favourable conditions. All this rouses discontent among local inhabitants. It is hard to call the existing economic system stable, despite of few foci of modernisation, because a change of administration or disloyal actions of large tenants lead, as a rule, to land rearrangement.

The Chechen Republic represents a special case. In addition to the moratorium on land privatisation, which predetermined the transformation of collective farms into public and municipal enterprises, the factor of minefields left after hostilities is important here: their area in the republic's plains is estimated at 1500 ha.

The land issue has also become a major problem when adopting economic development programmes that envisage the allocation of plots for residential development and the creation of new investment sites. In many cases, this has led to ethnopolitical conflict. The Kumyks and Nogais of Dagestan opposed the "divestment of their ethnic lands" (in Uchkent, Manaskent, and Kyakhulyai), appealing to the threat of "destruction" of their ethnic culture as the result of its erosion by an "alien" population. The Balkars (in Bezengi and Elbrus) raised an outcry against transferring "their" lands to the construction of a ski resort, justifying this with cultural arguments as well. The inhabitants of the suburban Kumyk village of Tarki did not agree to its inclusion into the limits of Makhachkala; neither did the Balkar villages of Belaya Rechka and Khasan'ya agree with their inclusion into the limits of Nal'chik. We can add a tangle of unresolved problems associated with the deportation and repatriation of peoples in Soviet times and migrations, which led to radical transformations in the ethnic composition of the population.

Unlike in lowland and foothill territories of the North Caucasus, the solution to the land issue in mountainous areas acquired new forms. When rural communities had transformed into *jamias*, the *local restitution of land ownership rights* occurred under Sharia law with the participation of the imam. In some cases, lands were distributed "by inheritance" or "by lot". Restitution, which rarely agrees with Russian legislation, also generated numerous conflicts, since lands could simultaneously be considered the property of a rural or tribal community, a family, or an ethnic group. Meanwhile, the leaders of the *jamias* show great interest in managing the local economy; this does not always elicit the support of the population, which prefers them not to participate in such administrative matters. The local authorities and, in a number of cases, the few surviving *kolkhozes* in the persons of their managers compete with *jamias* in economic and social influence in their districts and settlements. This struggle results in a "squeezing" of one private business by another, and the consequent destruction of the existing economy.

The cumulative effect of the above factors has led to the polarisation of the land use system in the North Caucasus: it is dominated by either large producers or personal subsidiary farms.[16] Most experts agree that, without the formation of a fully fledged institution of land ownership and its legislative and infrastructural support on the part of the government, the land issue will remain a factor that will constantly destabilise the situation.

Financial basis and the shadow economy

At first glance, the North Caucasus can seem a dynamic and intensively developing region, although burdened with numerous problems. Statistically it is a very poor, backward, and subsidised periphery. One of the causes of the inconsistency in evaluations is the extreme polarisation of the situation in the entire NCFD, as well as inside its republics. According to official statistics, in 2012–2014 the share of federal transfers in the budgets of the North Caucasus republics varied from 56 percent in Kabardino-Balkaria and North Ossetia-Alania to 81–85 percent in Chechnya and Ingushetia. In Stavropol krai, this indicator was about 30 percent.[17] The existing situation is usually explained by the region's poor economic development, the insufficiency of the taxation

Transformation and local modernisation   89

base, the undervaluation of taxable property, the inefficiency of tax and payment collection, and the presence of tax benefits. However, the above facts also characterise the majority of Russian regions. Nevertheless, the total per capita tax and nontax incomes there, as a rule, are between two to four times higher than in all the NCFD republics. Only Stavropol krai achieves the national average.

The same striking differences exist in the structure of tax revenues as well. The basis for the consolidated budgets of the Russian federal subjects (about 70 percent of tax and nontax incomes) comprises three taxes—corporate profit tax, personal income tax (PIT), and property tax. As a rule, the revenues from profit tax are higher than those from property tax (in oil-and-gas producing regions, more than twice as much), and their total contribution to the regional budget exceeds the PIT share. The situation in the NCFD is the opposite: with a small absolute size of the PIT, its share exceeds two-thirds of budgetary tax incomes. In 2014, the PIT share was 82 percent in the Chechen Republic and about 40 percent in Stavropol krai.[18]

The republics see this situation as negative: the PIT is mainly collected from budgetary organisations. The closed circulation of budgetary funds is unable to secure economic growth even under conditions where the per capita incomes of consolidated budgets of the North Caucasus regions, taking into account the federal transfers, are at a level typical for the Russian regions, 30,000–50,000 rubles per person (about €600 to €1,000 according to the average weighted 2014 exchange rate). The main way out is seen in the development of the tax base. Chechnya dreams of recovering its oil-producing and oil-refining industries. Other republics speak more about the development of tourism, commercial agriculture, and the processing industry. All projects bump into the shortage of investments, marketing difficulties, and the supply of raw materials for production.

However, the underdevelopment of the tax base is just the tip of the iceberg of the NCFD republics' problems. The local experts whom we questioned confirmed that, if economic activity, from renting property (land plots, buildings, and apartments) to the operation of large businesses, had come out of the shadows, the PIT share in the republican budgets would have decreased to the level of Stavropol krai. The attitude to tax evasion is ambivalent in the region.

First, it is stressed that business plays an active role in the economic development of the republics, despite its weak effect on the formation of regional budgets. Money goes not into the budget but into a new business project. *Second*, business is an important employer, even if we speak about "shadow" hiring. In an excess-labour region, like the North Caucasus, employment without labour contracts and payments to social and pension funds is seen as a lesser evil than real unemployment, especially among the young. The population trades on this situation by working and simultaneously drawing unemployment compensation.

The same ambiguous situation exists in the case of property taxes. The issues of land ownership, land surveys, and the inclusion of land-plots into

90 V.A. Kolosov et al.

the public register have not been resolved in any of the NCFD subjects. The population does not strive to register property, let alone to pay property taxes. *First*, there is a problem with the current owners of homes and surrounding grounds: one person may own several homes where various members of the family clan live. *Second*, traditionally, the youngest son inherits the parental home, but, as long as the parents are alive, any other family members may live in it, while the youngest son may, for example, have moved to Moscow or Tyumen. In addition, it can be the eldest son who has built the home for his parents. Clashes arising between compliance with Russian legislation and tradition lead to the protraction of property registration. In the case of land plots, especially in suburban districts, the situation is even more complex due to the collision of not only family but also intergroup interests (clan, ethnic, and so on). *Finally*, a modest rent received from letting property, rather than incomes or savings, often functions as a financial "safety cushion" for the population, and, as a rule, is used for daily needs. Therefore, a rent decrease as a result of paying property tax is perceived as a reduction of current living standards.

The policy of "reconciliation" with the shadow economy and tax evasion when resolving tactical problems (mitigating social tension, increasing personal incomes, minimising costs, and so on) drives the NCFD regions into a strategic trap, securing their reputation as financially dependent on federal transfers, and unattractive for investments. The preservation of high unemployment indicators with a high level of self-employment and low indicators of tax revenues under lively business activities create the wrong idea of the potential and internal resources for modernisation and development.

"Anchor" investment projects

In the past decade, federal policy in the North Caucasus has aimed at compensating for the consequences of the Chechen wars, eliminating destabilising factors, gaining the social support of the population, and stimulating modernisation and economic growth. Major criticisms vis-à-vis the policy conducted on the part of Russian and international experts pertained to its costliness, unrealistic project implementation timeframes, institutional problems, and conflicts between local businesses and large investors.[19] From 2012 through 2014, the region's investment portfolio numbered over 30 projects in the agroindustrial complex, tourism, the manufacture of building materials, small-scale power generation, and transport infrastructure, totaling 1.2 trillion rubles. Potential investors and conditions and scope of government support were assigned to each project (Figure 4.1). Special attention was given to the tourism–recreation cluster—the resorts of Arkhyz, Veduchi, Elbrus-Bezengi, Mamison, Lagonaki, Matlasu, Tsori, the Caspian coast, and the Caucasian Mineralnye Vody Region.

Transformation and local modernisation 91

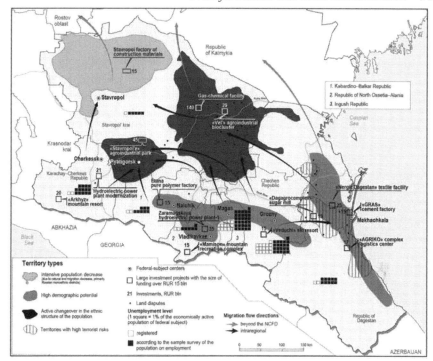

Figure 4.1 "Anchor" investment projects in the North Caucasus

When making decisions on whether to include projects into the investment programme, experts faced a number of problems. First, there was the low quality of project preparation in the activity of regional lobbies, who wished to obtain government guarantees to implement their own business interests. Second, there was the uncertainty with the land issue and the absence of the necessary land-cadaster documents. For example, in Dombai, a mountain resort actively developed back in Soviet times, no legally "pure" land plot was found; therefore, when selecting priority projects, the decision was made in favour of Arkhyz. However, strong resistance sprang up there among the local population, who traditionally engaged in cattle grazing. Third, there was the underdevelopment of the institutional framework, and the strong dependence of investors on personal arrangements and the interests of regional and municipal administrations.

Contrary to expectations, the population did not support large investments. The local elites started actively to implement them, seeing the priority of local development in them, which created problems for local small businesses. Many local entrepreneurs associate their dissatisfaction with the current state of "their" affairs with nonmarket competition and administrative protectionism. The local entrepreneurs, as well as inhabitants, fear that large players will

92   V.A. Kolosov et al.

move them to the background As a result, the expected investments yield an unexpected effect: they slow down social "lifts" and provoke social tension and population outflows.

Criticising the approach to the development of the North Caucasus used by the federal authorities and large businesses, many experts justifiably point to the need to build the local population and business into the process of forming investment clusters, and to take account of land and clan relations. This thesis, however, has not been elaborated in detail. It is totally unclear how to combine the ideology of transparency, which is the basis of public–private partnerships, and traditional practices based on corruption and privileged relations. However, the experience of large projects implemented successfully in the North Caucasus (for example, the Derways automobile factory in Karachay–Cherkesia) demonstrates the abandonment of traditional clan relations and the use of current social practices. It matches some well-known provisions of modernisation theory – on the one hand, a possibility of partial modernisation embracing only some sectors of economy and specific strata of society, and on another hand, the need for flexible social structures and social context necessary for adopting technological innovations as a condition of modernisation.[20]

Local development and obstacles to its progress

In the post-Soviet years, private initiative played a prominent role in the region's development, except in Chechnya, where government investments were still the main source of funding. Clusters developed in rural districts and specialised in the commodity production of grains, vegetables (cabbage, potatoes, onions, tomatoes), fruits (apricots, grapes), and honey; bull-calf fattening; and raising sheep and poultry. Numerous manufacturing units and workshops appeared in the cities, producing footwear, furniture, and clothing (Figure 4.2). These clusters are based on small "informal" family businesses. They contribute to the growth of well-being, the creation of new industries, and the modernisation of existing businesses; in other words, they contribute to solving strategic problems set at the federal level. These clusters fostered new competences in the field of agrarian technologies, as well as marketing; but, most importantly, they favoured an entrepreneurial environment, open to innovations and potentially capable of propelling economic development in the entire region. This is quite comparable with enterprises in some areas of northeastern and central Italy that have become the global centres of production of a number of high-quality consumer goods.

The development of clusters encourages optimism as most experts regard support for local businesses as the way out of economic stagnation. However, this is open to doubt. Success stories involved primarily private backyards, small-scale production, or the service sphere, and have not transformed into regional development. A model under which a small producer invests his labour and receives an income but does not pay taxes and transfers economic

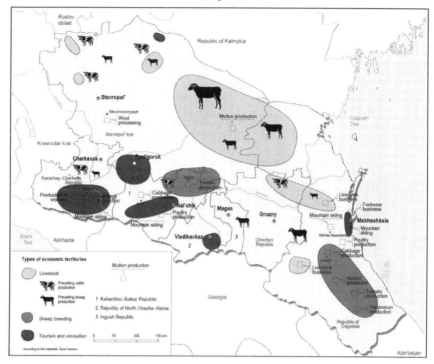

Figure 4.2 Nodal modernisation in the North Caucasus

risks and infrastructural problems to government bodies is very fragile and vulnerable. Social guarantees are lacking; the competitiveness of products is weak; incomes are often of a seasonal nature, vary greatly depending on a changing demand and do not yield a multiplicative effect. This is reflected in the indicators of socioeconomic development of the NCFD: the region counts among the major laggards in the Russian Federation and, at the same time, stands out for its massive shadow economy. In fact, local agents of development, even if they succeed, take into account only their personal or group interests. This is encouraged by:

- *ethnic mobilisation*, which does not allow "outsiders" to enter into one's own territories;
- *competition between secular and religious systems of values*: alternative ideas of the region's future affect the nature of economic relations and business rules;
- a *multitude of de facto legal systems ("polyjuridism")*: simultaneous use of Russian legislation, *adats*, and sharia, to which the population resorts depending on the situation;
- *absence of cooperation* in solving the problems of territorial development;

94   *V.A. Kolosov et al.*

- *low level of interpersonal trust;*
- *grassroots and top-level corruption.*

This study shows that practically everywhere the logic of economic rationality, which presupposes the creation of an attractive and transparent environment for business, is at odds with the regional culture and traditions. The standard tools of modernisation (the creation of new jobs, the increase in the educational level, the quality of life, and so on) are not sufficient in these conditions. Tailor-made strategies are required not only to invest in the material sphere or human capital, but also to affect the values shared by people. We discuss hereafter the key factors affecting any development projects in the North Caucasus.

The most severe problem of the North Caucasus is corruption, which has become an integral part of the way of life and has turned into a "regulator" of social relations. Grassroots corruption is widespread in education, health care, and public and municipal services. It is considered impolite to reject a relative's request, for example, to help pass an examination or enter a higher educational institution if one has levers of influence. People use their connections to illegally produce documents entitling them to various public benefits (disability benefits, maternity capital, and so on). Corruption is not only connected to budgetary transfers from the federal centre;[21] it also develops through any human contact with the administration. It is difficult and in some cases even impossible to get a position in a state-funded institution without a bribe or services for the person who makes employment decisions. Bribery is connected to the provision of municipal and public services, primarily when processing documents of ownership rights, acquiring information, and opening a business. Most of the population in the North Caucasus believes that the level of corruption is increasing (Table 4.1).

Nevertheless, our survey shows that if corruption is not identified or criticised, people are reluctant to uncover it. Many actions that would be

Table 4.1 Do you think the level of corruption in your region is decreasing, increasing, or not changing?

	NCFD	Dagestan	Ingushetia	KB	KCh	NO-A	Chechnya
Decreasing	5	3	9	7	2	6	10
Increasing	41	54	36	34	50	25	31
Not changing	46	38	54	51	40	55	48
I do not know	8	5	1	8	8	14	11

Source: S. R. Khaikin and N. P. Popov, "Problemy Severnogo Kavkaza i effektivnost' gosudarstvennoi politiki v otsenkakh mestnogo naseleniia (Problems of North Caucasus and efficiency of state policy in local population assessments)", *Politeia*, No. 4, 173 (2012).

Transformation and local modernisation 95

deemed illegal or morally unjustified in Central Russia are not perceived as such in the North Caucasus. Embezzlement, tampering, bribing officials, and some other criminal acts by officials or businesspeople are assessed as crimes, but many grassroots transactions are regarded as fair. In addition, both the direct execution of official duties and legal abuses are paid for. For people, corruption proper is only the intemperate enrichment of officials. Abuse of power "in one's own favour" is impeached, but similar actions in favour of family, relatives, friends, or fellow villagers are regarded as appropriate. Grassroots corruption is seen as a custom that provides equal access to deficient resources or the social infrastructure. Hence this leads to the idea of "good authority", one that does not interfere with people "solving" their problems but is efficient enough to accumulate resources necessary for this.

Since they regard corruption as an attribute of the upper layers of the federal and regional authorities, or the consequence of imperfect legislation, or even a Soviet legacy, people do not associate it with their own behavioural mindsets. Double standards with regard to corruption greatly hinder populational support for anticorruption policy. At the same time, since corruption in the upper echelons of power is perceived by all as an obvious evil, this entails resorting to "fair" legal systems as an alternative to state legislation (sharia, *adats*).

"Polyjuridism", the simultaneous effect of two or more legal systems, has always been typical of the North Caucasus. In tsarist days, the choice between state legislation and other legal norms was regulated by Russian subordinate acts. In Soviet times, official legislation did not have a monopoly either. In the first years of Soviet power, which hoped to bring "working Muslims" to its side, sharia was supported to the detriment of *adat*,[22] which was considered a relic of the past. From the late 1920s, the practice of sharia law started to be forbidden. In the 1970s, a revived interest in popular traditions made attitudes to *adat* more tolerant. In post-Soviet years, when it became clear that the existing legislation was not quite adequate for new economic realities, the importance of sharia and *adat* in the life of North Caucasus society grew tremendously. Formal legal institutions and, in particular, courts turned into an arena of struggle between interest groups which relied on different resources, such as ethnicity, clan and community alliances, affiliation with the Sufi Brotherhood or a community of believers, "native" inhabitants of a village or district, and so on. Modes of conflict resolution and ways of forcing people to fulfill decisions raised doubts as to their legitimacy and often ended in stalemate.[23]

Legal uncertainty was amplified by radical shifts in the composition of the populations of large cities. The massive outflow of Russians and other "non-titular" nations was compensated by the inflow of highland and rural populations. Former ruralists, as well as other citizens, tried to rely on traditional (alternative) legal institutions. At the same time, there has been no clear-cut differentiation between the jurisdictions of the institutions. Therefore, there has been not so much a return to historically prominent legal systems as their hybridisation, understood as the blending of official and alternative norms. A specific market of institutions developed,[24] which allowed individuals to choose the rules of the game, and the beneficiaries of this system gradually emerged.[25] Sharia and traditional law were exercised contrary to the state laws they conflicted with. As the polls in the North Caucasus republics show, almost two-thirds of the local population believe that in conditions when secular law contradicts faith, it may not be observed. People who think that Russian laws should be observed in any case are much fewer in number (20 percent).[26]

The insufficient effectiveness of state institutions (primarily courts, which do not comply with legal norms but with informal rules in order to protect "insiders" under any circumstances) and the lack of regulation in the sphere of ownership and labour relations lead to a situation in which people prefer to resolve disputes through imams or *alims* (experts in sharia). A high level of trust in religious authorities ensures the legitimacy of their verdicts. Similar mechanisms of social control over the execution of decisions can be found in the case of *adats*: the guarantor here is the rural community or *jamia*.

Yet it would be a mistake to think that sharia and *adats* are partially or fully ousting Russian legislation. The degree of strength of "polyjuridism" in the NCFD republics differs greatly from region to region: alternative norms are most frequently used in Dagestan, Chechnya, and Ingushetia, but even there their effect spreads only to individual aspects of social and ownership relations.[27] However, we should not ignore the fact that the sharpest competition between legal systems unfolds in the loci of modernisation, that is on territories or in cities affected by local initiatives. On the one hand, participants in these initiatives are vitally interested in reducing risks and legal uncertainty, protecting their property and businesses, and capitalising their assets.[28] This explains why even unbelievers use sharia norms to resolve disputes. On the other hand, both Islamic leaders and *jamias* are interested in expanding their influence and control on local businesses and personal incomes. Among local agents of development who need state regulation of relations between legal systems are farmers, small and medium businesspeople socialised in towns, who do not have the same social capital as the members of rural communities, and villagers who raise the issues of restoring the institutions of *waqf* land use, distributing former *kolkhoz* and *sovkhoz* lands, the rights of relatives, neighbours, and outsiders (when community members sell or rent out their land shares).[29]

Conclusion

Owing to the complexity and patchiness of geographical and social conditions, including the ethnic composition of the population, and a high proneness to conflicts of the interests of various groups, the processes of modernisation in the North Caucasus differ specifically from other regions of Russia. Various forms of modernisation—demographic, sociocultural, technological, and institutional—manifest themselves in various territories in different combinations and degrees, and often conflict with one another. Thus,

Transformation and local modernisation 97

regional development programmes call for the population to remain situated in the mountains despite excessive labour resources and the growing spatial and social mobility of the population. The causes of excess labour are, in turn, the unfinished demographic transition, technological modernisation, and economic downfall. Differences between lowland and mountainous territories are still very noticeable, although they have been smoothed out recently. The post-Soviet archaisation of the economy, social structures, and relations blends to differing extents with modernisation and leads to a fantastic plexus of archaic elements and innovations.

The rapid development of entrepreneurial activities and private initiatives in the North Caucasus coincides with the presence of multiple local communities that preserve a deep allegiance to traditional values and culture. Such a combination inevitably generates contradictions. Striving to resolve them, North Caucasus society sees a way out either in amplifying the regulating role of the secular state represented by the federal centre and its programmes of regional development, or in religion, various forms of Islam, which are becoming increasingly popular, especially among young people. The complexity of this situation requires not only taking into account local realities, but also searching for common points of reference in opposite processes, identifying the nerve that would make the economic and cultural mechanisms of society work in unison. Only then may we hope that the successes of private and entrepreneurial initiative will contribute to the modernisation of the region, and federal projects will yield the anticipated effects. What actions are possible to that end?

First, as our study has shown, North Caucasus society clearly shows a moral need for honesty, fairness, justice, and law observance. This is the field on which Islam competes successfully with the Russian state. However, the same ethical principles are important for the implementation of any investment projects. Business implies social responsibility, transparency, public utility, and respect for the labour and property of others. In the Russian context, the desire to act within these rules is limited by corruption, the unreliability of law enforcement, and defects in the court system. Protection against embezzlers of state property implies a reduction in the number of participants in projects to a narrow circle of honest and rock-solid individuals. Local agents of development are, as a rule, not included in this list. It is clear that such a situation is perceived as discriminating and unfair. It results in the undermining of trust in the state and an increase in the number of "closed-access" institutions, which directly contradicts the principles of transparency in doing business. To overcome this situation, support for the bottom level of justice is necessary through the mechanisms of reputational control and the introduction of "polyjuridism" into the legal framework.

Second, the idea of modernity is associated with the values of self-expression and independence, which are, to a greater extent, typical of individualist societies. In collectivist cultures, self-realisation is also associated with independence in decisions and the presence of choice. The North Caucasus

98 *V.A. Kolosov et al.*

witnesses three strategies of achieving self-realisation: (a) a career "at home," the success of which depends on the combination of family position and personal qualities; (b) migration as a means of social mobility, and (c) conversion to "new" Islam. If the first two roads, associated with a number of socio-economic limitations, require a wealth of knowledge, experience, and personal efforts, the third road is open to all, providing for status and individual self-realisation. The lawfulness of this choice is justified by the "putridity" of the existing social order. The recognition of its ruin entails the need to rebuild society on new moral foundations. Structurally, this narrative is very close to the one of modernisation; it also draws the contours of the future and stigmatises the present, but there are drastic differences. "New" Islam does not offer a programme on how to resolve existing social and economic problems, and does not provide answers to human needs associated with a realisation of the value of individual lives. However, the actions of the Russian state in this respect look rather inarticulate. The deficit of opportunities for self-realisation, which originates in the post-Soviet years, has persisted since the 1990s. Therefore, any actions of the state that expand the freedom of choice on life's journey, including support for entrepreneurship, will contribute to mitigating the contradiction between the pursuit of self-realisation and the impossibility to implement it in actual conditions. Women, who strive to expand their rights and better the future for children, appear as a natural ally of the secular state here.

Third, the notion of *connections* is central to traditional, as well as to modern, societies, despite the difference in the nature of interactions and their interpretations. Of greatest importance are, in the former case, connections that ensure internal cohesion, and, in the latter case, connections that create conditions for building "bridges" between social groups and societies. The first does not exclude the second: various forms of social capital do not only exist simultaneously but depend on one another. This finds its expression in the parallel manifestation of phenomena such as collaboration and rivalry, differentiation and integration, competition and cooperation. If we look from this perspective at the problem of divergence between federal and local efforts aimed at the development of the North Caucasus, it will become clear that this is caused not so much by the crudity of federal projects but rather by the absence of a coordinating link. Big business is unable to interact directly with private backyards and urban petty producers due to the difference in scales and the insufficient reliability of small economic agents. There is the need for a mediator who would compensate for these two drawbacks. These functions can be performed by local cooperation, protecting the interests of "one's own" producers, and promoting their products and services in the market. This means that solving the problems of coordinated development requires not only an institutional infrastructure but also trust in it, the scarcest product in Russian society. Organisational

Transformation and local modernisation 99

support is necessary to create cooperatives capable of making local agents of development competitive. This is a tremendous challenge since social solidarity in North Caucasus society goes hand-in-hand with suspiciousness and distrust in neighbours.

Notes

1 Parts of the following publication are used in this chapter: V.A. Kolosov, O.I. Vendina, A.A. Gritsenko, O.B. Glezer, M.V. Zotova, A.B. Sebentsov and A.B. Panin, "Economic and Social Reforms in the North Caucasus: Goals, Limitations, Problems, and Results." *Regional Research of Russia*, 2017, Vol. 7, No. 3, pp. 259–270.
2 Khalidov D. Severnyi Kavkaz, *Shto delat'? Sistemnyi analiz, nazrevshie mery i aktualnye proekty* [*North Caucasus: What is to be Done? A System Analysis, Imminent Measures and Actual Projects*]. Moscow: RGGU, 2010; I.V. Starodubrovskaya, ed., *Severnyi Kavkaz: modernizatsionnyi vyzov* [*North Caucasus: The Challenge of Modernization*]. Moscow: Delo, 2011; S.M. Markedonov, *Severnyi Kavkaz: modernizatsionnye perspectivy bespokoinogo regiona* [*North Caucasus: The Perspectives of a Disturbing Region's Modernization*]. *Neprikosnovennyi Zapas*, 2011, No. 1, pp. 62–69; D. Sokolov, Kh. Magomedov and N. Silaev, "Istochniki konfliktov i razvitia na Severnom Kavkaze." *Doklad Kavkazskogo Tsentra proektnykh reshenii.* Moscow: Kavkazskii uzel, 2013. Access: www.kavkaz-uzel.ru/articles/222451/.
3 Z.M. Abdulagatov, *Islamskoe massovoe soznanie postsovetskoi Rossii* [*Islamic Mass Consciousness in Post-Soviet Russia*]. Makhachkala: Alef, 2013.
4 T.G. Nefedova, *Selskoe Stavropolie glazami moskovskogo geografa* [*The Countryside of Stavropol Krai by the Eyes of a Moscow Geographer*]. Stavropol: SGU, 2012.
5 V.S. Bobrovnikov, "Arkheologia stroitel'stva islamskikh traditsii v dagestanskom kolkhoze [The archeology of construction of Islamic traditions in a Dagestani kolkhoz]," in *Konfessia, imperia, natsia: religia i problema raznoobrazia v istorii postsovetskogo prostranstva* [*Confession, Empire, Nation: Religion and the Problem of Diversity in the History of the Post-Soviet Space*]. Moscow: Ab Imperio, 2012, pp. 404–433.
6 V.A. Tishkov, ed., *Rossiiskii Kavkaz* [*The Russian Caucasus*]. Moscow: FGNU Rosinformagrotekh, 2007.
7 Kh. V. Dzutsev, F.B. Tsogoeva, L.T. Khetagurova and A.R. Gabueva, "Religioznye mezhethnicheskie orientatsii naselenia republic Severo-Kavkazskogo federalnogo okruga Rossiikoi Federatsii [Religious interethnic orientations of the population of the republics of the North Caucasian Federal District of the Russian Federation]." *Teorii i problemy politiheskikh issledovanii* [*Theories and Problems of Political Studies*], 2015, Nos 4–5, pp. 24–41; M. Ya. Yakh'yaev, "Islam v politicheskikh i sotsiokulturnykh protsessakh na Severnom Kavakaze [Islam in political and sociocultural processes in the North Caucasus]." *Islamovedenie* [*Islamic Studies*], 2014, No. 1, pp. 86–90.
8 M. Ya. Yakh'yaev, Op. cit.; A. Malashenko, *Islamskii faktor na Severnom Kavkaze* [*Islamic Factor in the Northern Caucasus*]. Moscow: Gendal'f, 2001.
9 L.D. Gudkov, B.V. Dubin, N.A. Zorskaya, O.S. Konstantinova, and M.A. Plotko, "Situatsia na Severnom Kavkaze: popytka pilotnoho issledobania v piati respublikakh [Situation in the North Caucasus: an attempt of pilot research in five republics]." *Vestnik obshchestvennogo mnenia. Dannye. Analiz. Diskussii* [*Herald of Public Opinion. Data. Analysis. Discussions*], 2012, Nos 3–4, pp. 25–70; Kh. V. Dzutsev et al., Op. cit.; Z.M. Abdulagatov, *Islamskoe massovoe soznanie v*

100 *V.A. Kolosov et al.*

postsovetskoi Rossii [*Islamic Mass Consciousness of Post-Soviet Russia*]. Makhachkala: IIAE DNTs RAN, 2013.

10 A.S. Antipova, "Tsennosti islama i svetskoe gosudarstvo v sotsiologicheskom izmerenii [The values of Islam and a secular state in a sociological dimension]." *Sociologicheskie issledovnia* [*Sociological Studies*], 2007, No. 3, pp. 111–118.

11 A.G. Levinson, "Kavkazskie problemy v narrativakh zhitelei Kavkaza i drugikh chastei Rossii [Caucasus problems in the narratives of the inhabitants of Caucasus and other parts of Russia]." *Obshchestvennoe mnenie. Dannye. Analiz. Diskussii* [*Herald of Public Opinion. Data. Analysis. Discussions*], 2012, Nos 3–4, pp. 78–89; L.D. Gudkov, B.V. Dubin et al., Op. cit.

12 S.R. Khaikin and N.P. Popov, "Protestnye nastroenia na Severnom Kavkaze: obshchee i chastnoe (chast II) [Protest moods in Northern Caucasus: the general and the particular (part II)]." *Monitoring obshchetvennogo mnenia: ekonomicheskie I sotsialnye peremeny* [*Monitoring Public Opinion: Economic and Social Changes*], 2012, No. 5, pp. 59–74.

13 E. Hobsbawm and T. Ranger, eds, *The Invention of Tradition*. Cambridge: Cambridge University Press, 2003.

14 "The North Caucasus: the challenge of integration", International Crisis Group (www.crisisgroup.org). European Reports Nos 220, 221, 226 and 237; D. Sokolov, Kh. Magomedov and N. Silaev, "Istochniki konfliktov i razvitia na Severnom Kavkaze [The Sources of Development's Conflicts in the North Caucasus]." *Doklad Kavkazskogo Tsentra proektnykh reshenii* [*Report of the Caucasian Centre of Project's Solutions*]. Moscow: Kakazskii uzel, 2013. Access: www.kavkaz-uzel. ru/articles/222451/.

15 *Kutan* was initially a camp of shepherds on a winter pasture. In Soviet times, Dagestani *kolkhozes* in the mountains received lands in the valleys for grazing, which gradually turned *kutans* into 145 permanent settlements with a population of almost 80,000 people, with schools and libraries, but without an official status. The *kutan* inhabitants are constantly facing problems of home and land registration, pension entitlement, social benefits, and so on.

16 *Selskoe khoziaistvo, okhota i okhotnichye khoziaistvo, lesovodstvo v Rossii* [*Agriculture, Hunting and Hunting Economy, Forestry in Russia*]. Moscow: Rosstat, 2015. Access: www.gks.ru/bgd/regl/b15_38/Main.htm.

17 *Regiony Rossii: sotsialno-ekonomicheskie pokazateli* [*Regions of Russia: Socio-Economic Indicators*]. Moscow: Rosstat, 2015. Access: www.gks.ru/free_doc/doc_ 2015/region/reg-pok15.pdf.

18 Regiony Rossii. Op. cit.

19 D. Khalidov, Op. Cit.; I.V. Starodubrovskaya, ed., Op. Cit.; S.M. Markedonov, Op. Cit; "The North Caucasus: The Challenges of Integration (IV): Economic and Social Imperatives." Report of the International Crisis Group No. 237 (Europe). 7 July 2015, p. ii. Access: www.crisisgroup.org/en/regions/europe/north-caucasus/ 237-north-caucasus-the-challenges-of-integration-iv-economic-and-social-impera tives.aspx?alt_lang=ru.

20 D.E. Apter, *The Politics of Modernization*. Chicago: The University of Chicago Press, 1965.

21 "Chechnya: The internal abroad." Report of the International Crisis Group, 2015. Access: www.kavkaz-uzel.eu/articles/264772/.

22 As a rule, Muslim legal culture associates *sharia* with consideration of civil issues, and *adat* is communal, *tukkhum* law, which dates back to pre-Islamic legal norms and regulates relations within a family and clan.

23 E. Varshaver and E. Kruglova, "'Koalitsionnyi klinch' protiv islmaskogo poriadka. Dinamika rynkov razreshenia sporov v Dagestane ['Coalitional clinch' vs. Islamic order. The market of institutions related to dispute resolution in Dagestan]." *Ekonomicheskaia politika* [*Economic Policy*], 2015, Vol. 10, No. 3, pp. 89–112.

24 S. Pejovich, "The market for institution versus the strong hand of the state: the case of Eastern Europe," in B. Dallago and L. Mittone, eds, *Economic Institutions, Markets, and Competition*. Cheltenham: Edward Elgar, 1996, pp. 111–126; D.C. North, J.J. Wallis and B.R. Weingast, *Violence and Social Orders: A Conceptual Framework for Interpreting Recorded Human History*. Cambridge: Cambridge University Press, 2009; V. L. Tambovtsev, *Ekonomicheskaia teoria institutsional'nykh izmenenii* [*Economic Theory of Institutional Changes*]. Moscow: Teis, 2005.

25 K. Kazenin, "Perspektivy institutsional'nogo podkhoda k yavleniu poliyuridizma (na primere Severnogo Kavkaza) [Perspectives of the institutional approach to legal pluralism: the case of North Caucasus]." *Ekonomicheskaia Politika* [*Economic Policy*], 2014, Vol. 19, No. 3, pp. 178–198.

26 Z. M. Abdulagatov, *Islamskoe massovoe soznanie v postsovetskoi Rossii* [*Islamic Mass Consciousness of Post-Soviet Russia*]. Makhachkala: IIAE DNTs RAN, 2013.

27 K. Kazenin, "Severnyi Kavkaz: realizatsii strategii sotsialno-ekonomicheskogo razvitia meshayut zemel'nye otnoshenia [The North Caucasus: the implementation of a strategy of socioeconomic development is hindered by land conflicts in cities]." *Ekonomicheskoe razvitie Rossii* [*Economic Development of Russia*], 2015, Vol. 22, No. 12, pp. 122–125.

28 D. Sokolov, "'Kormlenie Kavkaza' ili ochagovaia modernizatsia? ['Feeding the Caucasus' or focal modernization?]." *Informatsionnoe agentstvo REGNUM*, Stavropol, 25 October 2011. Access: https://regnum.ru/news/1459527.html?forprint.

29 I. Starodubrovskaya and K. Kazenin, Op. cit.

5 The making of groups, boundaries and cleavages in the South Caucasus

From macro to micro dynamics

Giulia Prelz Oltramonti

Introduction

Until 1991, the geopolitical map of the Caucasus looked fairly straightforward. One long border divided the Soviet Union from its southern neighbours and, internally, administrative boundaries parcelled the territory into Soviet Socialist Republics (SSR), Autonomous SSR and Autonomous Oblasts. The whole territory belonged to a large integrated economic space – the Soviet Union – that had no borders or customs fracturing it. The Russian language, officially operating as a lingua franca, attenuated linguistic divides and relegated other languages to the homeland (with the exception of Georgian, which was preserved as Georgia's official language). This does not mean that significant cleavages were absent in the region; it is enough to mention the institutionalisation of nationality through ethno-politics and *korenizatsiya* (Tishkov, 1997; Dean Martin, 2001). It was reflected on people's IDs, through folklore and in internal politics.

Soviet boundaries were unquestionably disturbed with the fall of the USSR, and even earlier. The relaxation of internal control allowed for the voicing of claims to reshape boundaries in the late 1980s in unprecedented ways. Previously, national representatives had voiced their requests through institutional hierarchies, while the last years of the USSR saw a burgeoning of public mobilisations (Cheterian, 2009; Jones, 2012). Since then, dividing lines on maps of the Caucasus have multiplied at a considerable speed. National borders were established *de jure* by the three newly independent states, Armenia, Azerbaijan and Georgia, and, almost at once, *de facto* borders were superimposed resulting from the conflicts in Nagorno-Karabakh (1991–1994), South Ossetia (1991–1992) and Abkhazia (1992–1993). Ethnic cleavages surfaced even in instances where they did not turn into fully fledged separatist conflicts, such as in the Georgian region of Samstkhe-Javakheti. Some borderlands escaped the control of central governments and maintained full autonomy until the mid-2000s, such as Svaneti or Adjara in Georgia.

While national and geopolitical transformations are the most easily identifiable changes, shifting cleavages across the region have occurred in a multiplicity of areas. Economic, commercial and security structures have overlapped with those of external actors. Promoting increased cooperation between the states of the South Caucasus was presented by its western partners as a key means to overcome the region's conflicts through building interdependence and trust and creating non-zero-sum forms of sovereignty that can facilitate decentralised, federal and confederal solutions to the region's territorial conflicts (Boonstra and Melvin, 2011). However, the advent of a new phase of integration in the Caucasus – with Armenia in the Eurasian Economic Union, Georgia linked to the EU and Azerbaijan pursuing its own course outside larger integration projects – leaves the region even more divided and less open to regional cooperation (Melvin and Prelz Oltramonti, 2015).

The economies of the South Caucasus have become highly fragmented as a consequence of closed borders, differing natural resources endowments and diverging geopolitical orientations and support from external actors. The new dynamic of integration of local economies with trading blocs outside the region further undercuts efforts to maintain economic ties between the three countries. Legal frameworks, which affect citizenship status and the ability to cross borders and migrate, have evolved in different directions. Even identities (linguistic, religious, ethnic) have been shaped by the events taking place in the last quarter of a century. Some boundaries disappeared – or shifted – as a result of government interventions and external influence. But mostly, these changes created boundaries where none previously existed – or seemed to exist.

This chapter focuses on the production of and cleavages between boundaries in the Caucasus. Our focus on cleavages – and related borders and boundaries – derives from the recognition that by focusing on the category, on the group, on the entity, something is lost in terms of understanding who creates and shapes the category/group/entity. Bourdieu underlined that substantial power is involved in the crafting of identity categories that drawing boundaries involves - from the ability to 'impose the legitimate definition of the divisions of the social world and, thereby, to make and unmake groups' (Bourdieu, 1991, 221). As this making and unmaking of groups has been a key process that has defined the region in the last 25 years, significant attention should go into understanding the crafting of the divisions, their nature and their position, and identifying not only who gets included, but also who is excluded. When competing strategies of dividing the region exist, cleavages can appear between different areas of exclusion and inclusion. Whether as a result of these cleavages distinct groups emerge, or whether they are integrated into contiguous groups, and what determines the result, is explored in this chapter.

The chapter is composed of three parts. First, it traces the wide processes of border and boundary creation that have shaped the South Caucasus in the last quarter of a century. It covers the diverging trajectories of Armenia, Azerbaijan and Georgia, including their protracted conflicts, and the recent developments in terms of geopolitical and commercial integration of the region in wider institutional frameworks. It then reviews the literature on borders and boundaries, explaining why they should be treated as loci of

104 *Giulia Prelz Oltramonti*

power and constitute a central component of the analysis of power dynamics in the region. Third, it dissects the narrower case of the boundaries straddling the Inguri River. It shows how the aforementioned boundaries can broadly overlap with local ones without coinciding, and how this in turn creates additional cleavages that severely impact on the borderlands' populations while, in parallel, creating opportunities for a variety of actors. This last part is supported by an extensive doctoral study on the exploitation of economic leverage in conflict protraction (Prelz Oltramonti, 2015). It obtained the views of various stakeholders and their interpretation of the mechanisms involved and included 66 open-ended, semi-structured interviews, which complemented the accounts available in reports and previous studies on economies of conflict protraction. Interviews were carried out with states' and *de fa*cto states' representatives, including politicians and civil servants; civil society representatives and NGO workers; businessmen and other relevant stakeholders, such as residents of borderlands and IDPs. Journalists, academics and researchers were also consulted.[1] This final part provides an illustration of meso and micro dynamics in the making and unmaking of groups and in the defining of their boundaries. This structure is dictated by the necessity to take a large view of border and boundary policies – from macro to micro – so as to understand the complexity of the interactions and of the various levels of expression of power in dividing and creating groups and polities.

Regional dynamics: conflicts, commercial agreements, geopolitics and economic trajectories intertwined

Recent developments (and less recent ones which still bear significant consequences today) in terms of boundering processes in the South Caucasus are outlined here. There are three sets of boundaries that are worth pointing out, as they are the clear expression of power exercised by a multiplicity of actors: the *de facto* borders that resulted from the conflicts of the early 1990s; the boundaries of security structures and alliances that reflected the geopolitical tendencies of the state and *de facto* states of the South Caucasus; and the commercial boundaries that result from the disintegration of the regional economic space, as a result of internal dynamics and external influence. The first set of boundaries result from the separatist conflicts of the early 1990s and marked the map of the South Caucasus in addition to national borders established in 1991. The second and third sets, namely security and commercial boundaries, intertwine and find their latest expression in integration into wider regional institutions, resulting in a widening of the institutional gap among the three countries as a result of their adherence to different projects of economic integration. Georgia signed the Deep and Comprehensive Free Trade Agreement (DCFTA) with the EU on 27 June 2014. Armenia joined the Eurasian Economic Union (EEU) on 2 January

Groups, boundaries and cleavages 105

2015. Azerbaijan has avoided formal involvement in the two projects, while maintaining its sectoral and bilateral engagement with member countries of both Unions.

Conflict has been a defining feature of the region over the past 30 years. Independence for Georgia, Armenia and Azerbaijan in the early 1990s was accompanied by the emergence of the three major secessionist conflicts that had their roots in centre-region tensions within the Soviet federal system, ethno-linguistic and communal disputes and struggles for power and property as the Soviet Union broke up. Ceasefire agreements were eventually agreed and international conflict management mechanisms established. Peacekeeping missions involving local and Russian troops were deployed for the two conflicts in Georgia alongside international observer missions. The Nagorno-Karabakh conflict was to be resolved through the Organization for Security and Cooperation (OSCE) Minsk Group, with control over the ceasefire line remaining with the opposing parties. The ceasefire agreements did not translate into peace agreements: during the 1990s and much of the 2000s, the conflicts of the South Caucasus continued in conditions of no peace, no war. The unresolved conflicts of Abkhazia, South Ossetia and Nagorno-Karabakh remain to this day major security challenges for the region, continuously producing loci of friction, which in turn require containing potential escalations, as shown by the events of April 2016 in Nagorno-Karabakh. They are often used as destabilising elements in domestic politics (Broers, 2014), and they hamper economic development by creating closed borders and diverting resources.

While 'hot' conflict was largely absent throughout the late 1990s and 2000s, the conflicts were not static. Abkhazia, South Ossetia and Nagorno-Karabakh were consolidated, to differing extents, as *de facto* states.[2] These situations threw down a challenge to the very border category that, *de jure*, has remained a prerogative of Azerbaijan, Armenia and Georgia. While dividing lines between the Russian Federation on one side, and Abkhazia and South Ossetia on the other, have remained as part of as the Russia-Georgia border recognised by the international community, the status of the dividing lines between the *de facto* states and Georgia is less clear. Until 2008, the ceasefire lines of Abkhazia and South Ossetia remained fixed entities, patrolled respectively by a Commonwealth of Independent States (CIS) peacekeeping force stationed under the observation of a small United Nations Military Observer Mission, and a peacekeeping force of Ossetians, Russians and Georgians, monitored by a mission of the OSCE.

However, the term ceasefire line has limited scope in terms of what it involves. It concerns the field of security – a cessation of hostilities – but does not explain the multifaceted dynamics that shape relations between two neighbours. Ceasefire agreements usually lead to peace accords or a resumption of conflict. In some cases, however, ceasefire agreements can dictate the state of affairs for prolonged periods of time. Ceasefire lines can therefore evolve into highly securitised zones, such as the case of Nagorno-Karabakh, or into semi-permeable boundaries with low levels of violence, such as the case of Transdniestria. During prolonged stalemates, ceasefire lines acquire traits of borders with the exception of legal recognition under international law. In parallel to the denomination of Abkhazia, South Ossetia and Nagorno-Karabakh as *de facto* states, the long-lasting ceasefire lines can be referred to as their *de facto* borders (the symbolic importance of this appellation for the Abkhaz authorities is shown further in the chapter).

In addition to the internal separatist conflicts, and the ensuing creation of boundaries, the three countries have also become embroiled in intra-state frictions and the geopolitical scramble for influence in the South Caucasus. What had originally been localised disputes gradually solidified as state-to-state conflicts. Armenia and Azerbaijan became full-scale adversaries and Russia became more involved in the conflicts in Georgia. From the early 2000s, the Euro-Atlantic community has strengthened its presence in the South Caucasus. In this shifting context, the protracted conflicts took on regional security significance. The transformation of the 'frozen' conflicts of the South Caucasus was laid bare in the Russia-Georgia war of 2008, which concluded with Russia occupying the breakaway regions and recognising them as independent states. Multilateral efforts to manage the conflicts in Georgia collapsed when the UN and the OSCE withdrew their regional missions. The EU deployed its own monitoring mission and became a co-chair of the Geneva International Discussions on the Georgia conflicts.

Following the 2008 war, the EU's involvement in the South Caucasus was channelled into the Eastern Partnership (EaP). As a political framework, the EaP was designed to promote more effective engagement with the states in the South Caucasus and Eastern Europe and to increase its weight in foreign policy in its neighbourhood. In bilateral terms, this evolved into a roadmap for Association Agreements with Georgia and Armenia, which included a DCFTA. The EU and Georgia signed an Association Agreement in 2014.

While the EU was developing its integration agenda, a group of Eurasian states led by Russia was formulating its own regional initiative. A Customs Union of Belarus, Kazakhstan and Russia came into existence on 1 January 2010, built on the Eurasian Economic Community created in 2000 and modelled on the European Economic Community. In November 2011 Belarus, Kazakhstan, and Russia signed an agreement to establish the Eurasian Economic Union by 2015. The EEU aims to expand greatly the scope of the Customs Union by creating a single market for goods, services, capital and labour. In September 2013, following a meeting between the Presidents of Russia and Armenia, in which President Putin sought to leverage Russia's key security and economic support for Yerevan, Armenia opted not to conclude an EU Association Agreement, for which it had completed negotiations, and instead moved to join the EEU (Giragosian, 2014).

Azerbaijan entered into negotiations on an EU Association Agreement but ultimately opted not to conclude an agreement and also to stay outside the Eurasian Union (Alieva, 2015). Subsequently, relations with the EU have

Groups, boundaries and cleavages 107

deteriorated due to criticism by the European Parliament of the political and human rights situation in Azerbaijan, placing in question future EU-Azerbaijan cooperation (Mamadov, 2015). Thus by 2015, the three South Caucasian republics operate in three different economic and political spaces, while the three *de fa*cto states (Abkhazia, South Ossetia, Nagorno-Karabakh) are, although to differing degrees, integrated into the Eurasian Union. The competing projects of economic integration should be seen in the context of the diverging economies of the region, although the impacts of the accession of Armenia to the EEU and Georgia's signature of the DCFTA on the respective countries and on the region as a whole are not yet measurable. The economies of the South Caucasus are highly fragmented as a consequence of closed borders, differing natural resources endowments and diverging orientations that have increased since the end of the Soviet Union.

We have described above the fractionalisation of space along security, economic and commercial axes. It can be seen as a process of making and unmaking groups and alliances, and of excluding the other. How does this take place, however? The following section shows that borders and boundaries are complex entities, of which a thorough understanding is necessary in order to elucidate how macro-dynamics actually translate on the ground.

Borders and boundaries as loci of power

While border and boundary are terms used in everyday language, they need to be briefly discussed as a matter of clarity. What is implied when talking about borders and boundaries in the South Caucasus? And why does looking at borders and boundaries – between different commercial blocks, or de jure/ de facto entities for example – tell us something about the capacity of actors to establish and consolidate their own power on the ground?

Borders can be seen in terms of 'fixed, legal, geopolitical entities' (Goodhand, 2008). However, in case of conflict, permanence, legality and geopolitics may be tested by the course of events, by a change in the interpretation of international law, by differences among parties in interpretation, or by a change in international law itself, or in geopolitical factors: '[borders] are not a permanence but merely a staged claim to permanence' (Jackson, 2008, 269). Additionally, the permanence and the legality of the borders may fail to coincide.

While lacking the geopolitical implications of borders discussed above, boundaries have been seen as something that indicates bounds or limits, as the dividing lines at which something changes, and which separate areas of certain rules of behaviour (Migdal, 2004). Boundaries are where the differences between two different areas have to be bridged and, while arrangements might exist to smooth out this process, frictions might arise. We can identify a multiplicity of boundaries of different natures, covering all areas of social interactions regulated by codified and un-codified rules. They may span geopolitical and trade arrangements (as the ones described above) on a larger

108 *Giulia Prelz Oltramonti*

scale to very local dynamics of identity and administration, which will be outlined later in the chapter. Boundaries can be hardened or softened to suit various interests, a process defined as 'boundary activation' (Tilly, 2003). Borders can undergo similar processes. What happens when a border or a boundary is hardened or softened? Enquiry into the impact of the porosity of borders on stakeholders of border systems has initially verged mostly on identity through an anthropological lens (Flynn, 1997; Long and Villarreal, 1999; Donnan and Wilson, 1999). At the same time, a better understanding of political economic agendas in civil wars has led scholars to pay greater attention to war economies in their regional contexts (Berdal and Malone, 2000), thus including the transitional locations between state and region, namely borders and surrounding borderlands (Goodhand, 2008). While conventional liberal wisdom affirms that, when boundaries harden, opportunities are lost, studies have shown that reality is more multifaceted, with winners and losers arising from border activation. Jackson points out that, generally, borderlands create 'energies and opportunities arising from the contrasts and discontinuities that they both create and then police' (Jackson, 2008).

In order to understand the mechanisms behind such process, we should first elucidate the role of borders. Borders are first and foremost 'sites and symbols of power' (Donnan and Wilson, 1999, 1), key locations where the state asserts its authority, by staging border and customs posts and limiting the flows of people and goods that can cross. Because of the cost for crossing that the authority can impose, an incentive to cross the border is created: the service of moving goods (and people) across the regulated boundary can lead to profit making.

Donnan and Wilson assert that '[the] existence [of borders] as barriers to movement can simultaneously create reasons to cross them' (Donnan and Wilson, 1999, 87). To illustrate this statement, let us point out that, for the residents of the Gali and Samegrelo borderlands, described later in the chapter, commerce through dividing lines often represents one of the few ways to make a living. For the private sector, borders represent a hurdle (in terms of logistics and finances) but also an opportunity to increase profits from additional services. For administrations and law enforcement agencies, borders are the line along which taxation can be extracted, whether officially or unofficially (in other words, bribes). Stakeholders of border systems are therefore extremely numerous and diverse.

Mobility through borders is a prized asset that influences the livelihoods and the economies of the regions surrounding them. On both sides of *de jure* or *de facto* borders, borderlands[3] are often characterised by a weaker presence of official authorities, due to their distance from the capital and the power that stakeholders of border systems can harness through the exploitation of opportunities created by the very existence of borders. As areas where all opportunities created by the cleavage are exploited, borderlands often become 'spaces of avoidance, where much that goes on is less than fully legal – in fact, they have a comparative advantage in illegality' (Goodhand, 2008, 234). While this is most apparent when transnational criminal networks are

Groups, boundaries and cleavages 109

involved, 'smuggling' also concerns residents of borderlands who make a living out of unsanctioned trade of agricultural products, commodities or consumer goods in small quantities.

In fact, the scrutiny that has been recently paid to the phenomenon of globalisation and enhanced communication technologies has also led to an additional understanding of borders, morphing from 'space of places' to 'space of flows' (Castells, 2011). While the argument that flows and mobility across borders in a globalised world transcend territorial borders may not be applicable to the cases under scrutiny here (Rumford, 2006), since they have remained for the most part outside of the globalised routes of information and exchange, this approach has the advantage of drawing attention to the element of flows. Instead of merely dividing the two sides, whoever controls a border regulates the passage of people and goods between the two sides, thus wielding considerable power. The phenomena described above are far from abstract ones and are manifested on the ground. Having covered the regional dynamics of boundaries creation in the South Caucasus in the first part of the chapter, the following section shows how geopolitical power is expressed territorially through the management of a particular checkpoint on the Inguri River.

Zooming in: the territoriality of the boundaries straddling the Inguri River

The boundaries enumerated in the first part of the chapter are the expression of power politics in a range of fields (geopolitical, military, economic and so on). While on maps they can appear as large strokes of colour, it is important to remember that they possess their own territoriality. Customs posts and customs police, together with the corollary infrastructure, denote the expression of various actors' power over the management of trade and their ability to control – and capture, through taxation – resources. Similarly, a ceasefire line is manned by a multiplicity of actors, who are willing to resort to the use of force to express and enshrine their position, as seen recently in Nagorno-Karabakh. A whole range of non-human displays of force – bases, barriers, barbed wire – serve a similar purpose, adding to the deployment of military personnel.

To illustrate what is meant by the territoriality of boundaries, it is useful to describe a specific case of micro-dynamics of *de facto* border post management. This example is drawn from a wider study on Russia's bordering and de-bordering practices in Abkhazia (Prelz Oltramonti 2016a) and focuses on a particular segment of the Abkhaz-Georgian ceasefire line in 2012, namely the only checkpoint officially open to transit on the Abkhaz side of Inguri River.

Starting from October 2012, Russian troops and de facto Abkhaz border guards were to man jointly the checkpoint on the Inguri River, with no changes to be made to schedules and operating principles of the checkpoint (which on the Abkhaz side of the river had been manned by Abkhaz personnel since 1993).[4] Passage of people and goods was to be granted on the basis of valid documents (whether Abkhaz IDs or foreign passports, requiring

110 *Giulia Prelz Oltramonti*

visas, with the exception of a few nationalities). However, changes in the implementation of the rules of transit, as well as in the management of the *de facto* border facilities meant that the difference between pre-2012 and post-2012 was as stark as ever. Abkhaz *de facto* authorities and border guards had previously applied a large margin of discretion in their management of their *de facto* border post, while informal transactions (bribes) and personal relationships eased the passage of both goods and people.[5] Russian military personnel, on the other hand, clearly distanced themselves from the civilians that wanted to cross.

The physical layout of the checkpoint was altered so as to create more distance between the various parts of the checkpoint. Incoming civilians were stopped as they stepped off the bridge across the Inguri by a Russian soldier who communicated by radio with the main area of the checkpoint, further afield, and who seemingly had no discretionary power to let them proceed. Civilians could then be left waiting for long periods of time, unable to establish for how long or why. When workers of international organisations crossed the bridge by car, they would be given priority to go through the checkpoint, while the processing of pedestrians stopped for up to an hour. The reason offered for such stoppage was that of 'processing the paperwork of the cars', though the passage of the cars themselves and checking the papers of vehicles and officials took an average of 10 minutes.[6] Once permitted to proceed, in small groups, civilians walked through a fenced tunnel all the way to the window in the main area of the checkpoint. There, Russian officials checked documents, and allowed or barred entrance. Abkhaz *de facto* authorities, while present, did not take part in the process.

The section of the boundary described here is part of the ceasefire line established in December 1993 along the Inguri River, which became, throughout the years, an entrenched *de facto* border; the process accelerated after the 2008 war and the Russian recognition of Abkhaz independence. However, even the exercise of qualifying this boundary is fraught with controversy and, as will be apparent below, immediately confronts the reader with the practices and discourses that constitute this case. This is partly due to the fact that the different appellations of the boundary carry significant implications in terms of recognition and interpretation of events. But this is also due to the fact that, as shown below, multiple boundaries do not overlap but are the object of a struggle for preponderance.

The *de facto* border along the Inguri, which, for Georgia, remains an internal Administrative Boundary Line (ABL), was established as the result of the Abkhaz-Georgian war of 1992–1993. From its onset, it reflected the tactical results of the conflict between Sukhumi and Tbilisi: that is the Abkhaz victory on the ground and their control over the entire territory of the former Abkhaz ASSR with the exception of the Kodori Valley. It also reflected the key role played by the Russian Federation in brokering the ceasefire agreement and as a key player in the diplomatic efforts to resolve the conflict in the following years. The return of refugees and displaced persons[7] was a pillar of the quadripartite

Groups, boundaries and cleavages 111

agreement signed by Georgia, Abkhazia, Russia and the UN in December 1993, which also included the pledge not to use force and to establish a UN Monitoring mission (UNOMIG) (Diasamidze 2003a). However, the decision to deploy a UN Peacekeeping mission was made dependent on the progress in the talks between the two sides, and hence never came into being. Instead, a CIS peacekeeping operation was established in April 1994, manned mostly by Russian personnel (Diasamidze 2003b). Crucially, in 2008 the CIS peacekeepers acted as the vanguards of the Russian troops advancing through Abkhazia (Blank, 2007, 5).

The Inguri ceasefire line, then, can be seen since 1994 as a locus of power for both the Abkhaz army, which had pushed its military campaign in 1993 all the way to it and which manned it until 2008, guaranteeing the southern border of the *de facto* Abkhaz state, and for the Russian one, with its presence on the ground reflecting its role as the power broker.

Denoting the importance of the symbolism of maintaining the control over the *de facto* border, Abkhaz authorities and border guards manned the checkpoint on the bridge over the Inguri River until October 2012. When Russian troops took over, the event received no coverage in the Abkhaz press and residents of Sukhumi and northern Abkhazia remained unaware of the shift for a few weeks. They would argue, as late as early November 2012, that the control of the checkpoint over the Inguri Bridge was a clear sign of Abkhaz independence vis-à-vis Russia, and that the stationing of Russian troops along the ceasefire line was no more than the result of a bilateral agreement, which increased Abkhaz security.[8] In other words, manning the main, and increasingly sole, point of passage along the Inguri River, and therefore controlling one's *de facto* borders, was presented as a proof of Abkhaz sovereignty.

In 2016, this military boundary along the Inguri denotes the extent of Russia's military and geopolitical expansion into the south-western Caucasus. It is worth noting, however, that in commercial terms, the Inguri River is the locus of a very different arrangement. While geopolitically Russia's and Europe's spheres of interest collide there (with the Abkhaz government staunchly pro-Russian, and the Georgian one pro-Western, albeit variably), the same is not true for the institutional framework aimed at promoting commercial integration. On the one hand, as Georgia has signed a DCFTA with the EU, Abkhazia is nominally part of the deal – although Tbilisi's lack of territorial control over Abkhazia means that the implementation in that region (and South Ossetia) is postponed.[9] So, in practice, goods produced on the Southern side of the Inguri River are expected to have preferential access to the EU market, on the basis of wide-ranging legal approximation with EU standards, while those produced on its northern side remain – officially – in limbo with regard to export towards the EU. On the other hand, Abkhazia has not become a member of the EEU, as all EEU's members aside from Russia do not recognise its independence. So the goods produced in Abkhazia are exported to Russia on the basis of a bilateral agreement between the two countries that stops short from including Abkhazia in a wider free-trade area.

112 *Giulia Prelz Oltramonti*

Finally, as Georgia considers Abkhazia part of its national territory and hence refuses to establish customs along the Inguri, the commercial boundary is therefore only a matter of concern for Abkhaz authorities.

It is to the Abkhaz authorities that this arrangement poses most problems. With security and commercial boundaries that do not coincide, Abkhazia finds itself in a cleavage between boundaries. On the one hand, it is excluded by a group (the EEU) to which it aspires in order to enhance its economic viability and which would provide official recognition by a multinational regulatory body. On the other hand, it is *de jure* included in a legal framework that maintains Georgia's territorial integrity as a cornerstone.

Shaping ethnicity to suit geopolitics: tinkering with yet another boundary

The Abkhaz authorities' response is to stress the boundary along the Inguri, and is actively trying to match the ceasefire line with geopolitical, commercial and other boundaries. But, as explained above, the inclusion in/exclusion from the EU and EEU frameworks is not actually in line with their geopolitical affiliation. As Abkhazia is *de jure* included in the DCFTA with the EU and excluded from the EEU, the boundary that determines its commercial arrangements runs north of Abkhazia along the Psou River and lumps Abkhazia together with Georgia in terms of how the two main regional actors (Russia and the EU) legally relate to it, regarding trade and inclusion into their supra-national structures.

In addition to these security and commercial boundaries, however, there is a plethora of parallel and competing boundaries that do not suit simplified cartographic mappings depicting the north-western Caucasus as a Russia-Abkhazia-Georgia streamlined affair. It is worth mentioning that, like most boundaries, they are far from static and immune from pressure from a variety of actors.

Far from being a unitary and homogeneous entity, Abkhazia is criss-crossed by multiple geographic, social and ethnic divisions. The most significant split, however, is the one between the eastern district of Gali[10] (and neighbouring areas of the Ochamchira and Tkvarcheli districts) and the rest of Abkhazia. Not only was the Gali district affected by the war in 1993, but it also remained subject to high levels of insecurity – comparatively higher than in the rest of Abkhazia – and isolation from the rest of Abkhazia throughout the 1990s and 2000s. Notably, when speaking about the 1993–2008 economy of Abkhazia, interviewees (whether residents or specialists) in Sukhumi never included the Gali district in their considerations and, when questioned about it, were surprised that the topic came up. This is not to say that there were no similarities between the district of Gali and the rest of Abkhazia, and it is interesting to notice that the approach was often different when talking about post-2008 dynamics, reflecting a process of integration of the Gali district within Abkhazia, which was non-existent before the Russo-Georgian war of 2008.

Inhabited almost exclusively by Georgians/Mingrelians,[11] the region has been the theatre of constant migrations in and out of its boundaries since the end of the Soviet Union. The main wave of displacement took place in 1993, followed in the mid-1990s by a wave of spontaneous return to the Gali district. Officially only the Georgians/Mingrelians who did not flee in 1993 were allowed to reside in the Gali district, yet the flow of tens of thousands of returnees back into Abkhazia was tacitly tolerated by the Abkhaz *de facto* authorities. Other movements of populations were caused by insecurity and renewed conflict: as a consequence of the escalation between Georgian paramilitaries and Abkhaz forces in 1998, some 35,000–40,000 returnees – almost all of the Georgian/Mingrelian population – fled the Gali district a second time (Trier et al., 2010, 35). Nevertheless, an even larger number returned in the early 2000s, with estimates that range from 45,000 (UNHCR) to 55,000 (Abkhaz authorities) (Trier et al., 2010, 35).

The difficulty of establishing precise estimates for the 'returnee' phenomenon (for which no common definition has been devised) partly depends on the seasonal nature of part of these migratory patterns: IDPs resident in Samegrelo during the winter would cross the Inguri River for the agricultural season and stay in the Gali district until the harvest. Some would cross the Inguri far more often, while for others it would be more convenient to split families, with working-age members living in the pre-displacement villages, tilling the land, while children lived and studied in Zugdidi.

In fact the ceasefire line (CFL), or ABL, along the Inguri, which has a key meaning in security terms and a symbolism for the Abkhaz authorities, meant little in terms of ethnic terms. The population on either side had strong links and widely spoke Mingrelian. This justifies a detour into the complexities of Mingrelian identity. Mingrelians are members of communal group belonging to the wider Georgian ethnic group traditionally inhabiting Mingrelia/Samegrelo.[12] The degree of separation between Mingrelians and Georgians, however, is a matter of contention. Abkhaz consider that a large segment of Mingrelians in Abkhazia is composed of former Abkhaz who underwent a process of Georgianisation during the Soviet Union. Self-identification varies considerably with how they are identified by others. The issue of Mingrelian identity has been extensively covered by Broers, who shows that it varies throughout socio-economic and geographical contexts and according to historical trajectories of respondents, varying from proud self-identification as Mingrelian and a renaissance of Mingrelian culture and use of the language, to a dismissal of Mingrelian identity, seen as a Russian-inspired strategy of divide and rule (Broers, 2012). He also points out that, far from being exclusionary, Mingrelian identities largely coexist with Georgian and Russian ones.

There has been a visible effort, in the last 25 years, to match ethnic boundaries with the security boundary running along the Inguri. The attempt by Abkhazia's *de facto* authorities to institutionalise the Mingrelian language in the 1990s is clearly in line with the political goal of tracing a line between

114 *Giulia Prelz Oltramonti*

the Gali district on the one side and Samegrelo on the other, or in other words of dividing a community that straddled both sides of the CFL.

This trend was accentuated after 2008. Abkhaz authorities in Sukhumi invested, in terms both of infrastructure and institutions, in the integration of the Gali district – previously seen as little more than an insecure borderland where illicit business was rife – into wider Abkhazia. It is interesting to notice that people and officials in Sukhumi mention the Gali district only with regard to the post-2008 period; in other words, since 2008 the Gali district and its 'Mingrelian' residents are included in imaginary realm of what is understood as Abkhazia by the other Abkhaz residents. It is worth noting that, to be included in the group, the residents of the Gali district are always and exclusively referred to as 'Mingrelians', never Georgians. 'Georgians' are those who inhabit Georgia, who might have fled during the 1992–1993 war and who are outright excluded from Abkhazia, been denied return or even a visa to visit family.

What this reflects is the attempt to create a polity with overlapping external boundaries of different natures. While Abkhazia is too diverse ethnically to create an ethnically homogeneous entity (Trier et al., 2010), what can be done is to define a boundary of exclusion that divides those who belong, the 'Mingrelians', and those who do not, the 'Georgians'. The largely disenfranchised Georgians/Mingrelians of the Gali district (Prelz Oltramonti, 2016b), who privately disclose complex multiple identities and strong links with family, friends and institutions in Samegrelo, are little more than pawns in a context where more powerful actors are at work in making groups that serve their interests.

Conclusion

From the macro to the micro levels, the South Caucasus is being fragmented in a variety of ways. As noted previously, however, the boundaries that the actors involved are setting do not always overlap. Cleavages between boundaries are thus created. The cases developed above allow us to understand better their characteristics and to answer the three following questions: what are the consequences of the creation of cleavages between boundaries of different natures? What does it mean to be caught in such cleavages between different expressions of power? And what opportunities are created by the actors shaping these boundaries?

This chapter has shown that there are a variety of ways to build groups/ establish boundaries between communities, and that it is necessary to look at them in unison. Too often, studies of this kind focus on one aspect of border and boundary making (whether trade, security, identity politics, but as discrete phenomena). The result is that the mismatch between the different lines is lost, and the analysis of borderlands becomes a dualistic affair between in and out, failing to take into consideration the both ins and outs can be multiple, variously combined, and interacting complexly. Falling in a cleavage between different sorts of boundaries shows the inability of a given actor to

Groups, boundaries and cleavages 115

set and manage its own overlapping boundaries, and therefore being subject to, and unable to sway, a more powerful actor's agency. In the case analysed in this chapter, external agency meant that Abkhazia was excluded by a series of arrangements – the EEU, as well as the club of internationally recognised states – to which it aspired.

At the same time, exclusion from something might mean forceful inclusion into another group. When boundaries are drawn, they might include a given area or polity in spite of the expressed will of its people or leadership. Abkhaz authorities have to reckon with the fact that, *de jure*, they are part of Georgia and its DCFTA with the EU. Georgians/Mingrelians, on the other hand, are drawn into the Abkhaz polity notwithstanding their long-held cross-Inguri identity and commercial links, as Abkhazia strengthens its *de facto* border along the CFL.

It is worth underlining that, as borders and boundaries are spaces of flows, these patterns of forceful inclusion and exclusion are not only about the creation of boundaries but also their potential hardening, thereby limiting the flow. By imposing a boundary, an actor signals its ability to manage it and to determine who crosses. The power that boundaries denote is not only that of exclusion from a particular group, but also that of regulating passage between the two sides. In the wide commercial arena of the South Caucasus, this sort of power is now, in additional to national governments and local custom officials, in the hands of the EU and the EEU. The Russian military affirms its presence by manning the checkpoint on the Inguri River. In both cases, the goal is not to seal hermetically the boundary, but to establish control over key components of flows (regulatory frameworks, custom posts). In that context, power derives from being able to set the rules by which all others must abide.

Finally, if shaping boundaries is an expression of power, actors re-state their power and their ability to shape relations by setting non-overlapping boundaries. Russia's position of power is expressed repeatedly – at the Psou and Inguri Rivers. Far from being twists of fate, cleavages are the purposeful results of policy choices made by the most powerful actors on the ground. Others may try to fill these cleavages but lack the necessary clout to succeed. Abkhazia aspires to overlapping external boundaries in order to reinforce its sense of in versus out and to establish itself as a polity with clearly determined boundaries. But as various forces have been vying for control and influence in the South Caucasus over the last 25 years, their expressions of power have formed an extraordinarily fragmented map of the region and a web of non-overlapping boundaries of various kinds that impact on the movement of people and goods, as well as their identities, their sense of belonging and their coping strategies.

Notes

1 The interviews were conducted mainly in 2012 (but also in the summer of 2009 and January 2015) in Tbilisi, Sukhumi, Gagra and the districts of Shida Kartli, Samegrelo, and Gali. Some additional interviews were conducted in Western Europe, while a small minority were carried out over the phone or via e-mail.

116 *Giulia Prelz Oltramonti*

2 These entities could be defined as states under the 1933 Montevideo Convention, albeit if considering 'relations with other states' not only in terms of diplomatic relations (but also i.e. commercial): 'The state as a person of international law should possess the following qualifications: a permanent population; a defined territory; government; and capacity to enter into relations with the other states' (The Avalon Project). However, the concept of statehood has customarily become linked to recognition by the international community, hence the definition of such entities in terms of *de facto* states. The appellation 'de facto state' is therefore understood as a state-like entity that lacks international recognition (Pegg, 1998; Lynch, 2004; Francis, 2011). There is no absolute consensus on the characterisation of these political entities. They are alternatively called 'quasi-states' (Kolstø, 2006; Baev, 1998), 'unrecognised states' (King, 2001), and 'pseudo-states' (Kolossov & O'Loughlin 1998).

3 Goodhand uses the term borderland as 'non-state space' and differentiates between three distinct types of borderlands (Goodhand, 2008, 193).

4 Interview with Alexandr Stranichkin, de facto Vice-Prime Minister of Abkhazia, October 2012, Sukhumi.

5 Interview with hazelnut traders, October 2012, Gali; interview residents of Gali district, along the Inguri River, November 2012, Gali district.

6 Own observations, October and November 2012.

7 Displaced populations are referred to IDPs by Georgians and refugees by Abkhaz, reflecting differences in how they see the ceasefire line: an internal administrative boundary for the former, an international border for the latter.

8 Interview residents of Gagra, November 2012, Gagra.

9 'Association Agreement between the European Union and the European Atomic Energy Community and their Member States, of the one part, and Georgia, of the other part'. *Official Journal of the European Union*, http://eeas.europa.eu/georgia/pdf/eu-ge_aa-dcfta_en.pdf.

10 The Gali district is the Southernmost district of Abkhazia, stretching from the Greater Caucasus range to the Black Sea, and straddling the Inguri River on its Southern flank. However, references to the district of Gali is fraught with dangers, as its boundaries were redesigned in 1995 by the *de facto* authorities. Part of the former district of Gali was included in the newly established district of Tkvarcheli, reducing the territory of the Gali district but also of the Ochamchira district. Both Gali and Tkvarcheli districts are inhabited by Georgian/ Mingrelian majorities, though in the case of Gali almost exclusively so. Hence, when referring to the district of Gali, there is an understanding that phenomena affecting it do not stop at the *de facto* administrative border between the two districts, but often involve the neighbouring areas of the Tkvarcheli district too.

11 This chapter refers to the Georgian and Mingrelian populations residing in, and displaced from, the Gali district, and Abkhazia more widely, as Georgian/ Mingrelian, reflecting the different appellations with which they are referred to by Abkhaz de facto and Georgian authorities, and, most importantly, with which they self-identified alternatively and, sometimes, interchangeably. This does not imply that all the Georgian population in Abkhazia was Mingrelian; this appellation allows for the possibility of the people designated to be one or the other, or both. However, it is worth noting that, very generally, a majority of Georgian/ Mingrelian city, and especially Sukhumi, dwellers would identify as Georgians, while Mingrelians constituted the majority in rural areas and in the Gali district.

12 Samegrelo is a region in Western Georgia, neighbouring Abkhazia. Its capital is Zugdidi. Together with Tbilisi, it was the centre of the Georgian civil war during which supporters of the first (ethnically Mingrelian) President Gamsakhurdia clashed with the forces that ousted him.

Bibliography

Alieva, Leila, 2015. 'The Eastern Partnership: the view from Azerbaijan', European Council on Foreign Relations, 19 May, www.ecfr.eu/article/commentary_azerbaijan 3023.

Baev, P., 1998. 'Peacekeeping and conflict management in Eurasia'. In Allison, A. and Bluth, C. (eds), *Security Dilemmas in Russia and Eurasia*, London: Royal Institute of International Affairs.

Berdal, M. and D. Malone, 2000. *Greed and Grievance: Economic Agendas in Civil Wars*, Boulder: Lynne Rienner.

Blank, Stephen, 2007. 'The values gap between Moscow and the West: the sovereignty issue', *Acque e Terre*, 6, p. 5.

Boonstra, Jos and Neil Melvin, 2011. 'Challenging the South Caucasus Security Deficit', FRIDE Working Paper 108 (April 2011), p. 17, http://fride.org/download/ WP108_South_Caucasus_Eng.pdf.

Bourdieu, P. 1991. *Language and Symbolic Power*, Cambridge: Harvard University Press.

Broers, L., 2012. '"Two sons of one mother": nested identities and centre-periphery politics in post-Soviet Georgia'. In Schönle, A. (ed.), *When the Elephant Broke Out of the Zoo: A Festschrift for Donald Rayfield*, Stanford: Stanford University Press, pp. 234–267.

Broers, Laurence, 2014. 'From "frozen conflict" to enduring rivalry: reassessing the Nagorny Karabakh conflict', *Nationalities Papers*, 43(4).

Castells, Manuel, 2011. *The Rise of the Network Society: The Information Age: Economy, Society, and Culture*, Oxford: Blackwell Publishers.

Cheterian, V., 2009. *War and Peace in the Caucasus: Russia's Troubled Frontier*, London: C Hurst & Co Publishers.

Dean Martin, Terry, 2001. *The Affirmative Action Empire: Nations and Nationalism in the Soviet Union*, Ithaca and London: Cornell University Press.

Diasamidze, T., 2003a. 'Memorandum of understanding between the Georgian and the Abkhaz sides at the negotiations in Geneva. 1 December 1993', In Diasamidze, T. (ed.), *Regional Conflicts in Georgia – the Autonomous Oblast of South Ossetia, the Autonomous SSR of Abkhazia, 1989–2002: The Collection of Political-legal Acts*, Tbilisi: Regionalism Research Centre.

Diasamidze, T. 2003b. 'Statement of the Council of the CIS Heads of states on conducting operations of peacekeeping in the zone of the Georgian-Abkhaz conflict. 15 April 1994', In Diasamidze, T. (ed.), *Regional Conflicts in Georgia – the Autonomous Oblast of South Ossetia, the Autonomous SSR of Abkhazia, 1989–2002: The Collection of Political-legal Acts*, Tbilisi: Regionalism Research Centre, 2003.

Donnan, H. and T. Wilson, 1999. *Borders: Frontiers of Identity, Nation and State*, Oxford: Berg.

European Union, 2014. 'Association Agreement between the European Union and the European Atomic Energy Community and their Member States, of the one part, and Georgia, of the other part', *Official Journal of the European Union*, 57(30) August.

Flynn, D. K. 1997. '"We are the border": identity, exchange, and the state along the Bénin-Nigeria border', *American Ethnologist*, 24(2).

Francis, C., 2011. *Conflict Resolution and Status: The Case of Georgia and Abkhazia*, Brussels: VUBpress.

118 *Giulia Prelz Oltramonti*

Giragosian, Richard, 2014. 'Armenia's Strategic U-turn', European Council on Foreign Relations, 22 April, www.ecfr.eu/page/-/ECFR99_ARMENIA_MEMO_AW.pdf.

Goodhand, J., 2008. 'War, peace and the places in between: why borderlands are central'. In *Whose Peace? Critical Perspectives on the Political Economy of Peacebuilding*, Basingstoke and New York: Palgrave Macmillan.

Human Rights Watch, 2011. 'Living in Limbo: Rights of Ethnic Georgian Returnees to the Gali District of Abkhazia', www.hrw.org/report/2011/07/15/living-limbo/rights-ethnic-georgians-returnees-gali-district-abkhazia.

Jackson, S. 2008. 'Potential Difference: Internal Borderlands in Africa'. In *Whose Peace? Critical Perspectives on the Political Economy of Peace-building*, Basingstoke and NY: Palgrave Macmillan.

Jones, S., 2012. *Georgia: A Political History since Independence: Nation, State and Democracy, 1991–2003*, London: I.B. Tauris.

King, C., 2001. 'The benefits of ethnic war: understanding Eurasia's unrecognized states', *World Politics*, 53(04).

Kolossov, V. and J. O'Loughlin, 1998. 'Pseudo-states as harbingers of a new geopolitics: the example of the Trans-Dniester Moldovan Republic (TMR)', *Geopolitics*, 3(1).

Kolstø, P., 2006. 'The sustainability and future of unrecognized quasi-states', *Journal of Peace Research*, 43(6).

Long, N. and M. Villarreal, 1999. 'Small Product, Big Issues: Value Contestations and Cultural Identities in Cross-border Commodity Networks'. In B. Meyer and P. Geschiere (eds), *Globalization and Identity: Dialectics of Flow and Closure*, Oxford: Blackwell.

Lynch, D., 2004. *Engaging Eurasia's separatist states: unresolved conflicts and de facto states*, Washington, D.C.: US Institute of Peace Press.

Mamadov, Eldar, 2015. 'EU and Azerbaijan: Breaking Up or Muddling Through?', Eurasianet.org, 16 September, www.eurasianet.org/node/75116.

Manasyan, Heghine, 2015. 'New Trajectories Of Integration In the Caucasus: The Challenges For Conflict and Security', Presentation at the seminar 'New trajectories of integration in the Caucasus: the challenges for conflicts and security' (organized in the CASCADE framework with the Stockholm International Peace Research Institute (SIPRI) and the Georgian Foundation for Strategic and International Studies (GFSIS)), Tbilisi, 2 June.

Melvin, Neil and Giulia Prelz Oltramonti, 2011. 'Managing Conflict and Integration in the South Caucasus: A Challenge for the European Union', SIPRI-CASCADE policy paper, November, www.cascade-caucasus.eu/wp-content/uploads/2015/11/D7.1-Conflict-and-integration.pdf.

Migdal, J. S., 2004. *Boundaries and Belonging: States and Societies in the Struggle to Shape Identities and Local Practices*, Cambridge: Cambridge University Press.

Pegg, S., 1998. *International Society and the De Facto State*, Aldershot: Ashgate.

Prelz Oltramonti, Giulia, 2015. 'The exploitation of economic leverage in conflict protraction: modes and aims. The cases of South Ossetia and Abkhazia (1992–2008)', PhD in Political Science, defended at the Université libre de Bruxelles, 20 October.

Prelz Oltramonti, Giulia, 2016a. 'Southbound Russia: processes of bordering and debordering between 1993 and 2013', *Connexe: les espaces post communistes en question(s)*, Brussels-Geneva.

Prelz Oltramonti, G., 2016b. 'Securing disenfranchisement through violence and isolation: the case of Georgians/Mingrelians in the district of Gali', *Conflict, Security and Development*, 16(3), 2.

Pugh, M. and N. Cooper, 2004. *War Economies in a Regional Context: Challenges of Transformation*, London: Lynne Rienner.

Rahmanov, Farhad, 2015. 'New Trajectories Of Integration In the Caucasus: The Challenges For Conflict and Security', presentation at the seminar 'New trajectories of integration in the Caucasus: the challenges for conflicts and security' (organized in the CASCADE framework with the Stockholm International Peace Research Institute (SIPRI) and the Georgian Foundation for Strategic and International Studies (GFSIS)), Tbilisi, 2 June.

Rumford, Chris, 2006. 'Theorizing borders', *European Journal of Social Theory*, 9(2).

The Avalon Project, 2011. 'Convention on Rights and Duties of States (Inter-American); December 26, 1933', http://avalon.law.yale.edu/20th_century/intam03.asp.

Tilly, C., 2003. *The Politics of Collective Violence*, Cambridge: Cambridge University Press.

Tishkov, Valery, 1997. *Ethnicity, Nationalism and Conflict in and After the Soviet Union: The Mind Aflame*, London: Sage.

Trier, T., Lohm, H. and Szakonyi, D., 2010. *Under Siege: Inter-ethnic Relations in Abkhazia*, New York: Columbia University Press.

6 Arctic labour migration, vulnerability, and social change in the South Caucasus

The case of Azerbaijanis in the polar cities of Murmansk and Norilsk

Sophie Hohmann[1]

Introduction and methodology

The collapse of the USSR, and with it its unique economic and social system, generated transformations in all spheres of the former Soviet societies. The reconfiguration of mobility (economic migration, environmental migration, forced displacement, exile) involved a set of new situations and migration strategies. Labour migration appeared as an alternative to the disintegration of the social system and the loss of Soviet social benefits. The increasing flow of migrant workers from the South Caucasus and Central Asia, who left mainly to try their luck in the Russian Federation, reflects socioeconomic and political changes unprecedented in this geographical area. Mobility during Soviet times occurred in a different historical and administrative framework because of the absence of political borders between Soviet republics. A completely new situation emerged after 1991, necessitating a legal framework for collaboration between states in a context of major crises.[2] New patterns of labour migration, temporary or circular (Mühlfried, 2014; Ivakhnyuk & Iontsev, 2012), emerged from the late 1990s as a new paradigm for Russia (Figures 6.1a and b and 6.2). The migrants' countries of origin also suffered from unprecedented transformations inherent to the construction of a new social order.

Migration from the southern USSR successor states and the regional geopolitical situation must be studied in the context of the crises that marked the 1990s as well as of the economic crisis in Russia. The flows of migrant workers from the South Caucasus can generally be dated back earlier than those from Central Asia, though the latter are quantitatively important (Figures 6.1a and 6.1b). Research on migration in Russia offers both empirical and theoretical contributions on issues as diverse as migration strategies, demographics, the impact of remittances on households, the reconfiguration of gender relations, migration of women, re-qualification through migration, ethnicisation of economic niches and health and social risks, as well as religious issues, radicalisation, inter-ethnic relations, xenophobia and nationalism and regional cooperation policies.

Migration, vulnerability, and change 121

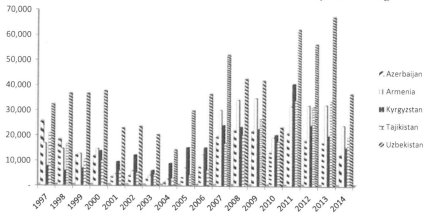

Figure 6.1a Nodal modernisation in the North Caucasus
Source: FMS database. www.gks.ru/wps/wcm/connect/rosstat_main/rosstat/ru/population/demography/#

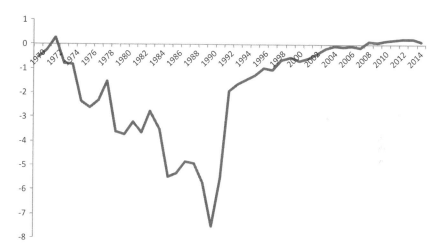

Figure 6.1b Net migration rate per 1,000 persons, Azerbaijan
Source: State Statistical Committee of the Republic of Azerbaijan. www.azstat.org

This chapter analyses the migration process from the Republic of Azerbaijan, a state rich in oil and hydrocarbons, yet unable to fulfil its role as a state ensuring social protections for its people and satisfying the demands of the internal job market. The issue of organisational strategies of migrants after 1991 will be examined by taking a broad historical perspective, in order better to understand continuities as well as ruptures caused by the collapse of the

122 *Sophie Hohmann*

USSR, and to study the networks that continue to support the migrants. The regionalisation of labour migration requires an analysis of its trajectory, and that of migrants' professional careers, considered here from a sociological and cross-cultural standpoint. The transgenerational study of migrants will allow us to recognise the geographical and temporal dimension of their trajectories, while being attentive to different historical periods of migration. The chapter contributes to sociological research through the analysis of universal ideal-types of economic migration. The strategies elaborated by migrants intersect and coincide: they are complex and require an analysis based on their migration routes, while framing available contextual data (historical, demographic and anthropological).

The research is based on a series of interviews, discussions and observations in the field conducted in Azerbaijan and in Russia.[3] Fieldwork was carried out during the summer of 2015 in the Russian North[4] to study Azerbaijani migrant worker networks in the polar region, and to conduct an analysis of the trajectories of migrants in a longer historical perspective in order to grasp the temporal and lattice dimensions. I found that labour migrants from Azerbaijan living in Murmansk or Norilsk were almost all from the Massali, Lenkaran and Lerik regions located in southern Azerbaijan, and this observation was confirmed by several interviews with scholars in Baku. I organised a second period of fieldwork in the Arctic city of Murmansk in March 2016[5] among the labour migrants identified above, and among Azeri 'first-migrants', who came to the North during Soviet times as army personnel and students (Antoine & al., 1987; Vivier, 2006; Hohmann, 2012).[6] I focused on polar migration and the everyday life of migrants from Azerbaijan, as well as demographic changes in the Arctic cities. I organised meetings and conducted interviews with local authorities, with migrants from Azerbaijan, with representatives of those in the Azeri diaspora who arrived during the Soviet period, with representatives of the Norilsk Nickel Consortium (I was able to visit factories in Norilsk, and mines in Talnakh and Kaierkan) and with Muslim religious authorities. I collected material on migration processes, on life histories and migrants' strategies from Azerbaijan at various periods of time. I also collected information and conducted interviews on the transformations of the labour market in the Russian Far North for a better understanding of the migration policy in arctic mono-cities. Finally, changing the perspective from the South (where I conducted work earlier) to the North allowed me to think about a new geography of 'centres' and 'margins' in the context of contemporary Russia.

We will see below how labour migration arose as an alternative to the weaknesses of social and economic policies in Azerbaijan and became a new social norm in face of a neo-patrimonial state. Moreover, I will highlight the plural process of migration and question trajectories that, although they are not statistically representative, deserve to be addressed because of their specific history of connections with the Russian Arctic since the creation of the great Soviet polar cities. This research also helps us to think about the timing

Migration, vulnerability, and change   123

of migrations in a longer-term frame, and as a story of margins included in the Soviet era as a continuous space, in a design very different from current boundaries. I will highlight the periodisation of Azerbaijani migration, which will allow me to analyse their careers as a response to vulnerabilities and the desire to perpetuate a social order established and codified 'here' (in Azerbaijan) while working 'there' (in Russia).

Migration to the extreme North and the reconstruction of the socio-economic field in Azerbaijan

Labour migration: a global response to vulnerabilities

Migration from Azerbaijan, as from other countries in the South Caucasus, goes back to ancient times and intensified following the conflicts in Nagorno-Karabakh (Mouradian, 1988; Papazian, 2010) and in Abkhazia and Ossetia (Merlin & Serrano, 2010; Serrano, 2007). The end of the Soviet Union led to new trajectories for migrants, mainly based on the search for work.

In terms of migration flows, the South Caucasus countries do not top the list: the Central Asian countries remain the main providers of manpower to Russia (Figures 6.3, 6.4). Nevertheless, migration from Azerbaijan is interesting to study (Dermendzhieva, 2011) and its long time-period allows one to provide a perspective on several generations of migrants (Hohmann et al., 2016). By the end of the nineteenth century Azeri engineers, who had acquired valuable know-how thanks to the discovery of oil in their country, were sent from Baku to Tyumen to participate in the beginnings of oil extraction in this region, where they are still present today. Alongside the petty trade sector, students, technicians and especially oil sector engineers supplemented other waves of migrants. Their contribution to the oil industry is a source of great pride for the Azeris, especially those in the diaspora (Braux, 2014). In the years 1970–1980, Heydar Aliyev increased the quota of Azeri students allowed to go study in higher education institutions of the USSR. However, students and engineers were obliged to enroll in the *orgnabor* system, aimed at organising internal migration by distributing migrants across large industrial projects of the Soviet era. This allowed the state to control their movements through the residence permit (*propiska*).[7] Thousands of young Azerbaijanis went to study in Russia at that time (Rumyantsev, 2014). Trade monopolies by certain social groups is a well-known phenomenon and is found both in the regionalisation and in the ethnicisation of markets: during the Soviet era, Azerbaijanis thus controlled nearly 80 percent of the Soviet flower market, in addition to their strong presence on many other markets (Yunus, 2003). The collapse of the USSR upset this balance, and the Nagorno-Karabakh conflict led to a huge wave of refugees, with over 800,000 internally displaced persons. Economic niches occupied by migrants have evolved over time; markets became more segmented and the construction sector became more attractive to economic migrants (Figures 6.1a and b and 6.2).

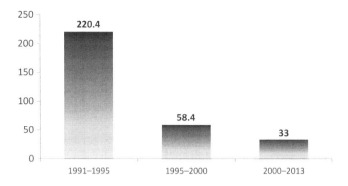

Figure 6.2 Number of migrants who left Azerbaijan per period (in thousands)
Source: State Statistical Committee of the Republic of Azerbaijan. www.azstat.org

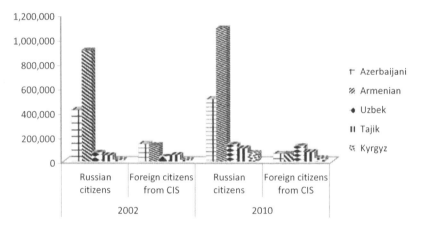

Figure 6.3 Ethnicity according to Russian or foreign citizenship of the CIS countries
Source: State Statistical Committee of the Republic of Azerbaijan. www.gks.ru/free_doc/new_site/perepis2010/perepis_itogi1612.htm www.perepis2002.ru/index.html?id=1

Country of origin	May 2014	March 2016
Armenia	491,501	464,884
Azerbaijan	600,096	445,575
Kyrgyzstan	539,108	905,659
Tajikistan	1,137,939	863,426
Ukraine	1,606,186	2,501784
Uzbekistan	2,509,998	1,762,364

Figure 6.4 Foreign citizens on the territory of the Russian Federation (aggregate data)
Source: Federal Migration Service (FMS): www.fms.gov.ru/about/statistics/data

The 2003 oil boom enabled Azerbaijan to restore living standards and economic independence following difficult years in the immediate post-Soviet period, while at the same time closing the public space and strengthening authoritarianism-neopatrimonialism (Laruelle, 2012a). This involves capturing political and economic power and its symbols and patronage of powerful informal networks and is reflected in particular by the predatory appropriation of resources, especially hydrocarbons, by the clans in power.

The social sector is now the poor relation in Azerbaijan. Despite increased spending in the 2000s due to a rapidly growing budget, inequalities persist because investments were ultimately low in the social sector. As elsewhere in the former USSR, albeit to varying degrees, the transition from a planned to a market economy has not been without damage and has affected the health and social sectors especially severely, while public spending on infrastructure, national defence and government services increased over the same period. Spending for social security decreased from 23.7 percent of total expenditures in 2003 to 11.6 percent in 2009; for education, over the 2005–2012 period expenditure amounted to 2.8 percent of GDP and is estimated in 2016 at 2.5 percent of GDP (Guliyev, 2016); for public health, spending was around 5 percent of GDP in 2016. The representations of the public health system became very negative irrespective of the interviewee's generation (based on observations and interviews by the author since 2011 in Azerbaijan, in Baku, Guba, Minguetchevir, Sheki). Above all, the fall in oil prices and the depreciation of the ruble (estimated at 80 percent according to the Center for Economic and Social Development in early 2015; interview in January 2015, Baku) led to a very negative situation in the labour market in Russia, including a pause in, or a definitive abandonment of, major construction projects. Transfers from Russia decreased significantly, which also affected the domestic economy. Besides, a new Russian Federation law[8] came into force on 1 January 2015 for migrant workers, stipulating the requirement to buy a licence and other obligations such as to pass an exam on Russian language and civilisation; this will certainly not hinder the inflow of informal workers and may even exacerbate it.

In addition, the crisis in Russia is reflected by a tendency to return Azerbaijani migrant workers, which may generate tensions in the Azerbaijani labour market. Since January 2015, over 70,000 migrants returned home, according to official data, and according to unofficial sources (CESD) the numbers could be much higher. As a migrant Azeri worker from Sheki commented: 'Why currently stay in Russia for work, when the ruble has fallen so much; it's no longer profitable for us'. Still, others do remain in Russia. I will analyse the careers and trajectories of migrants from Azerbaijan in the Russian Great North, in Murmansk region, in the Tajmir peninsula, Norilsk and Dudinka, to shed light on their original routes, characterised by an historical anchor and accompanied by geographic and professional logics.

126 *Sophie Hohmann*

Topography and temporality of migration to polar cities: case studies of Murmansk and Norilsk

The history of human settlement in the Murmansk region is much older than that in Norilsk. The assimilation (*osvoenie*) of this Northern region involved the significant intermingling, from the seventeenth century onwards, of early Russian settlers – the 'Pomoris' – with the indigenous Saami, whose presence is attested in this area for over 10,000 years. In particular, the construction of the railway in 1916 required a large workforce, and Murmansk soon became a typical product of Soviet industrialisation, with its industry, port and military bases. By contrast, the Norilsk-Nickel Kombinat was only created in 1935 by prisoners from the Norillag labour camp, before Norilsk acquired city status in 1953. The Murmansk region nevertheless followed the development of the same industries as Norilsk: extraction of nickel, copper, apatite, palladium, platinum and other semi-precious and precious minerals, as well as hydrocarbons. It also included a strong fishing sector, which ranked second in Russia: Murmansk was one of the most important Russian ports by the 1950s.

The industrial complexes developed with the first five-year plans, and most monocities[9] go back to the early 1930s. A city is considered a monocity when 25 percent of its population works in its primary industry, more than 50 percent of total town production is generated by this industry and more than 20 percent of the municipal budget is dependent on it (Didyk, 2014; Laruelle, Hohmann, Burtseva, 2016). All kinds of people have been working in the Murmansk region, originally hostile to mankind: people specially resettled (the *spetspereselentsy*, mostly kulaks), the Gulag prisoners (approximately 10,000 persons in the 1930s), but also volunteers. Mass industrialisation and the destruction of the peasantry in Central Russia led many people to migrate to the Kola Peninsula. 'Canadianisation'[10] did not take place in this region, contrary to the expectations of the authorities (Fedorov, 2009). A proactive strategy was adopted, including the establishment in 1932 of polar allowances that contributed to these populations staying longer (Fedorov, 2014). Moreover, the strategic impact of the presence of the Northern Fleet, and of the northern road to the Arctic – developed by the central government – contributed to the industrial and strategic conquest of the North, as a new frontier with strong resonances in the mental universe of the population.

This led to a demographic boom: Murmansk grew from 11,400 inhabitants in 1928 to 117,000 in 1939 (Fedorov, 2009). Completely destroyed and devastated during the Second World War, its industry rose again afterwards, and new waves of migrants helped rebuild the city: they found work in the industrial complexes and in the mines. Murmansk became the largest city located beyond the Arctic Circle, with 472,274 inhabitants in the 1989 census. Several waves of migrants occurred in the 1960s and 1970–1980, often with the romantic pioneer's idea of contributing to the continuity of the 'conquest' of the polar areas, and a willingness to accept the challenge of making the city a utopia.[11] The 1970s was a golden age: it was very prestigious to work in the

Migration, vulnerability, and change 127

North, and for that it was imperative to have an invitation and two letters of recommendation. This partly explains the high rate of out-migration to Murmansk in this period, even though the Brezhnev era of stagnation (*zastoi*) was already under way. The system was already disintegrating due to the suppression of economic reform, the war in Afghanistan and the development of an informal economy; this continued under Gorbachev and led to deteriorating living standards and hopes.

New frontiers, ancient migrations and reshaping of the urban landscape

After the collapse of the USSR, the liberalisation of prices in February 1992 (Heleniak, 1999) and the accompanying policy of economic shock therapy had lasting effects on the economy and the social and economic history of this polar region. The decentralisation of the federal budget to the regions very quickly changed the economies of the entire territory, especially in the monocities (Dydyk, 2014), which were very dependent on funds provided by a planned economy. This would lead to massive depopulation in the far North (Heleniak, 1999): why stay and work in areas hostile to humans without further financial and social compensations? The return of populations to the 'continental' homeland was combined with the process of 'westward drift' that was observed in Russia after the fall of the USSR. This resulted in an increase of the average age of the population in the arctic regions: the young working-age population had gone, leaving room for an ageing population (Mkrttchian, 2005). Between 1991 and 2012, the Murmansk region lost a third of its inhabitants (Bardileva & Portsel, 2014), transforming the urban world and its industrial landscape and generating a reconfiguration of professional solidarity and social fabric.[12] Norilsk has lost 35 percent of its population compared with the last Soviet census of 1989,[13] and it is these migration flows that reconfigured the demographic dynamics in the 1990s and 2000s. Populations of young migrants, who came alone or with their families, have changed the age structure of Norilsk, reflecting a younger population, since most migrants have not had time to grow old (Kašnitskij, 2014). The most salient example is the autonomous district of Yamalo-Nenets, where there has been a population growth generated by the influx of migrants who settled with their families and who have higher fertility than the average for Russians and the Nenets.

These big circumpolar cities witnessed an intensifying flow of migrant workers from the predominantly rural former Southern Soviet republics, Central Asia and South Caucasus, in the late 1990s, a trend that accelerated in the 2000s (Hohmann & al., 2014; Dermendzhieva, 2011). The Arctic region became an economically attractive region for people without prospects or plagued by uncertain political situations. However, this attraction did not occur by chance, and the territorial and economic anchor of Azerbaijanis (among other nationalities; see Figures 6.5 and 6.6) attests to reticularity,[14] allowing the development of the current recomposition of different professional niches.

128 *Sophie Hohmann*

Territorialisation of plural economic niches and generational trajectories

Despite this very unfavourable situation, there was no perforation of the urban space, and no district became comprehensively deserted in the Murmansk region. Besides the key areas related to mining of minerals, Murmansk preserved some diversification, which monocities could not do: food industries, services, transport companies and logistics necessitated by the proximity to the port and to the railway, as well as the administration of the region and the municipality.

The history of mobility in the Murmansk region, and also in the more recent city of Norilsk (1953), is interesting for several reasons. It provides information on population structures, on social stratification and on the transformation of the migration landscape according to historical and socio-economic processes. It also demonstrates collective journeys among migrants from various countries of the former Soviet space. These itineraries can be analysed through the prism of a sociological career perspective (Becker, 1985), but also through a generational prism. This approach allows one to decipher transformations over time, beyond the networks and professional sectors concerned, and to take into account the motivations and constraints of individuals who moved. Indeed, the different 'generations' of migrants (in its ideal-typical meaning), can reveal characteristics of their own,[15] encompassing through their modes of functioning the disruption of the established social order and socio-historical processes. This reading grid can address the issue of migration from a generational angle by taking the generation as a group of migrants (in this case immigrants) who belong to the same generation mode.

Social processes are subject to extreme fluctuations, and, accordingly, new paradigms emerged with the collapse of the USSR. Some nationalities from countries in the south of the former USSR would arrive in exponential numbers in the Murmansk region and Norilsk in order to find work; in the late 1980s the local population started to record a notable deficit, that would continue to widen in 1990–2000. However, it is important to emphasise here that the flow of migrants from the South Caucasus, as with those from Central Asia, can be linked clearly to mobility experiences during Soviet times and even before. These earlier experiences are also used as a bridge for compatriots and family, and allow one to identify the establishment of professional niches around nationalities. Considering these processes from a sociological angle of career trajectories, two broad categories can be identified from these 'newcomer' migrants: military service and work.

Migration for military service

The Murmansk region is one of the most militarised regions of Russia and hosts several military bases in closed cities (*ZATO*) – Aleksandrovsk, Severomorsk, Olenegorsk, Zaozersk, Ostrovnoi, Vidyaevo – where the Northern

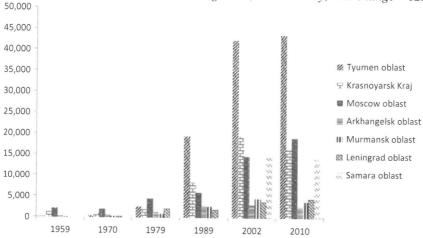

Figure 6.5 Number of Azerbaijani inhabitants in various regions of Russia according to censuses (Rosstat). www.gks.ru/free_doc/new_site/ (for censuses 2002 and 2010)
Source: http://demoscope.ru/weekly/ssp(for censuses 1959, 1979, 1989)

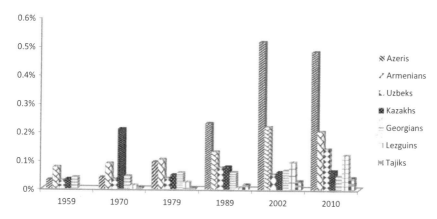

Figure 6.6 Ethnic groups from Caucasus and Central Asia in Murmansk oblast according to censuses (Rosstat). www.gks.ru/free_doc/new_site/ (censuses 2002 and 2010)
Source: http://demoscope.ru/weekly/ssp(for censuses 1959, 1979, 1989)

fleet is concentrated. The need for servicemen on the bases, as well as in the Northern fleet, represents a significant niche for migrants. Among the interviewed persons of Azeri origin[16], many were born in the 1950–1980 period and were sent to the Murmansk region to do their military service. Many Armenians were also sent, in particular those who were studying at the Baku naval military school before the end of the 1980s. There was also a high prestige

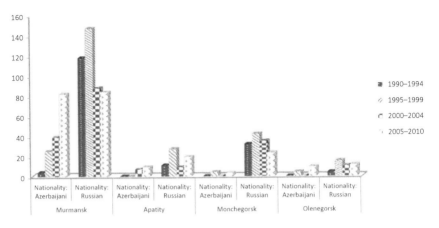

Figure 6.7 Distribution of Azerbaijani inhabitants, by cohort (year of move) and nationality (Russian or Azerbaijani) in Murmansk, Apatity (the second largest city in the region) and two monocities (Monchegorsk and Olenegorsk, both in Kola Peninsula)

Source: Rosstat. Calculation by the author. www.gks.ru/free_doc/new_site/perepis2010/perepis_itogi1612.htm

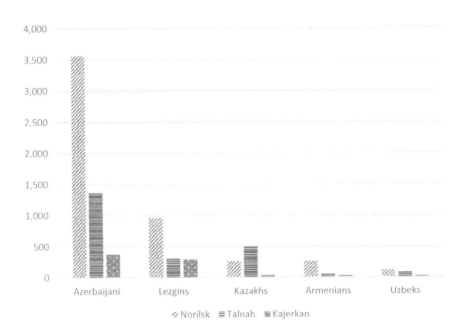

Figure 6.8 Nationalities from Southern Caucasus and Central Asia living in Norilsk and its satellites (Census 2010)
Source: www.gks.ru/free_doc/new_site/perepis2010/perepis_itogi1612.htm

Migration, vulnerability, and change 131

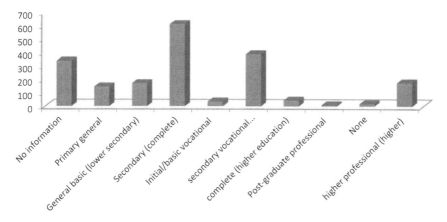

Figure 6.9 Level of educational attainment among Azerbaijani inhabitants of Murmansk city (Census 2010)
Source: www.gks.ru/free_doc/new_site/perepis2010/perepis_itogi1612.htm

associated with work in the Northern Fleet for those who were admitted. Some stayed on as contract workers, others found work in another sphere and remained. One of them was Reza[17], a person born in 1950 in the region of Astara, a Talysh, even if he declared himself Azerbaijani in the last Russian census of 2010:

> All that did not exist before the collapse of the USSR; at the time there was no Talysh or Azeri, it was the Union of Soviet Socialist Republics ... I feel above all a Soviet citizen even if all this is over ... I came here in Murmansk to do my military service in 1972, I was sent to Severomorsk (a closed city), I served in the fleet of submariners and then I joined in the fleet as a contract worker before entering the security forces of the MVD, the Ministry of Interior in Murmansk in 1990 ... I cannot stand the cold, I've never been able to bear it, but I prefer to stay in the North even though I love my country of origin... it's too hard there, and here we are family, three of my four children are here in the area and they have a job, my youngest daughter is in 5th grade and works well in school, that's what counts...
>
> (Interview in Murmansk, March 2016)

The army allows one to acquire social status (Jones, 1990), to build social networks, and for those who decided to do their military service in Murmansk after 1991 it was a way to get Russian citizenship. Azeris did not necessarily intend to stay after their military service, but the socio-political context of the late 1980s and early 1990s for those who had completed their military service (generation born in the 1960s–1970s) in the USSR and

132 *Sophie Hohmann*

Azerbaijan SSR encouraged them to remain in the North. The intention is therefore to be questioned through various exogenous parameters, and not only the endogenous ones. The same phenomenon was observed in Norilsk (Figures 6.8 and 6.9): there is no chance of professional mobility, and military service could be one of the starting points for a career in a city or mono-city of the North. Likewise, having studied at an institute specialising in metal-lurgy or mining was also an important reason, as we shall see below.

Migration for work: territoriality and social ties

Migration for work is at the heart of the conquest of the Great Russian north, which evokes mental representations of a heroic frontier or 'pioneer' region. The industrial conquest of the Murmansk region started with a labour force of essentially Slavic origin. After the Second World War, and with a huge need for reconstruction, there was an influx of Ukrainians and Belarusians, now the two largest nationalities after the Russians in the Murmansk region. These national-ities quickly found a professional niche in the extractive industries in the Mur-mansk region. Job opportunities were not lacking in the 1950s; the Komsomol were characterised by an intense relation to industrial development in these pioneer areas hostile to man. Many Ukrainians who worked as miners in the Donbas or who trained in specialised institutions in metallurgy stayed to work in the North. In addition, financial incentives, such as the specific subsidies in the North (*severnye nadbavki* or *poliarki*), were introduced in 1932 and represented significant financial incentives, as well as the 'nordicity coefficients' introduced in the 1960s, which increased salaries according to remoteness (this incentive also applied in the East and the South of Russia, such as the Chita region) as well as various social benefits, such as 21 days' paid leave from the company.

The South Caucasus nationalities (Armenians and Azerbaijanis especially) have a long tradition of mobility in Russia, including in the North (as oil work-ers, engineers, geologists, experts, students, traders, fish plants, ports). In Azer-baijan, one of the main reasons for a high rate of out-migration to Russia was the dire economic conditions and food provision of population in rural areas in the late 1960s. Seeking a better life, many people began to leave the Azerbaijani SSR for Russia in large numbers. Thus, the difference between immigration and out-migration for Azerbaijan reached 26,000 people by the mid-1980s, a fourfold increase compared with 1970. Since the majority of migrants were young people, it created a demographic problem in Azerbaijan.

Azerbaijanis[18] are the first nationality of the country's post-Soviet South to settle in the Murmansk region, as in the other polar regions (see Figures 6.6, 6.7 and 6.8), and remain very active. Many migrants came temporarily as part of seasonal migration for a few months to sell their products, or as those who found themselves on major construction projects in the 1980s, such as the famous *stroiotryadi*, or as those who played and continue to play a car-dinal role in the organisation and consolidation of post-Soviet migration strategies elsewhere in Russia (Rahmonova-Schwarz, 2010, Sahadeo, 2012).

Migration, vulnerability, and change 133

The end of the USSR transformed the economic relationships, and mobility patterns were reconfigured. Nevertheless, the economic niches, even if they changed after 1991, were marked by a long history and the 'ethnicisation' of economic sectors. Azerbaijanis who once sold fruit and vegetables on the market or in small shops became managers or directors of entire supermarket chains (like the *Evroros* chain in the Kola Peninsula) or took control of wholesale markets and became major entrepreneurs (observations in the summer of 2015 and the winter of 2016 in Murmansk, and the summer of 2015 in Norilsk and Dudinka). A new migrant 'aristocracy' was born, covering the generations of Azerbaijanis arriving before the end of the USSR and those aggregated to the niches developed during the Soviet era (see Figure 6.9 on the level of education among Azeris in Murmansk). Moreover, niches became more pluri-ethnic, establishing new relationships of trust with other nationalities, such as Uzbeks and Tajiks, because 'they do not drink and they work well' (interviews with Azerbaijanis in Murmansk). At the last Russian census of 2010, Azerbaijani nationals constituted 42 percent of all Southern nationalities of the former Soviet Union in the Murmansk region, Armenians 18 percent and Uzbeks 12 percent (about 7,000 Uzbeks with or without residence permit).[19]

Embedded reticular migration

Prioritisation of ethnic niches, in addition to their regionalisation, is a reality that reflects economic as well as social and cultural issues. In Murmansk, Azerbaijanis traditionally working in fruit and vegetables wholesale markets are mainly from the southern regions of Azerbaijan (Massali, Astara and Lenkaran[20]). Even in Soviet times, Azeri traders in Russia were from these regions, but also from the North East of Azerbaijan (Gusar and Khachmaz, mainly populated by Lezgins) because of their ancestral know-how in this business. The collapse of the agricultural economy and the disappearance of collective and state farms hit rural market gardens very hard, including many compatriots now found in Murmansk. It was in the 1990s that commercial 'shuttle' (*chelnok*) migrations back and forth developed as a survival strategy. These migrations, typical of the early post-Soviet period, helped building networks that would establish the current professional niches in the field of business.

Moreover, the Nagorno-Karabakh conflict resulted in flows of Azeri migrants to Russia in general, and to the North in particular, in the late 1980s and early 1990s. The lack of living space for the internally displaced Azerbaijanis (which in 2016 still account for 6 percent of Azerbaijan's total population) led them to find better living conditions beyond the borders of their country. Many Azerbaijani people who lived in the border provinces of Karabakh, for example in the completely devastated Agdam region, left their homes. Nowadays, Azerbaijanis from Agdam are found in Murmansk, working in clothing markets. Markets became more segmented after the

134 *Sophie Hohmann*

disappearance of the Soviet Union, but the economic niches they represent maintained themselves, based on the long-standing and solid reputation of Azerbaijanis in this sector. In the service sector, as mentioned above, some became heads of shopping centres; the general manager of *Evroros* is an Azerbaijani who received medical training in Baku and re-oriented himself towards business. Restaurants and cafes are also attractive niches. This network of shopping centres is protected by various networks that overlap more or less formally (personal observations in the field). Finally, one also finds students specialising in engineering or other areas popular with industrial complexes such as mineral extraction, prolonging a tradition established during Soviet times.[21]

For newcomers, Murmansk (as other circumpolar cities) is a city like no other. There, life develops in a logic of insularity that is unique to people living in the Great North, evoking the continent (*materik*) as a distant country, another land. Adaptation and representations of migrants differ with respect to the far North and the polar cold. Eduard, 34, a native of Massali, who arrived in Murmansk in 1996 (his father began trading in Murmansk in 1987), still remembers the shock at arrival on the tarmac, the biting cold:

> For me, the north is the cold. The polar night is pure hell. At first, one expects to see the sun and one understands that it will not come ... In contrast, the polar day is paradise! I just love it! And I like skiing, I love snow, I know everyone does not like it, but I do! One thing is certain, the North requires being prepared, and it's not easy.

Vugar, aged 32, also from Massali, arrived in the late 2000s, and evokes its tropism for sea fishing:

> I do not have Russian citizenship yet, and I would like to go to the sea ... I used to go fishing there (in Azerbaijan), I lived close to the Caspian, I love the sea ... I would like to become a fisherman but not on big boats rather on small trawlers for crabs, all kinds of fish, but not more than a week at sea. But to go out to the sea, you need citizenship ... for me the North is the sea, it is fishing, and when I arrived here I had not thought of all that, I was not sure where I would find myself... and then there are the people, and the Azeris will tell you they have the wrong course because of the cold and everything, but in fact they get quickly attached to the North, and to the people from the North, here it is very unusual ...
> (Interview in Murmansk, March 2015)

They are obviously marked by the fierce climate and the geographical isolation from the rest of Russia, but they also integrate quickly into the symbolic and physical domination of the industrial complex, the mono-industries and mono-cities. Some manage to integrate the access to status with a higher qualification, and this gives migrants a more heroic character on old 'pioneer'

Migration, vulnerability, and change 135

fronts. Through their own professional and personal journey of migrants who left the Caucasus to 'realise themselves' in the North, they renew the myth of the pioneer, and adapt to post-Soviet conditions of market economy and free movement.[22]

Role of diaspora associations in the reconstruction of social networks

The strategies implemented by post-Soviet Azeri migrants to access the labour market are facilitated by the fact that the diaspora has been particularly well established in Murmansk since Soviet times. Afil Guseinov is the head of the Azerbaijani diaspora in the Murmansk region through its representative function of the branch of the All-Russian Azerbaijani Congress (VAK) for the Murmansk region.[23] Afil is as the ideal type of the second generation of Azeris arrived in Russia. Born in 1966 in Nakhichevan[24], he was called up for military service in the Murmansk region in 1983, where he returned after studying law elsewhere (Sevastopol and Moscow). Afil is very active in administrative assistance to Azerbaijani migrants, and also at other social and economic levels. According to him, the number of Azerbaijani migrants decreased from 20,000 in 2013 to 13,000 (aggregate data) in 2015, since many have left because of the crisis.[25] The association led by Afil is working closely with AZIA, established in 2008 by an Uzbek diaspora leader, Paridokhon Nasirova, born in 1960 in Andijan. Both diaspora associations have developed a strong experience of managing various aspects of social, economic and security life of migrants.

Being secure in the Great North: representations of the Kola Peninsula, between stability and security

Despite the remoteness of the region, the Kola Peninsula is traditionally characterised as a magnet for migrant workers who came from other republics of the former USSR or from Moscow and St. Petersburg. Interesting results from the biographical interviews conducted in Murmansk, and language tests for migrants organised by the University of Murmansk between 2013 and 2015[26] showed that migrants have developed strategies of consolidation in the Russian North. Over a third of migrants opted for the temporary entry visa, or for the residence visa, although tests are more difficult than those for getting a business licence. The local office of the FMS in Murmansk confirms that every year between 5,000 and 7,000 foreigners obtain a residence permit for five years with a residence permit or a temporary visa for three years, bringing them into the category of permanent residents of the Russian Federation. Over the 2011–2014 period, trends in the number of foreign members of the CIS obtaining a temporary residence permit was growing (Federal Migration Service data reports 2011, 2012 and 2013).[27] The motivation for such a choice is explained by the fact that the certificate to obtain a higher status (registration and residence permit) gives

136 Sophie Hohmann

one the right to live on Russian territory for three years, whereas the certificate for obtaining the licence (valid only one year) gives only the right to work.

According to anthropologist Elena Zmeeva from the Social Science Research Centre in Barents/Apatity (MGGU), the reasons guiding the choice of migrants to the Kola Peninsula are essentially economic and political, and are linked to conflict in their country or region of origin. However, these choices are also explained by the presence of relatives, compatriots and the absence of conflict (Razumova, 2004), and security and stability of employment, which characterise this northern region (Zmeeva, 2011) (Figure 6.7). In addition, there are few illegal workers in Murmansk and the Murmansk region, as in Norilsk. These highly monitored cities are hardly liveable in without a legal status and various on-site observations show this well. As soon as they arrive, migrants are looking for ways to pass language tests to obtain a work permit or a licence. They are aware that their legal status is a way to circumvent risk, or to avoid finding themselves struggling in informal criminal networks, which is in fact a reality for some of them (personal observations and interviews in Norilsk in July 2015 and in Murmansk in March 2016).

The results of our in-depth, biographical interviews conducted in March 2016 confirm investigations conducted by the Social Science Centre Apatity (MGGU) with 900 Caucasians (North and South) since January 2015, and the findings of Olga Zmeeva (2011).[28] The economic factor ranks first in the responses: ability to find work, opportunities in the labour market, earning more money, work to finance a wedding, a house, buying a land plot. However, this does not imply that the choices are limited to the Kola Peninsula, as everywhere in Russia the main motivations for migration are economic. So there is something else that guides the choice of migrants to this polar region of Russia (as to other places elsewhere, such as the Yamal peninsula in Tyumen region). Why do migrants come to work in Murmansk? What are their motivations? This question was posed to each migrant entering the survey: the main motivation was clearly the presence of relatives, friends, or peers: 'I have a brother who works here', 'my mother lives here / I came to see her', 'my father lived here for 10 years', 'a friend told me that I could work here' are fragments of recurrent answers during these interviews. The importance of belonging to a clan or a sub-clan is also highlighted in this survey as an important variable. Several levels intervene in the labour market and employment: Azerbaijanis employers, as well the Uzbeks, claim that they make their choice primarily among their countrymen.

Thus, a 'socio-ethnic' stratification is looming through the organisation of recruitment and horizontal strategies between Caucasian and Central Asian ethnic groups such as Tajiks and Uzbeks. They all are well informed through the media and other means of communication: mobile phones, Internet/Skype, announcements on TV and so on. Moreover, an important element for explaining the choices of migrants in this region is the presentation of the

Migration, vulnerability, and change   137

Kola Peninsula as a 'space or zone without ethnic conflict' (Razumova 2004). The Murmansk region is characterised by a high level of ethnic tolerance, and this is one of the major reasons why migrants make this choice, especially those who suffered earlier from ethnic conflicts, such as Nagorno-Karabakh, the two Chechen wars, the Osh massacres in Central Asia's Kyrgyzstan, and, more recently, the war in Ukraine. Stability in Murmansk can be explained by the history of its settlement, its military history, Soviet legacy, the city and region's industrial history, but also by the importance of local cultural interactions, as briefly described above. Indeed, socio-cultural adaptation of populations in North Russia was a necessary condition for successful integration into the regional ethnic community and, therefore, for a process of acculturation.

Another important parameter also explains the attraction of the Murmansk region for migrants: good relations with the local population, with employers, with the owners of apartments rented by migrants. Many migrants speak of their employers with respect and vice versa. The willingness of companies to protect stability of employment and, by extension, their productivity in a region where overall security prevails, and where administrative rules are followed, can result in good care for migrants (language tests, support for getting administrative documents, insurance policy) by the employer himself. Of course, the situation behind the scenes is different, as everywhere, as employees of FMS testify (interviews in Murmansk, 12 July 2015). Nevertheless, migrants put forward emotional comfort in work and everyday life, the quality of human relationships in business, the public health system, the stores and the presence of the police as arguments for choosing this region.

Finally, turning to the opinions and representations of the non-migrant inhabitants of Murmansk, they are divided and reflect in some ways European reactions, especially since the beginning of the migration crisis and the war in Syria. The study of and participation in social networks (such as Facebook and *V kontakte*) show very mixed reactions to the creation of an adaptation centre for children of migrants in Murmansk. The Murmansk region had already been shaken socially by the arrival of thousands of Ukrainian migrants fleeing the Donbas conflict, and when an 'Arctic road' (a corridor on the Russian-Norwegian border) suddenly emerged in September 2015 for refugees fleeing the southern Mediterranean basin (Hohmann & Laruelle, 2016a), local scholars following migration issues (such as Zmeeva from the Kola Research Center in Apatity) noticed a rise in xenophobic discourses among the Russian population. As in Western Europe, refugees, migrant workers and their children became conflated in the minds of people. Russian propaganda based on rejection of 'others' further affected the tolerance of the inhabitants of Murmansk, who did not make such judgments before and accepted Azeris and Central Asians as the only persons able to conduct trade, sell good fruits and vegetables and open 'exotic' restaurants, in continuation of what already existed during Soviet times. The 'Arctic road'

138 *Sophie Hohmann*

refugee crisis quickly came to a halt because of the closure of the Norwegian border with Russia, after refugees had been well informed about the impossibility of reaching Norway; the perception of Murmansk peninsula as a secure, peaceful place for inhabitants, both non-migrant and migrant, survived.

Conclusion

Generations of people born in the Soviet Union between 1950 and 1970 perform an important function in the formation of current migration processes in Russia, but also in the shaping of the meaning of migration and its possibilities. They are characterised as intermediate generations, and provide a major reticular dimension in which to view the new generations of migrants. Through this analysis, mechanisms underlying a systematic arrangement of social relations aimed at preventing social insecurity are revealed (Castel, 2003). As demonstrated above, diaspora associations help guarantee a form of 'global' security. Here, the concept of 'embeddedness' developed by Granovetter (1973; 1985) allows one to consider economic exchanges without isolating them from social relations. However, it is clear that the networks composed of parents and compatriots – especially among Azerbaijanis present in the Murmansk region since Soviet times – are crucial to supporting the access of migrants to the labour market, and to controlling newcomers and establishing trans-generational networks. Moreover, understanding the migration process through the sociological lens of generation modes allow us to show universal characteristics in places where the historical construction of empires (Russian or French for example) and their socioeconomic conditions explain these migratory processes.

The capital integration into networks and the development of interpersonal relationships provide opportunities for migrants to broaden their fields of contractual opportunities and to lose the initial stress of migration. The dynamic conditions of 'social embeddedness' of these practices strongly affect the contractual path of migrants by allowing them to access those arrangements deemed most interesting to them. Networks are mostly based on the principle of reciprocity, which implies the existence of symmetrical entities (Polanyi, 1983) reciprocity being defined as a double but not instantaneous transfer. The counter-party, or a reciprocal transfer (such as an airfare or transportation fee funded by the migrant's family against a later transfer of money, or setting up a small business to run a family and community waterwheel), will depend on the existing tension in the group, on social pressure, on the social obligation to give back which, in turn, can lead to exclusion from the group in case of non-fulfilment of the obligation or counter-obligation. The results of this study about the complex individual and collective strategies that integrate migration as a resource but also as a risk, and the choice of the Murmansk region, demonstrate overall strategies aimed at risk-avoidance.

It follows from this study that labour migration is a major social fact in the Caucasian landscape in response to social and civil insecurity. This alternative

Migration, vulnerability, and change 139

is a means of informal solidarity (Lautier, 2004), a kind of insurance against risk, through which migrants can develop new forms of mobilisation against poverty, a response to the mismanagement of states, to the loss of the 'welfare state' (loss of safety nets, demodernisation, predation of the means of production) and to the bankruptcy of the social status of the men in these patriarchal Caucasian societies: men were – and remain – the guarantors of the sustainability of the social and family order. Nevertheless, migration implies a dependency on the global situation, including on political and economic conditions in host countries, as we see today in Russia. They also depend on various forms of allegiance to migrant networks, and therefore on various loyalty systems that characterise these complex systems. In 'post-heroic' post-Soviet societies, assurances as to the survival of community, of family, and of relatives should be sought in a re-weaving of norms and networks that existed before the collapse of the USSR, reshaped in face of new global contingencies.

Notes

1 The author would like to thank warmly Professor Bruce Grant, New York University, for his very useful comments on a draft of this chapter.
2 In Azerbaijan, a State Migration Service modeled on the Russian FMS was established by a presidential decree of 19 March 2007. The government played an important role in stabilising it; in 2004, the Concept for State Migration Policy was adopted and in 2013 Azerbaijan was the first CIS country adopting a Migration Code, amalgamating all the existing laws and legal codes into one single overarching Act. As a result it is now much easier for migrants, as well as employers in hiring foreign migrants and understanding the issues on migration. The Act has also made the registration process (both for residency and employment reasons) simpler for migrants. Those with refugee status and successful asylum seekers are exempted from obtaining work permits should they find employment. The Act also provides incentives to foreign direct investors by granting three-year stay permit for anyone investing 500,000 manats ($322,000) into the economy. The Act was the first of its kind in the South Caucasus region (interview with an economist from CESD, Baku).
3 This research was funded by the CASCADE project and by the Norwegian Research Council, in partnership with George Washington University and the Institute of Barents (University of Tromsø) through the ARCSUS project (the Arctic Research Coordination Network Project: Building a Research Network for Promoting Arctic Urban Sustainability, funded by the National Science Foundations, for 2013–2017).
4 On the Kola peninsula (Murmansk city, Apatity, Zapoliarnij, Nikel, Monchegorsk, Kirovsk, Teriberka) and on the Tajmir Peninsula (Norilsk and Dudinka).
5 I conducted this fieldwork with Aleksandra Burtseva from the MGGU, Faculty of Humanities, Arctic Murmansk University.
6 I conducted in-depth interviews based on the AGEVEN biographical methodology, a chronological grid providing an efficient tool that allows one to date events precisely and to classify demographic events such as changes of places of residence, in marital status and other life cycle events. The method is very flexible, and one could add other events such as use of healthcare, history of legal status, economic and political events, natural catastrophes and legislation. Besides the AGEVEN

140 *Sophie Hohmann*

grid, I used a semi-structured questionnaire to record precise trajectories of labour migrants, strategies of families, changes of residence, life style in Russia, administrative issues, health care issues, legal status, transportation, sociability and economic niches.

7 The *orgnabor* system is now different because it deals only with international migration and involves only a few hundred people according to the FMS (Ivakhnyuk & Iontsev, 2012).

8 Federal law of 24 November 2014, No. 357-FZ, On amendments to the Federal Law on the Legal Status of Foreigners in the territory of the Russian Federation and other legislative acts of the Russian Federation.

9 The eight monocities of the Murmansk regions are Kirovsk, Kovdor, Zapoliarni Zori, Monchegorsk, Tumannyi, Zapoliarnyi, Revda, Nikel. Murmansk city was not a monocity, unlike Norilsk.

10 During the 1920s the authorities expected a 'natural' evolution of the region, referred to as 'Canadianisation', referring to the model of Canadian development. However, this policy quickly failed, as the region was hit by a large turnover of people not wanting to stay and consequently a low potential for the creation of a labour force.

11 Interview conducted with Oleg Kovas, Human Resources at Norilsk-Nickel, Zapolyarnyi-Nikel complex, 14 July 2015.

12 This was due to a lower birth rate and life expectancy than elsewhere: 63 years for men and 74 for women.

13 Yet, compared to other Arctic regions like Chukotka and Yakutia (Heleniak, 1999), it remains relatively untouched.

14 This sociological notion of reticular embedding in migration emphasises the importance of historical factors as well as that of social capital in the construction of migrant networks and careers.

15 Bourdieu and Sayad showed similar effects when analysing generations of Algerian migrants in France (Bourdieu & Sayad, 1974 and 1999).

16 Interviews in the markets in Murmansk in July 2015 and March 2016 with the Azerbaijani diaspora in restaurants and during the festival of Nowruz (Iranian New Year on 21 March) in Murmansk.

17 To ensure anonymity, identities were changed.

18 In the late 2010s, there are an estimated one million workers from Azerbaijan in the Russian Federation (source: IOM), and 60 percent of remittances would be for families living in rural Azerbaijan (source: FAO).

19 Interview with representative of the Central Asian Aid Organisation (AZIA), July 2015 in Murmansk.

20 The Massali region, mainly populated by Talysh, is a poor area. On Azeri migration, see Yunusov, 2003.

21 It is also noteworthy that in Soviet times, the compulsory allocation process (*raspredelenie*) of the labour force meant that one had to serve the state for five years after studies paid for by the state.

22 Interviews with migrants from Azerbaijan, Tajikistan and Uzbekistan, Norilsk, July 2015.

23 VAK was founded on 5 March 2001. The Murmansk branch of VAK was founded in 2004 but has actually worked only since 2008. There are other subsidiaries in Russia and VAK plays an important role in the administrative regulation of the Diaspora working with local authorities, and is responsible for the adaptation of local culture, Russian language exams, and coordination with national associations and organisations.

24 Nakhichevan is renowned for its elite and its intellectuals (the Aliev dynasty comes from Nakhichevan). Baku is also known for its aristocracy and its elites.

25 Interview with Afil Guseinov, 9 July 2015 in Murmansk.

Migration, vulnerability, and change 141

26 Interviews and personal observations in Murmansk, and during testing in Murmansk in March 2016.
27 Information collected by Alexandra Burtseva.
28 Zmeeva conducted a major survey in 2004–2005 in two samples: the inhabitants of several towns of the peninsula, and migrants from North and South Caucasus.

References

Ahmadov, I. (2016). 'Azerbaijan's New Macroeconomic Reality: How to Adapt to Low Oil Prices'. *Caucasus Analytical Digest*, 83, 21 April. www.css.ethz.ch/content/dam/ethz/special-interest/gess/cis/center-for-securities-studies/pdfs/CAD82.pdf.

Allahveranov, A. and Huseynov, E. (2013). 'Azerbaijan Country Study'. EuropAid. 130215/C/SER/Multi. Baku.

Antoine, P., Bry, X. and Diouf, P. D. (1987). 'La fiche AGEVEN: un outil pour la collecte des données rétrospectives', *Techniques d'enquête*, 13(2), 173–218.

Aslanli, K. (2016). 'Lower Oil Revenues, Higher Public Debt: the Fiscal Policy Implications of Low Oil Prices in Azerbaijan', *Caucasus Analytical Digest*, 83, 21 April. www.css.ethz.ch/content/dam/ethz/special-interest/gess/cis/center-for-securities-studies/pdfs/CAD82.pdf.

Bardileva, Y. P. and Portsel, A. K. (2014). 'Sovremennye demograficheskie vyzovy i ugrozy v Murmanskoi oblasti', in *Sovremennye vyzovy i ugrozy razvitiia v Murmanskoi oblasti: regional'nyi atlas*, Murmansk: Murmansk Gosudarstvennyi Pedagogicheskii Universitet.

Becker, H. S. (1985). *Outsiders. Etudes de sociologie de la déviance*, Paris: Métaillié, 248.

Boonstra, J. and Delcour, L. (2015). 'A broken region: evaluating EU policies in the South Caucasus', Policy Brief Cascade, FRIDE, No. 195, January.

Bourdieu, P. and Sayad, A. (1964). *Le déracinement, la crise de l'agriculture traditionnelle en Algérie*, Paris: Éditions de Minuit, 220.

Braux, A. (2014). *Moscou/Caucase: migrations et diasporas dans l'espace post-soviétique*, Paris: Petra, 346.

Castel, R. (2003). *L'insécurité sociale*, Paris: Seuil, 95.

CESD Research Group, 2012, 'Azerbaijan Economy Since Independence; Independent View, Baku, March'. http://cesd.az/new/wp-content/uploads/2012/03/Azerbaijan_Economy_Since_Independence1.pdf.

Chulkov, A. V. (1994). 'Naselenie i trudovye resursy v Noril'skom promyshlennom raione', *Sociologicheskie*, 7, 39–42.

Dermendzhieva, Z. (2011). 'Emigration from the South Caucasus: who goes abroad and what are the economic implications?', *Post-Communist Economies*, 23(3), 377–398.

Didyk, V. and Ryabova, L. (2014). 'Monogoroda Rossiiskoi Arktiki: strategii razvitiya (na primere Murmanskoi oblasti)', *Ekonomicheskie i sotsial'nye peremeny: fakty, tendentsii, prognoz*, 4(34), 84–99.

Fedorov, P. V. (2009). *Severnyi vektor v rossiiskoi istorii. Tsentr i kol'skoe zapoliaree v 16–20 vekov*, Murmansk: Murmansk Gosudarstvennyi Pedagogicheskii Universitet.

Fedorov, P. V. (2014). *Kul'turnye landshafty kol'skogo severa v usloviakh urbanizatsii (1931–1991 gg)*, Murmansk: Murmansk Gosudarstvennyi Pedagogicheskii Universitet.

142 *Sophie Hohmann*

Granovetter, M. S. (1973). 'The Strength of Weak Ties', *The American Journal of Sociology*, 78(6), 1360–1380.

Granovetter, M. S. (1985). 'Economic Action and Social Structure: The Problem of Embeddedness', *American Journal of Sociology*, 91(3), 481–510.

Guliyev, F. (2016). 'Azerbaijan: Low Oil Prices and their Social Impact', *Caucasus Analytical Digest*, 83, 21 April. www.css.ethz.ch/content/dam/ethz/special- interest/gess/cis/center-for-securities-studies/pdfs/CAD82.pdf.

Heleniak, T. (1999). 'Out-migration and Depopulation of the Russian North during the 1990s', *Post-Soviet Geography and Economics*, 40(3), 281–304.

Heleniak, T. (2008). 'Changing Settlement Patterns across the Russian North at the Turn of the Millennium', in M. Tykkyläinen and V. Rautio (eds), *Russia's Northern Regions on the Edge: Communities, Industries and Populations from Murmansk to Magadan*, Helsinki: Aleksanteri Institute, 25–52.

Heleniak, T. (2009). 'The Role of Attachment to Place in Migration Decisions of the Population of the Russian North', *Polar Geography*, 32(1), 31–60.

Heleniak, T. (2010). 'Population Change in the Periphery: Changing Migration Patterns in the Russian North', *Sibirica: Interdisciplinary Journal of Siberian Studies*, 9 (3), 17–18.

Hohmann, S. (2012). 'Processus migratoires et trajectoires de vie au Tadjikistan après la guerre civile. Application de la méthode AGEVEN auprès de travailleurs migrants dans sept villages autour de Douchanbe', *Migrations Société*, 24(141–142), 41–58.

Hohmann, S. and Laruelle, M. (2016a). 'From the Mediterranean to the Far North: A Refugees Corridor at the Russian-Norwegian Border', The Arctic Institute.org, 24 August.

Hohmann, S. and Laruelle, M. (2016b). 'Norilsk, ville polaire, cité du nickel', *Le Monde diplomatique*, July.

Hohmann, S., Laruelle, M. and Burtseva, A. (2016). 'Murmansk. Biography of a City and its Population Movements', in Laruelle, M. (ed.), *New Mobilities and Social Changes in Russia's Arctic Regions*, Abingdon: Routledge, 158–175.

Hohmann, S. and Lefèvre, C. (2014a). 'Measures of poverty in the Caucasus and Central Asia: international approaches and specificities of Southern countries of the former Soviet Union', in Hohmann, S., Mouradian, C., Serrano, S. and Thorez, J. (eds), *Development in Central Asia and the Caucasus: Migration, Democratisation and Inequality in the Post-Soviet Era*, London: I.B. Tauris, 183–211.

Hohmann, S. and Lefèvre, C. (2014b). 'Post-Soviet Transformations of Health Systems in the South Caucasus', *Central Asian Affairs*, 1, 48–70.

Hohmann, S., Mouradian, C., Serrano, S. and Thorez, J. (eds) (2014). *Development in Central Asia and the Caucasus: Migration, Democratisation and Inequality in the Post-Soviet Era*, London: I.B. Tauris, 288.

Ivakhnyuk, I. and Iontsev, V. (2012). 'The Role of Circular Migration in Russia', CARIM-EAST Explanatory Note 12/87, September.

Jones, E. (1990). 'Social Change and Civil-Military Relations', in Colton, Timothy J. and Gustaffson, Thane (eds), *Soldiers and the Soviet State*, Princeton: Princeton University Press.

Kašnitskij, I. (2014). *Vliânie migracii na demografitcheskuju strukturu v malyh territoriâh Rossii* (*Mémoire de master*), Moscow: Institut Demografii, VyShKa.

Laruelle, M. (2012a). 'Discussing Neopatrimonialism and Patronal Presidentialism in the Central Asian Context', *Demokratizatsiya*, 20(4), 301–324.

Migration, vulnerability, and change   143

Laruelle, M. (ed.) (2012b). *Migration and Social Upheaval as the Face of Globalization in Central Asia*, Boston: Brill.

Laruelle, M. (2014). *Russia's Arctic Strategies and the Future of the Far North*, New York: M.E. Sharpe.

Laruelle, M. and Rakishvaya, B. (eds) (2015). '"Pamyat" iz plameni Afganistana. Interv'yu s voinami–internatsionalistami Afganskoi voiny 1979–1989 godov', Central Asia Program Series No. 2, Astana, Washington, D.C. https://app.box.com/s/umser0gccid0n6cvrl51kuyrsc8ikm8b.

Lautier, B. (2004). *L'économie informelle dans le Tiers Monde*, Paris: La découverte, Print, Repères, 125.

Lewin, M. (2003). *Le siècle soviétique*, Paris: Fayard/Le monde diplomatique, 526.

Merlin, A. and Serrano, S. (eds) (2010). *Ordres et désordres dans le Caucase*, Brussels: Editions de l'Université de Bruxelles, 228.

Mouradian, C. (1988). 'Permanence de la famille arménienne', pp. 59–84 (in collaboration with Anahide Ter Minassian), in Basile Kerblay (ed.), *'Evolution des modèles familiaux dans les pays de l'est européen en en URSS'*, Paris, IMSECO, coll. 'Cultures et Sociétés de l'Est'.

Mkrtchyan, N. (2005). 'Migratsiya v Rossii: zapadnyi dreif', *Demoscope Weekly*, 185–186.

Mkrtchyan, N. and Karachurina, L. (2014). 'Migratsiya v Rossii. Potoki i tsentry prityazheniia', *Demoscope Weekly*, 21 April–4 May, 595–596.

Mühlfried, F. (2014). 'Let's flow! Circular migration and transhumant mobility among the Tushetians of Georgia', *Caucasus Survey*, 2(1–2), 1–13.

Parente, G., Shilklomanov, N. and Streletskiy, D. (2012). 'Living in the New North: Migration to and from Russian Arctic Cities', *FOCUS on Geography*, fall, 77–89.

Papazian, T. (2010). 'Nœud gordien ou rocher de Sisyphe? Le conflit du Haut-Karabagh dans les stratégies des chefs d'Etat de l'Arménie postsoviétique', pp. 171–195, in Merlin, A. and Serrano, S. (eds), *Ordres et désordres dans le Caucase*, Bruxelles: Editions de l'Université de Bruxelles.

Polanyj, K. (1983). *La grande transformation. Aux origines politiques et économiques de notre temps*, Paris: Gallimard, 476.

Rahmonova-Schwarz, D. (2010). 'Migrations during the Soviet Period and in the Early Years of USSR's Dissolution: A Focus on Central Asia', *Revue européenne des migrations internationales*, 26(3), 9–30.

Razumova, I. (2004). 'Severnyi "migratsionnyj tekst" postsovetskoi Rossii, Etnokul' turnye protsessy na Kol'skom Severe. Apatity, Izd-vo Kol'skogo nauchnogo centra Regional'naâ akademiâ nauk (RAN).

Revich, B. et al. (2014). 'Sociodemographic Limitations of the Sustainable Development of Murmansk Region', *Studies on Russian Economic Development*, 25(2), 201–206.

Rumyantsev, S. (2014). *Migratsiya i diasporastroitel'stvo v postsovetskom Azerbaidzhane*, Natsional'naya Akademiya Nauk Azerbaidzhana, Institut filosofii i prava, Baku, 'Sabah', 165.

Sahadeo, J. (2012). 'Soviet Blacks and Place Making in Leningrad and Moscow', *Slavic Review*, 71(2), 331–358.

Sayad, A. (1999). *La double absence: des illusions de l'émigré aux souffrances de l'immigré*, Paris: Editions du Seuil, 448.

Scott, J. C. (1976). *The Moral Economy of the Peasant: Rebellion and Subsistence in Southeast Asia*, New Haven: Yale University Press, 246.

144 *Sophie Hohmann*

Serrano, S. (2007). *La Géorgie. Sortie d'empire*, Paris : CNRS Editions.

Thompson, E. P. (1991). *The Moral Economy Reviewed, Customs in Common*, London: The Merlin Press, 259–351.

Vivier, G. (2006). 'Comment collecter des biographies? De la fiche Ageven aux grilles biographiques, Principes de collecte et Innovations récentes', *Actes du colloque de l'Association Internationale des Démographes de Langue Française 'Population et travail'*, Aveiro, 119–131.

Yalçin-Heckmann, L. (2010). *The Return of Private Property. Rural Life after Agrarian Reform in the Republic of Azerbaijan*, Halle Studies in the Anthropology of Eurasia, LIT Verlag, 225.

Yunusov, A. (2003). 'Etnicheskie i migratsionnye protsessy v postsovetskom Azerbajdzhane', http://migrocenter.ru/publ/trud_m/06.php.

Yunusov, A. (2013). 'CARIM East-Consortium for Applied Research on International Migration, Integration in Azerbaijan's Migration Processes', CARIM-East Research Report 09, 22.

Yurchak, A. (2006). *Everything was Forever, Until it was No More – The Last Soviet Generation*, Princeton and Oxford: Princeton University Press, 341.

Zmeeva, E. (2011). *Novyi dom, vdali ot rodiny: etnicheskie migranty na Kol'skom Severe*. Apatity: Izd-vo Kol'skogo nauchnogo tsentra RAN, 95.

7 Armenian volunteer fighters in the Nagorno-Karabakh conflict

An eye on narrative trajectories in a no-war no-peace situation

Aude Merlin and Taline Papazian

We would like to thank warmly Anne Le Huérou, Derek Averre, Kevork Oskanian, Neil Melvin, Christophe Wasinski, Xavier Follebouckt, Marielle Debos, Vahram Ter-Matevosyan and Anis Memon for their valuable input. Their help contributed substantially to improve this chapter. We also want to thank Natalia Voutova for her help in Yerevan. We are grateful to the Université libre de Bruxelles (ULB) for extending financial support to this publication.

Introduction

In April 2016 the 'Four-Day War' erupted in Karabakh.[1] This short but brutal bout of hostilities was one more manifestation, if any were needed, of the unstable situation – 'neither war nor peace' – that has reigned in Karabakh since the cease-fire in 1994. It is a clear reminder that the conflict that erupted in 1988 has never truly been resolved, resulting in a 'frozen situation' (Broers, 2013a). The OSCE Minsk Group offered proposals at regular intervals throughout the 1990s and 2000s, only to be met with a refusal by one party or the other to compromise. The irrelevance of the expression 'frozen conflict' – that had already been challenged by growing cease-fire violations since 2014 – is no longer questionable. Instead, the term 'unresolved conflicts' is now often preferred to describe such seemingly intractable post-Soviet conflicts characterized by varying but constant degree of intensity of military operations. While the 2016 war signals an abrupt break in the low-intensity conflict going on since the 1994 cease-fire, leading to the identification of two distinct wars, on the long-run it primarily underscores a continuum of instability.[2]

The Karabakh status quo, on the other hand, could actually be described as frozen. Since 1994, Karabakh has displayed many features of a *de facto* state[3] (Broers, Iskandaryan and Minasyan, 2015). After developing a strategy of openly claiming 'unification' with Armenia, Karabakh chose to declare its independence in 1991 and has continued to demand the recognition of this status following the military victory of 1994.[4] Even if Karabakh has remained totally outside Azerbaijani control ever since the cease-fire of 1994, Baku reckons that it still belongs to Azerbaijan.

146 *Aude Merlin and Taline Papazian*

By immersing ourselves in a particular societal response – the engagement of volunteer fighters from Armenia in the Karabakh war in 1988–1994 and again in April–May 2016 when military confrontations were at their peak[5] – we attempt to re-explore motivations for the conflict over a period of more than 25 years, which encompasses an entire generational cycle. Our research question deals with how war veterans remember and tell about their war experience against the backdrop of the 2016 warring peak. It aims at analysing the subjective meaning of voluntary engagement and the perception/labelling of the conflict by volunteers. The purpose of this chapter is to offer some insights on the features of that particular societal response (volunteering) in a situation of politically non-resolved and militarily never-ending conflict and the effects that situation produces on their trajectories. At this point in our investigation, we are providing a preliminary analysis of the qualitative data collected during two fieldworks in Armenia (June 2016 and January 2017), following an inductive approach.

We worked through 20 single and group semi-open interviews.[6] By navigating our way through various channels that led to a 'snowballing' effect of participation, we were able to interview a variety of people: some 'old-timers', members of organizations for the assistance of former combatants, the head and the vice-head of the *Yerkrapah* Union of volunteers ('defenders of the land'), former combatants who became career soldiers, members of a special *djogad* [battalion] (the *Ardziv Mahabart* battalion of those 'condemned to death'), and of *Osoby polk* [special battalion], a professional soldier who defected from the Soviet Army to join the front, a former GRU soldier become a field agent during the war, two women, and a television reporter/documentary filmmaker who had reported on the Karabakh war in 1992–1994. We also conducted two complementary interviews with close relatives of former combatants (the widow of a 'lost' volunteer and the son of a soldier who died in combat). The diversity of their sociological profiles was particularly enriching, and we placed great importance on the meaning that the participants gave to their actions, taking a Weberian[7] perspective of interpretive approach to the participants, which means that we focus on their rationale as 'actors', without any prejudgment towards them. The list of people interviewed has no statistical weight in terms of representativeness, but the qualitative material that it represents provides us with the heuristic elements that we will develop subsequently.

The manner in which hundreds of veterans voluntarily enlisted again in April 2016 and the subsequent weeks,[8] and the testimonies we were able to gather from them, have enlightened us on their perception of the conflict and their role within it over a long no-war no-peace period. It would naturally be necessary to complete this investigation with a symmetric enquiry of the perceptions and experiences of Azerbaijani ex-combatants who participated in the same conflict.

Becoming a combatant: singular trajectories within a collective sociopolitical history

Our interviews clearly show that the experience of the war in 2016 unleashed vivid memories of the events of 1988–1994. Those memories followed two narrative paths: one picking up key events that marked the outbreak of war in Karabakh, and the other traveling the road of personal histories of 'becoming a combatant', the latter process stemming, as the stories make clear, from the intersection of an objective situation and a subjective process of involvement into the fighting. A striking example of this combination is reflected in the question of the beginning of the war. For each volunteer, dating the start of the war is necessarily caught up in this dual narration: in the absence of any general mobilization, the former combatants describe their entry into the war as a mix of informal improvization and a logic of collective action.

Two dimensions coexist. One is the collective sociopolitical fabric of history, within which a number of events remain in the memories as critical junctures. In this interlacing of events, where objective facts meet individual decisions, one event is common to the narratives of all former Armenian fighters we interviewed: the Sumgait events of February 1988 where 32 Armenians were killed and 197 injured in the span of a three-day pogrom in Azerbaijan.[9] It is mentioned as an event of collective significance holding a predominant place in the beginning of the war, one it indeed gained from a political point of view as well (Papazian, 2016). Strikingly enough, the term Sumgait is sometimes used by the interviewees as a generic expression encompassing several such instances that took place in Azerbaijan between 1988 and 1990.[10] The other is the individual representation of events, particularly in a society where access to information was highly controlled by the state, according to which actors date the beginning of their war subjectively. Thus each participant's actual experience offers first-hand information, and the aggregate of these experiences outlines a collective history, emphasizing the autonomy of societal rationales over political ones.

One way of dating the outbreak of war: Sumgait

> It started immediately after Sumgait. The most important thing is how the whole of the Armenian people rose up. In '88, on the 28th of February – that's the most important thing. It started after Sumgait. And then the Armenian people rose up and their foremost demand was: Nagorno-Karabakh.
> (Gegam, born in 1961, president of *Osoby polk* – special detachment, an organization for ex-combatants from this detachment)

All of our respondents insist on the catalysing effect that the events of Sumgait had on their own engagement,[11] as the sign of a watershed after which it was impossible to remain neutral or continue to put one's faith in political mobilization. While demonstrations were experienced as important places and times for socialization, they were often presented in an inverse chronology to that of actual facts: memory reorganizes the logic of past events, since after the massacres of Sumgait participation in demonstrations did not intensify numerically but rather took on a new significance. By going to demonstrations, people tried, sometimes haphazardly, to become involved on the military front and not simply the political one. Demonstrations were no longer simply an occasion for chanting *Miatsum* (unification), but also a space where people created ties, signed on to lists, let others know that they were ready to set off, by reaffirming Karabakh's claims. But our participants' memories were often jumbled, with some people attributing the demands for independence of Nagorno-Karabakh to that period, when in fact they would only be formalized in slogans in 1991 when the strategy of unification was abandoned in favour of a bid for independence. That is how Manvel, a former soldier who is currently active in a veterans' assistance organization, associates the gatherings in the square of the Opera house after Sumgait to the demands for Karabakh's independence.

> Yes, like all normal people, everyone stood up and went to the Opera… and demanded Artsakh's[12] independence, because…
>> (Manvel, member of a veterans' organization, Yerevan, 7 June 2016)

At the political level, the pogroms played a role in accelerating attempts to form militarized groups ready to leave for the front. As soon as 1988, the Karabakh committee decided to set up *yerkrapah djogadner* [*lit.* armed groups of guardians of the country] (Papazian, 2016). Simultaneously, the Armenian National Movement (ANM), leading the demonstrations in favour of Karabakh's inclusion within Soviet Armenia's territory, radicalized its defiance towards Soviet power and started to claim sovereignty. The most significant decision in that regard was the creation of a defence committee in 1990 headed by Vazgen Sargsyan.[13] The committee's mission was to try to supervise the formation and dispatching of *djogads*, informal armed groups comprised between 15 and a couple of dozen men, mounting to a maximum of 5,000 persons in the whole Republic. Since Armenia was still part of the Soviet Union, that mission was all but official.[14] The various conflicts in the Caucasus exhibit some of these same commonalities: individuals towards the war, in a mix of informal groups of fighters, attempts at self-organization and formalization by the burgeoning political forces.[15]

Committed volunteers, improvised fighters

The absence of a declaration of war as well as of an established state produced a situation where spontaneity and improvization prevailed in the formation of groups of *djogad*. There is a sort of shortcut in people's memories that led from demonstrations to the formation of *djogad*.

> At the beginning. When there were meetings, I stayed there for several days. I took part. There were guys who were all the same age, or about the same age. From the depths of their souls, they were all eager to join Karabakh. And then we started setting up detachments, *djogads*.

As Gamavoragan? [As volunteers?]
Yes. Gamavoragan. [As volunteers].
(…)
We gathered altogether. Nobody knew each other. We didn't know who the others were, they didn't know who I was, we just met at a meeting and set up a detachment.

(Manvel, member of a veterans' organization, Yerevan, 7 June 2016)

The way arms were acquired was typical of the improvization reigning in the late 1980s to early 1990s period when the Soviet system was gradually disintegrating before new states had been institutionalized. Weapons were gathered from any available source and by any means: storming garrisons, buying, swapping, corruption. These same practices can be seen at work in Abkhazia and Chechnya: becoming a combatant was part of a context of economic disorganization that resulted from the perestroika reforms, in conjunction with the logic of privatising and weakening the Soviet state (Beissinger and Young, 2002). So we can discern a varied 'fighter's kit': some went scavenging amongst the weapons of village hunters, some in garrisons that had been forced, some criss-crossed the Caucasus to stockpile arms:

There were no automatic weapons. We had hunting rifles…
Where did the weapons come from? From homes?
Sure.
Are there weapons in every house?
No, not in every one.
Did you know where to look?
Naturally.
Did you ask neighbours? Relatives?
Friends. Neighbours. Anywhere.

(Armen, vice-president of a local *Yerkrapah* branch, Dilijan,
3 June 2016)

Ruben is a former Soviet officer who defected in order to form a group of combatants and reach the border between Armenia and Azerbaijan in 1990. He recalls both how he organized his group of combatants and what weapons they had when they went off to fight:

So you got these eight people together in 1989? At the beginning of the year? And after that, what did you do in concrete terms? Where did you get weapons? What strategy did you use?
Weapons… Yes, we had weapons… well, I mean hunting rifles, and later on we got our hands on small calibre rifles from the DOSAAF (the Soviet Volunteer Society for Cooperation with the Army, Aviation, and Fleet). Then we took weapons from the Azeris.[16]

(Ruben, former Soviet officer, Yerevan, 7 June 2016)

150   *Aude Merlin and Taline Papazian*

Their combat experience before volunteering to fight was often quite varied. Most of the people we interviewed had done their military service during the Soviet period, but some still learned in the field. Gegam concedes that everyone in his *djogad* learned to fight that way – simply by fighting.

> *Did those 36 guys know how to fight?*
> They learned.
> *In the field?*
> You know, we all learned in the field.
> (Gegam, *Osoby polk*, veterans' organization, Yerevan, 7 June 2016)

'Political scheming' *versus* 'noble fighting'

The stories we gathered from Armenian ex-combatants place great importance on etiquette in the conduct of warfare. Whether this reflects reality or a myth, the fact that they mention this topic at all is interesting. Experience in fact shows that warfare, wherever it takes place, pushes all boundaries: anyone can end up perpetrating acts of barbarity. Topics which one comes across when interviewing *gamavoragan* are: fighting for one's land, one's people, one's nation; fighting only in self-defence; respecting the laws of warfare and rules pertaining to prisoners and their rights; situating one's own battle within the long collective history and justifying it partly on the basis of past traumas – these are the basic elements of their stories.

Memory and personal memories of the genocide of Armenians (1915–1918) are omnipresent in veterans' narratives of their engagement in the Karabakh conflict. Family memories and/or national history are often called on to assimilate fighting for Karabakh as a just cause.

> We knew what happened in 1915. And when Artsakh war started I gathered my *djogad* and fought from dusk to dawn. (…) My *nom de guerre* is 'Black Tulip'. Not because I am Alain Delon.[17] But because when Turks massacred our ancestors in 1915, black tulips came through the soil on which they fell.
> (Sasun Mikaelyan, former commandant and politician, Hrasdan,
> 14 January 2017)

Contrasting with the moral justification of war, disdain for politics or geopolitics comes across very often in the interviews, some of them consider opportunistic and dirty, an attitude widespread in the ex-Soviet space. The world depicted in these conversations is neatly divided into two camps: one worthy of engagement, and the other not. Vova, a former GRU officer and member of a secret intelligence group, shares his vision of the world in the following terms:

Volunteer fighters in Nagorno-Karabakh 151

Do you think politics is more dirty than war?
I consider that war is mud, blood and sweat, whereas politics is only muddy. Furthermore, war is a necessity, whereas one can very well live apart from politics. I don't meddle with politics. It is very disagreable for me to have any contact with people in politics. Some political forces offered me financial support, I refused.

(Vova, Yerevan, 13 January 2017)

The worthy harks back to romantic, chivalrous epics of disinterested sacrifice for a noble cause; the unworthy smells of lowly self-interest and corruption, of individuals and oligarchies who calculate for short-term gains. In other words, it is utopian to speak of the (noble) political translation of a military state of affairs (also noble), since politics to the point of view of veterans by definition is never a noble thing.

This dichotomy is found equally in domestic and international politics. The issue of Russia's role in local geopolitics reveals the way in which the Four-Day War has reawakened memories of the first war and its aftermath. A striking case in point was the veterans' view of the 1994 ceasefire, its temporality and consequences, a leitmotiv in our interviews. In May 1994, after three years of all-out military warfare, Russia brokered a cease-fire between the three belligerent parties: Armenia, Azerbaijan and Nagorno-Karabakh. Looking back, nearly every single one of our interviewees' narratives about the ceasefire of 1994 is tinged with a palpable bitterness. The common thread is Russia 'imposing'[18] the ceasefire, thus preventing the Armenian fighters from completing their task which, in the interviewees' fantasies, meant possibly going all the way to Baku or taking over Nakhichevan.

Did you have a feeling that the war was going to end?
No. Aliyev asked the Russians and they forced the Armenians to sign the ceasefire document.
Did you want the war to continue? For how much longer?
I don't know what our government thinks but these are historically Armenian territories and our historical border was at the river Kura. The war will not end until there is a natural border between Armenia and Azerbaijan.
I would like to concentrate on the fact that Aliyev asked the Russians to force the Armenians to stop.
Not forced but convinced.
So what do you think you should do? Continue the war?
Why didn't the USSR stop its offensive after it had reclaimed its borders and reached Berlin? Why should they? Their goal was to make Germany capitulate. So I don't understand why we stopped. It makes no sense.

(Gagik, a former member of *Ardziv Mahabarat*, Yerevan, 1 June 2016)

152 *Aude Merlin and Taline Papazian*

One can sense a deep bitterness at the web of patronage that binds Armenia, a country that depends on Moscow for its security (Minassian, 2008),[19] while Russia continues to sell arms to Azerbaijan.[20] This situation of 'neither war nor peace' has been in place for 22 years and is largely ascribed to Moscow's geopolitics of the status quo in the southern Caucasus, resulting in a plan of differentiated yet balanced support for both parties in the conflict. The Four-Day War has also reawakened their earlier sentiments regarding the *Koltso* in 1991, when the Soviet Army intervened by surrounding and deporting Armenian villages from the Karabakh oblast and its surroundings.[21]

> They were all against us; the Soviet Union was against us. There was even the whole *Koltso* operation where Soviet troops defended Azerbaijan. They gave them weapons, they fought against us, they made us outlaws and declared us separatists.
>
> (Ruben, a former Soviet officer, Yerevan, 7 June 2016)

The legitimacy that comes from having fought and contributed to the military victory in 1994 gives soldiers and former soldiers the right to criticise Russia. And their criticisms gain in strength since they themselves have not subsequently entered politics; the generally unfavourable perception of politics encourages a harshly critical stance. As such, Gagik is criticising not only 'Russia' but also the Armenian political elite when he vents his indignation at the fact that Nikolai Ryzhkov was awarded a hero's medal:

> Since 2004, Nikolai Ryzhkov has been the only person to receive a national hero's medal in Armenia. This is someone who has nothing to do with independent Armenia. He was the Prime Minister of the USSR in 1988 and lived in Gyumri for one month to evaluate the consequences of the earthquake. Nothing was even done. I don't understand the point in giving him a national hero's medal… If he had at least done something to help after the earthquake, then… maybe… but it's still a disaster area there. Why was he given a hero's medal but not the people who really deserved one? Why don't our current heroes like Armenak Urfanyan, Robert Abajyan, Kyaram Sloyan get national hero's medals?

Armenak Urfanyan, Kyaram Sloyan, Robert Abajyan and Andranik Zohrabyan were the first military casualties Armenians (from Armenia and NKR) suffered in the four-day war. They have been praised for their behaviour in battle and awarded several distinctions. By contrasting the merits of a former Soviet minister with those of young military officers and soldiers, the interviewee points out that, in his eyes, the highest distinction in the Republic should be given to people who sacrificed their lives for its sake. When glancing over more than 25 years of history of Armenia from the late Soviet years to current independence, the interviewee's landmark of appreciation of one's deed is action undertaken in the ongoing conflicting situation.

Volunteer fighters in Nagorno-Karabakh   153

For our sample of veterans, the main feature characterizing the last 25 years is permanent absence of peace: although the concept of 'peacelessness' does not exist, it would be appropriate to describe and analyse situations like the one over Karabakh where a cease-fire is theoretically holding on for decades, but in fact merely containing all-out warfare; instead, quasi every-day violations, regular more intense military peaks of activity and small-scale warring episodes take place. The expectations of veterans – and more largely of a sizeable portion of the Armenian society – are turned towards the next military peak,[22] a psychological state that can be coined of alert.

Unresolved conflict and the paradox of an ordinary state of alert seen through veterans' social trajectories

> Well, the ceasefire has been in place for 22 years, but every year, every month, every week we hear that they have killed, they have killed, they have killed... So is it a ceasefire? It is not. It is obviously war.
> (Armen, vice-president of the organization *Yerkrapah*, Dilijan, 3 June 2016)

These are the words of a former combatant who later became a career soldier in the Armenian Army after the 1988–1994 Karabakh war, and then the vice-president of the local *Yerkrapah* branch. They are indicative of the situation that is 'neither war, nor peace', which by and large characterizes all the so-called 'frozen' conflicts of the post-Soviet space (Merlin, 2017; Fischer, 2016). In the absence of a peace treaty and a deep-rooted resolution to the conflict, violence continues unabated on the frontline while the conflicting states – recognised and unrecognised – keep arming themselves and remaining permanently on alert. The absence of faith among states and, to a large degree, among societies, increases the degree of alienation of the two peoples.

After the Armenian military victory and the cease-fire of 1994, the question of statehood remained a determining factor in many respects, especially when compared with other military victories of non recognized would-be states in the post-Soviet space: Abkhazia and Chechnya. The issue of combatants' return to civilian life and especially of their disarmament epitomizes this. In stark contrast with Abkhazia after the cease-fire of 1993, and Chechnya after the cease-fire of 1996, the Armenian state endeavoured to systematically collect arms. In the case of Chechnya, almost all of the combatants held on to their weapons after Grozny was retaken in August 1996, and some of them immediately became spoilers of the fragile peace they wanted no part of (Merlin, 2012). As for Abkhazia, the separatists had no intention of requisitioning arms, since the idea seemed absurd and even meaningless in the absence of a peace treaty.[23] In the case of Armenia, however, there is a clear distinction to be made: while Karabakh is a non-recognized state, like Abkhazia, Armenia relies heavily on its identity as a state that is in the process of being built and that is recognized by the international community,

154   *Aude Merlin and Taline Papazian*

which makes a considerable difference and moulds the post-war period in an altogether different manner.

One thing that comes across in the interviews is that veterans see a continuum of war of varying intensity between 1994 and 2016, with the Four-Day War coming as a climax but not an ending in a long period of unfinished war. Among Armenian society at large, on the other hand, the dominant perception is more of a continuum of post-war stability that is interrupted by specific moments of greater violence. At the same time, the veterans are part of society so interactions and gaps exist in the evolution of these perceptions. In this section, we suggest that veterans' sociological trajectories – within the scope of our interviews which obviously offer a bias since nobody in our sample had turned into an outright marginal after the cease-fire – has a heuristic value to look at the notion of a state of alert: the social activities of a significant proportion of them emphasize both a reconversion of their skills in civilian life and the practical consequences of their representation of the Karabakh conflict as unfinished. In our sample, trajectories in the long cease-fire period of 25 years can be analysed as a reflection of a process of alert institutionalization on the level of the state but also its impregnation by individual practices.

Reinsertion of former fighters and the institutionalized state of alert

Several interviews point to a strong link between war experience as a combatant on the one hand, and enlisting in the Armenian army after the cease-fire on the other, a choice that interviewees report for significant numbers of their *djogad*'s comrades. This institutionalization of individual military trajectories in the post-war context contrasts with the informal paths leading to 'becoming a combatant' described earlier. Each of these individual paths follow on from the making of the Armenian independent state, first and foremost tangible in the state's handling of a military prerogative: the birth of the Armenian army came about precisely in a context of war, in accordance with a pattern that Charles Tilly has already analysed under the heading 'The State makes war and war makes the State' (Tilly, 1984; Blom, 2006; Papazian, 2010). But these former combatants were also determined to participate in the creation of a new army. In that sense, their decision to pursue a military career was an obvious move.

In addition to reconverting newly acquired skills in order to make a living – which obviously has a utility – we found there a strong desire on behalf of a former volunteer to transmit his/her ethical motivations and ideological principles to fellow comrades who became the next generation with time under cease-fire passing. Even more distantly related to war choices that appeared among interviewees such as making research on deceased young soldiers when being a mourning mother or becoming head of legal affairs in a municipality and thus 'strengthening the state' are consciously related to a desire to pass on what motivated an engagement of life and death through war and to

Volunteer fighters in Nagorno-Karabakh 155

keep that alive for them, for the society at large and for the youth especially. The arguments brought to explain this choice tend to be of a political, symbolic or historical nature; the economic reality is not immediately mentioned, and when it does come up, it is not used as an explanation.

So you came back in May of 1994 after handing over your weapons... What did you do? Did you have any plans?
I was obviously thinking about work.
What type of work specifically?
I continued in the military. I have 23 years of experience and now I'm a military instructor in the schools. We actually provide instruction to our youth before they reach draft age, so that when they leave for the army they know what to expect...
What if there had been no Karabakh war? Would your life have been different? Would you have done something else, or would you still have been a soldier?
I didn't want to be a soldier, but my great grandparents are from Muş and Van. They told us about what it was like back then... May the earth lie over them as soft as down. They told us about what happened in 1915 and afterwards.
Armen, when you enlisted after the war, was that something you wanted to do, or was there simply no other work to be found?
It was something I wanted to do. I wanted to transmit my experience and know-how to the kids who were going to do their military service. It worked. I had some good kids. We still keep in touch by phone nowadays and our families have become friends.

(Armen, vice-president of the local branch of *Yerkrapah*, Dilijan, 3 June 2016)

The way in which people began to enlist as professional soldiers in the burgeoning Armenian army sheds light on how the Armenian state itself came into being.

The double movement of demobilization and enlisting in the regular army takes a sequential form, with a clear break marking the combatants' return to civilian life, and another marking their entry into the life of professional soldiers.

Most of the people we interviewed still had a vivid memory of V. Sargsyan's role in that process. Manvel had this to say:

Do you know what Vazgen Sargsyan said? He said, 'It's good that you fought to get the lands of our ancestors back, but now it is time to build our army. In memory of those who sacrificed their blood, their strength to achieve victory. Now it's time to build the army.' And those of us who wanted to do that got involved.

(Manvel, veterans' association, Yerevan, 7 June 2016)

156 *Aude Merlin and Taline Papazian*

In fact, the move towards independence combined with the outbreak of war made the army an urgent necessity, as both a fundamental building block in the construction of a state and as a logical consequence of it. In reality, however, the gradual process of turning volunteers into experienced soldiers and then professional military officers was at work long before the cease-fire of 1994. It began during the war itself, in particular from 1992 onward (Papazian, 2016), when the Armenian Defence Minister, Vazgen Sargsyan, created the *Mahabart* ('condemned to death') battalion, laying the groundwork for the professionalization of volunteers. When Vazgen Manukyan took over the position in October 1992, he gradually reorganized volunteers through a system of contract and turnover: although payment was extremely low, the men were listed and the brigades were rationalized. In parallel, an army of conscript soldiers was built. The Armenian Army was thus formed during the war, and its formation was no doubt hastened by the war. On the state level, the daily concerns over security translated into giving institutional, financial and personnel priority to issues and agencies dealing with defence (Papazian, 2016). Strikingly, this state of permanent alert is also reflected in our interviews, not only in discourse but also in practice. For instance, a number of interviewees, old and young alike, mentioned being 'always ready' to depart, having for example a bag ready with military equipment, checking on their uniforms regularly, updating crisis related utilities, sometimes taking a couple of extra military classes, and so on.

The *Yerkrapah* Union, a case in point

The *Yerkrapah* Union's creation aimed more specifically at supporting the process of reintegration of war veterans and maintaining their engagement. The *Yerkrapah Gamavoragan Mioutiun* (Union of Volunteer Defenders of the land), is a union of volunteer combatants which was officially founded in July 1993 by Vazgen Sargsyan. It really took off once the cease-fire had proved stable: starting from 1995, V. Sargsyan emphasizes the absolute necessity for Armenia that 'the powder in the barrel remains dry'. (Papazian, 2016). Once again Defence Minister, he was concerned with offering a social space to all volunteers returning to civilian life, rewarding them socially and symbolically for their participation in the war, but also keeping an eye on them in order to avoid two pitfalls or tendencies in particular that he considered risky. The first was armed men returning to civilian life; the second was veterans forming political parties and turning Armenia into a military regime (Papazian, 2016).

The *Yerkrapah* gradually came to number some 6,000 former combatants within the war years. Several thousand more former soldiers swelled its ranks, although this figure cannot be verified. Some sources put their total numbers as high as 30,000 people in the beginning of the 2000s (De Waal, 2003). In any case, the *Yerkrapah Gamavoragan Mioutiun* has become a powerful political organization in Armenian public life. Other associations of former combatants also sprang up, some sources saying as many as several dozens, but the *Yerkrapah* Union is the most visible, powerful and active (Libaridian, 2003; De Waal, 2003). *Yerkrapah* are important in the question of transmission for their involvement in *badani* (youth) clubs where *Yerkrapah* members come to instruct teenage members.

Here is the testimony of the vice-president of the Dilijan branch of the *Yerkrapah*:

> *Can you explain what it means to be* Yerkrapah?
> We saw what happened in April (2016)... the Four-Day War. We were made for that, that's our reason for existing. When military operations take place, we're all together.
> *When was the* Yerkrapah *founded?*
> *Yerkrapah* was founded in 1989, well, for all intents and purposes in 1990.
> *By whom?*
> By our *Sparabed*[24] [Constable] Vazgen Sargsyan, of course.
> *What was the purpose?*
> The same purpose naturally.
> *How many members are there in the* Yerkrapah?
> Now? Umm, you'll have to excuse me but I don't know the exact number. But there's a new generation developing.
> *Do you have to have combat experience to become a member of the* Yerkrapah?
> Yes, of course, experience. But you also have to love your country first and foremost.
> *Are there people of all ages from every generation?*
> Of course.
> *Vazgen Sargsyan created the* Yerkrapah *Union, and after the war their ranks filled?*
> Yes, of course.
> *The people returning from the war joined the* Yerkrapah?
> They were already members.
> *What does it mean in concrete terms to be a member of the* Yerkrapah?
> *Does it mean going to schools and talking in front of the school children? Helping veterans? Or being a reserve force in case of war?*
> All of those things.

The seeming confusion of dates regarding the creation of the *Yerkrapah* in this excerpt actually points out how Armenian combatants were amalgamated from war volunteers to veterans and onto professional militaries whose tasks included teaching war skills in cadet schools and later on to young *Yerkrapah* members.

158 Aude Merlin and Taline Papazian

Making transmission their new mission: from the battlefield to the teaching ground, and back

Among our interviewees' trajectories of reconversion in the long run, one feature is striking: almost all of them chose to do something through which they could firstly relate to their war experience and secondly transmit it to others, generally younger people. This is done either through institutional channels such as the *badani Yerkrapah* [*Yerkrapah* youth] or through individual initiatives.

Concerning the first channel, the *Yerkrapah* Union founded a badani section in 1999 that really kick started in 2009. In 2014, a cooperation agreement was signed between the *Yerkrapah*, the Ministry of Education and the Ministry of Defence aiming at expanding the network of clubs, which are now partly funded on the state budget for education. As of 2014, there were 72 badani branches in Yerevan and the regions and in 2016, badani clubs were hosted in more than 1,400 regular schools throughout the country, gathering children and teenagers aged 12 to 18. Their claimed membership is 30,000.[25] The badani curriculum comprises practical lessons of military artfare grounded in an ideology of 'patriotic education'. The Zovouni school that we were able to visit[26] offers a particularly instructive glimpse at the way in which courses are conducted and in which history and geography are mustered, sometimes for fanciful –obviously partial to the Armenians – ends. The use of visuals in the classrooms illustrates a concern with long-term transmission, jumbling history, memory and war, as well as the territorial, political and institutional de facto integration of the Armenian state and the non-recognized entity of Karabakh. Hanging on the main wall is a map of 'the Republic of Armenia and the Republic of Mountainous Karabakh' united in a single territory.. Right underneath, a collage modeling *Tsitsernakaberd* – the Genocide Memorial in Yerevan – and the *anmorouk* flower – a forget-me-not chosen as the world-wide symbol marking the centennial of the event in 2015, made by the young *Yerkrapah*. And above, a large poster gathering photos and short biographies of the great military figures of the nineteenth and twentieth centuries: from famous *fedayis* (volunteer fighters) of the last century to the leaders of the First Republic (1918–1920) to the Second World War hero of the Soviet Union: Karabakh born Marshal Baghramyan. In a second classroom are five posters representing the principal actors and military operations of the four great moments: the *fedayi* movement (which here is called *hayduk*); operations from the First Republic, especially Sardarabad, a 1918 battle where ragged Armenian troops were able to prevent a conquest of Russian Armenia by the Turkish army; operations from the Second World War with emphasis on the role of Armenians within the war; and the Artsakh [Armenian for Karabakh] *azadamart* [liberation war], all illustrated through maps. To the right of these five posters are two smaller documents. One is an award given by the Ministry for Emergency Situations in 2013 to Artur Hovanisyan, the *badani* instructor of the school, for 'his work on patriotic

Volunteer fighters in Nagorno-Karabakh 159

military education and culture for the benefit of the sacrificed generation'. Below it, is the pledge the conscript makes when joining the Armenian armed forces.

The example of Vova, former GRU officer mentioned earlier, is typical of a private path of reconversion and transmission: after leaving the GRU – military intelligence department of the USSR – at the end of the 1980s Vova engaged in a secret group called 'Karabakh 2' which purpose was to collect up-to-date information on developments on the ground. Years after the war, in 2010, Vova founded a club called 'Art of staying alive' [*Vokhtch Menalou Arvest, VOMA*]. The VOMA is in fact a school where a number of instructors, including its founder, teach volunteers of all ages how to deal with crisis situations in their everyday life and more particularly in war times. The audience is mainly young (from 16 to 35), two thirds male but with increasing numbers of women. The total number of students is confidential; based on our fieldworks, we estimate its total (past and present) at more than 500. When interviewed, Vova reckoned that his private initiative is complementing the state's actions in that domain.[27] This initiative implicitly points out a defiance of the state's capacity to adequately cover all necessities dictated by the volatility of the conflict and the fragility of the cease-fire. Private initiatives thus become a way to complete the defence training provided by the state (military service) and by institutional large channels (*Yerkrapah*) to young (and less young) men and women, so that they acquire the potential of turning into voluntary combatant at any moment and the ideological principles sustaining their engagement. Overall, private initiatives of transmission speak of the daily integration of the state of alert in the Armenian society outside state channels.

Conclusion

The material we have been working on, albeit of no statistical or general value on combatant trajectories of Armenians in the Karabakh conflict, sheds lights on three dimensions. First: how major symbolic collective historical facts (Sumgait, the genocide of the Armenians) mould individual narratives of going at war. Second: the very concrete ways through which individuals would become fighters in the troubled ending of the Soviet Union in the South Caucasus, where a deliquescent Soviet state was leaving disorganized military structures but where no functional independent state was yet able to organize mobilization for war. Third, the representations of a long cease-fire period that is neither a genuine post-conflict era nor a viable peace and which impregnates bodies and souls with a permanent state of alert.

Preliminary results of our research on volunteers from Armenia in the Karabakh conflict are twofold. First, narratives of war veterans about their engagement, their memories of it, emphasize the troubled waters surrounding the temporality and quality of this conflict. On the one hand, there is the official political-military dating of the war: the Karabakh movement from 1988 onwards alongside low intensity conflict in Karabakh, including operation 'Ring' in 1991; then full out warfare starting with the break up of the Soviet Union in December 1991; and finally the post-1994 cease-fire period. The Four-Day War in 2016 did not break the tempo of unstable peacelessness, since another cease-fire was concluded after that episode which is just as inefficiently living up to its purpose. On the other, there are individual narratives showing a mixed picture with no clear sequence of events between peace and war, but a couple of striking events emerging from their memories. These two levels of narratives are bridged on numerous crossing-points where we have seen the individual narratives traveling. Although small, our sample displays noticeable homogeneity in perceiving the Karabakh war as one of defence of an endangered Armenian people in Azerbaijan, transposing Sumgait's Armenians faith in the Karabakh region of Soviet Azerbaijan.

Second, the issue of the conflict's temporality and quality is strenghtened by the post-cease-fire situation of peacelessness, tainted by all hues of the warfare palette, from ordinary cease-fire violations claiming a couple lives every week to the short but intense operations of the Four-Day War in 2016. To veterans interviewed in the aftermath of the Four-Day War, the situation is predominantly one of permanent instability and looming of resumption of hostilities we called a 'state of alert'. Far from being a conjunctural coincidence resulting from the events of April 2016, for many of them their practices testify that they indeed remain on alert. This feature is best exemplified through veterans who built their post-war lives in continuity with skills and know-how acquired in the war, particularly military officers and/or teachers, instructing young potential new volunteers. In our sample of interviewees, there were also young volunteers, albeit too few to be included in the present analysis. Nevertheless, let us signal that so far our interviews with young volunteers who joined the April war point out the relevance of the issues raised in this chapter concerning older veterans. On the eve of the 30th anniversary of the beginning of the Karabakh conflict, and as hostilities threaten to resume sooner rather than later (ICG report, June 2017), the interest of pursuing this investigation on the meanings of engagement to extend it to a full generational cycle remains high.

Interviews

Armine works as a legal expert in a ZAGS (public registry) in Dilijan, a city located in the north of Armenia. She fought actively during the war in Karabakh.

Zepiur is an instructor at the Tigran Mets military training centre. She left for the front lines during the Four-Day War.

Ruben is a former Soviet soldier who defected at the end of the 1980s (during the Soviet period) in order to enlist in Karabakh.

Volunteer fighters in Nagorno-Karabakh   161

Gagik was put in solitary confinement during his military service for arguing with an Azeri about the history of the Karabakh territory. He was a member of the 'special' *djogat Smertnik* (*Artsiv Mahabart*, those who are condemned to death). He currently teaches traditional Armenian dance in schools.

Gegam is a former commander of a *djogad* (group or detachment of fighters), who now runs 'The Special Regiment' (*Osoby polk* in Russian) an organization for former combatants, in Yerevan. He was seriously wounded. The interview was conducted in the organization's building with a group of combatants, in the 'Bangladesh' neighbourhood in Yerevan.

Tatul and **Manvel** are members of Gegam's organization (*Osoby polk*).

Born in 1972, **Armen** is the vice-president of the *Yerkrapah* ('the defenders of the land') in Dilijan. At the age of 16, he left with the partial consent of his parents and the gratitude of his schoolteacher. He enlisted in the Army when he returned from the war in 1994. He then 'naturally' left again in April 2016. He is married with two children.

Levon is from Dilijan. He began as a commander of a *djogad*, then became a career soldier, and finally became an instructor with the *Badani Yerkrapah* after retiring. He is a well-respected man with five children. He led his son Albert in the April 2016 conflict.

Erik is an 'independent' taxi driver: just like his volunteering during the war, he says that he transports whom he likes where he likes. He fought during the Karabakh war from 1988 to 1994, then left again in April 2016. He is photographed with the young conscripts and *gamavoragan* (volunteers).

'General' Manvel has been president of the *Yerkrapah* since the disappearance of their founder, Vazgen Sargsian. He combines the figure of a former fighter who once again set off to fight in April 2016, as well as of the local despot in his stronghold of Echmiadzin. He is a controversial figure in public opinion, both much-loved and often criticised.

'Mamigon' (assumed name) broadens the conventional image of a volunteer as he is not strictly speaking a former soldier even though he saw a lot of combat. He volunteered for special missions such as finding arms caches and transporting seized weapons.

Vagam, born in 1971, volunteer from the 1988–1994 war and member of the Dashnak Party.

Vardan Hovhanissian is a television journalist and a documentary filmmaker at Bars Media whose documentary *A Story of People in War and Peace* won an award at *Voske Tsiran*, the Yerevan film festival. As a television journalist, he covered the entire first war.

Vova Vartanov, former officer of GRU, founder of the VOMA ('Art of staying alive' club)

Arsen is a young Dashnak who set off in April 2016.

Hovik is the son of a soldier who died from war-related causes.

Silva is the wife of a volunteer soldier who was listed as missing in 1994.

162 *Aude Merlin and Taline Papazian*

Sasun Mikaelyan is a former commandant (of Sasun's *djogad*) and a politician.

Notes

1 Mainly with bombings of Talysh, Madaghis and Mardakert villages (east of NKR), and then Kazakhlar/Nuzger, Alkhanli/Fizuli (south), as well as Kapanli-Seysulan and Gulistan/Tonashen (north). Information collected and reported by Emil Sanamyan, independent analyst and journalist, on 23 April 2016. The complete timeline of events by Sanamyan is available on his blog: http://yandunts. blogspot.co.il/2016/04/april-2016-war-in-karabakh-chronology.html (accessed June 2017).
2 See: ICG, 'Nagorno-Karabakh's Gathering War Clouds', 1 June 2017, www.cri sisgroup.org, Report No. 244, Europe and Central Asia.
3 When compared to the legal definition of a state as established in the Montevideo convention, Nagorno-Karabakh lacks international recognition and arguably a permanently defined territory, this last point being part of the negotiation process. Because its independence has not been *de jure* recognised internationally, despite a growing number of states individually recognising the republic, particularly in the USA, Karabakh does not enjoy the benefits of complete sovereignty (Broers, Iskandaryan and Minasyan 2015).
4 In addition, the Nagorno-Karabakh Republic has undertaken a number of political and legal steps in order to acquire various attributes of statehood, most notably holding regular elections since 1996 and adopting a constitution in 2006 and a second one in 2017 renaming itself the Republic of Artsakh – the Armenian name of Karabakh.
5 Most sources mention several thousand Armenians leaving to fight in Karabakh in 2016. As a comparison, initial figures of volunteers at the beginning of the war at the end of the 1980s were roughly similar, around 5,000, organised into *djogad* (groups of combatants). As an estimate, the numbers of fighters from Karabakh *per se* run from just below 1,000 to a couple of thousand for the 2016 war. Field notes, June 2016.
6 Interviews were conducted in Armenian by Taline Papazian and in Russian by Aude Merlin.
7 Max Weber, *Economy and Society: An Outline of Interpretive Sociology* (1922), revised edition 1978, University of California Press.
8 Interviews with the deputy Minister of Defense and with the head of the department of social affairs of the Ministry of Defense, June 2016.
9 See Cheterian (2008), pp. 97–109.
10 Three anti-Armenian pogroms took place in the Soviet Republic of Azerbaijan: two in 1988, first in Sumgait then Kirovabad/Ganja, and one in January 1990 in Baku.
11 For an analysis of the link between the events of Sumgait and the Karabakh war, see V. Cheterian, 'Sumgait: the birth of Karabakh conflict', in *War and Peace in the Caucasus, Russia's Troubled Frontier*, Hurst, 2008, pp. 97 & ff.
12 'Artsakh' is the Armenian name of Karabakh.
13 See the chapter 'Violence physique et souveraineté politique', in Papazian, 2016.
14 For more in depth analysis of this political process, see chapter 'La guerre, épreuve de l'Etat', in Papazian, 2016.
15 Aude Merlin and Silvia Serrano, 'Repenser le lien entre Etats et violences au Caucase', *Dynamiques internationales*, 2012, http://dynamiques-internationales. com/wp-content/uploads/2016/01/DI6-Merlin-Serrano.pdf.

16 Weapons were often acquired on the battlefield. For more information on the different channels through which Armenia addressed serious shortage in weaponry the Karabakh war, see Papazian, 2016, chapter 'La guerre, épreuve de l'Etat'.
17 *Black Tulip* is a french film (shot by Christian Jaque in 1963) in which Alain Delon plays the lead role.
18 This is the word used by all of our respondents.
19 On Russia's defence support of Armenia, see Minassian, 2008: Armenia, a Russian Outpost in Caucasus? www.ifri.org/sites/default/files/atoms/files/ifri_RNV_minassian_Armenie_Russie_ANG_fevr2008.pdf.
20 The resentment towards Moscow has been growing rapidly in the last years, under the conjunction of several factors pointing out the unequal relationship between Russia and Armenia. Among the important facts, let us note: the use by Russia of its security leverage over Karabakh to make Armenia join the Customs Union in 2013; the murder of a family in Gyumri by a Russian soldier stationed in that city's military base in 2015; the continuous selling of large quantities of weapons to Azerbaijan ($3 billion in 2015).
21 Cheterian (2008), p. 121. *Koltso* (ring) is the name of a military operation conducted by the Soviet OMON and the 4th Soviet army stationed in Azerbaijan in the Spring of 1991 consisting of brutal displacement of Armenian populated areas inside the Nagorno-Karabakh oblast and in its surroundings. The unsaid reason for this brutal intervention of the Soviet army in Karabakh was to stop Armenia from pursuing an independence process launched the previous year. Armenia interpreted this act as an unsaid declaration of war but followed on its constitutional path towards independence. For more detailed analysis of political and military implications of operation *Koltso*, see Papazian, 2016, chapter 'La guerre, épreuve de l'Etat arménien'.
22 Marielle Debos (2016) coins the concept of 'interwar' (*entre-guerres*) to emphasize a situation where fighters keep waiting for the next episode of war in a long-lasting absence of peace in Chad.
23 Field notes, Abkhazia, Aude Merlin, January 2015, January 2017.
24 Honorary title that was given to Vazgen Sargsyan before his untimely death: although a civilian, Vazgen Sargsyan is considered as the lasting commander of the volunteers, and by extension the father of the Armenian army since it was built primarily on the volunteers' engagement in the war.
25 Information retrieved from the official website of the *Yerkrapah* Union (www.ekm.am) and given also by Manvel Grigoryan, at the time President of the Union, during an interview in June 2016.
26 Near Yerevan, June 2016 and February 2017.
27 Interview with Aude Merlin, January 2017, Yerevan.

Bibliography

Beissinger, Mark R., 2002. *Nationalist Mobilization and the Collapse of the Soviet State*, Cambridge: Cambridge University Press, p. 503.
Beissinger, Mark R. and Young, C. (eds), 2002. *Beyond State Crisis? Post-Colonial Africa and Post-Soviet Eurasia in Comparative Perspective*, Washington D.C.: Woodrow Wilson Center Press.
Berdal, Mats R., 1996. *Disarmament and Demobilisation after Civil Wars*, Oxford: Oxford University Press.
Berdal, Mats R. and Ucko, David H., 2009. *Reintegrating Armed Groups after Conflict: Politics, Violence and Transition*, Abingdon: Routledge.

164 *Aude Merlin and Taline Papazian*

Blom, Amélie, 2006. '"La guerre fait l'Etat": trajectoires extra-occidentales et privatisation de la violence', Centre d'étude en sciences sociales de la défense, www.aca demia.edu/27332609/C2SD-Guerre_fait_lEtat.pdf.

Broers, Laurence, 2013a. 'Recognising politics in unrecognised states: 20 years of enquiry into the de facto states of the South Caucasus', *Caucasus Survey*, 1(1), 59–74.

Broers, Laurence, 2013b. 'Cartographic exhibitionism? Visualizing the territory of Armenia and Karabakh, with Gerard Toal', *Problems of Post-Communism*, 60(3), May–June, 16–35.

Broers, Laurence, 2014a. 'From "frozen conflict" to enduring rivalry: reassessing the Nagorny Karabakh conflict', *Nationalities Papers*, 43(4), 556–576.

Broers, Laurence, 2014b. 'Mirrors to the World: The Claims to Legitimacy and International Recognition of De Facto States in the South Caucasus', *Brown Journal of International Affairs*, 20(2), spring/summer, 145–159.

Broers, Laurence, Iskandaryan, Aleksandr and Minasyan, Sergey (eds), 2015. *The Unrecognised Politics of De Facto States in the Post-Soviet Space*, *Caucasus Survey*, Caucasus Institute, ASCN, Yerevan.

Cheterian, Vicken, 2008. *War and Peace in the Caucasus: Russia's Troubled Frontier*, London: Hurst.

Cornell, S. E., 2011. *Azerbaijan Since Independence*, New York: ME Sharpe.

Darby, John, 2001. *The Effects of Violence on Peace Processes*, Washington, D.C.: United States Institute of Peace Press.

Darby, John, and MacGinty, Roger, 2008. *Contemporary Peacemaking: Conflict, Peace Processes and Post-War Reconstruction*, Basingstoke: Palgrave Macmillan.

De Waal, Thomas, 2003. *Black Garden, Armenia and Azerbaijan through Peace and War*, New York: NYU Press.

Debos, Marielle, 2016. *Living by the Gun in Chad: Combatants, Impunity and State Formation*, London: Zed Books.

Deriglazova, Larisa and Minasyan, Sergey, 2011. 'Nagorno-Karabakh: The Paradoxes of Strength and Weakness in an Asymmetric Conflict', *Caucasus Institute Research Papers*, 3, June, Yerevan Caucasus Institute, p. 104.

Donabedian, Patrick and Mutafian, Claude, 1991. *Artsakh: histoire du Karabagh*, Paris: SEVIG Press, p. 174.

Duclos, Nathalie (ed.), 2012. *War Veterans in Postwar Situations: Chechnya, Serbia, Turkey, Peru, and Côte d'Ivoire*, Basingstoke: Palgrave McMillan.

Fischer, Sabine (ed.), 2016. 'Not Frozen! The Unresolved Conflicts over Transnistria, Abkhazia, South Ossetia and Nagorno-Karabakh in Light of the Crisis over Ukraine', SWP Research Paper, www.swp-berlin.org/fileadmin/contents/products/research_papers/2016RP09_fhs.pdf.

Follebouckt, Xavier, 2012. *Les conflits gelés de l'espace postsoviétique. Genèse et enjeux*, Louvain-la-Neuve: Presses universitaires de Louvain.

Hannoyer, Jean, 1999. *Guerres civiles: économies de la violence, dimensions de civilité*, Paris: Karthala-CERMOC.

Hassner, Pierre and Marchal, Roland, 2003. *Guerres et sociétés: états et violence après la Guerre froide*, Paris: Éditions Karthala.

Hawk, Kathleen Hill, 2002. *Constructing the Stable State: Goals for Intervention and Peacebuilding*, Westport (CT): Praeger.

Holsti, Kalevi Jaakko, 1996. *The State, War, and the State of War*, Cambridge: Cambridge University Press.

Hovahnnisyan, Nikolay, 1999. *The Karabakh Problem: Factors, Criteria, Variants of Solution*, Yerevan: Zangak-97, p. 112.

ICG, 2017. 'Nagorno-Karabakh's Gathering War Clouds', June, Report No. 244, Europe and Central Asia: www.crisisgroup.org.

Kaldor, Mary ([1999] 3rd edition 2012). *New and Old Wars: Organized Violence in a Global Era*, Cambridge: Polity Press.

Kalyvas, Stathis, 2001. 'New and Old Civil Wars: A Valid Distinction?', *World Politics*, 54(1), 99–118.

Kalyvas, Stathis, 2005. 'The Remnants of War', *Perspectives on Politics*, 3(3), 692–693.

Kalyvas, Stathis, 2006. *The Logic of Violence in Civil War*, Cambridge and New York: Cambridge University Press.

Le Huérou, Anne, Merlin, Aude, Regamey, Amandine and Sieca-Kozlowski, Elisabeth (eds), 2014. *Chechnya at War and Beyond*, Abingdon: Routledge.

Libaridian, Gérard (ed.), 1991. *Armenia at the Crossroads: Democracy and Nationhood in the Postsoviet Era: Essays, Interviews and Speeches by the Leaders of the National Democratic Movement in Armenia*, Watertown (MA): Blue Crane Books, p. 170.

Libaridian, Gérard, 1999. *The Challenge of Statehood: Armenian Political Thinking since Independence*, Watertown (MA): Blue Crane Books, p. 162.

Libaridian, Gérard, 2004. *Modern Armenia: People, Nation, State*, New Brunswick (NJ): Transaction Publishers, p. 311.

Lindemann, Thomas and Saada, Julie (eds), 2012. 'Guerres et reconnaissance', *Cultures & conflits*, 87.

Linhardt, Dominique and Moreau de Bellaing, Cédric (eds), 2014. 'Ni guerre ni paix', *Politix*, 26(104).

Merlin, Aude, 2012, 'The Postwar Period in Chechnya: When Spoilers Jeopardize the Emerging Chechen State (1996–1999)' in N. Duclos (ed.), *War Veterans in Postwar Situations: Chechnya, Serbia, Turkey, Peru, and Côte d'Ivoire*, Basingstoke: Palgrave Mcmillan, pp. 219–240.

Merlin, Aude, 2017. 'Les conflits dits gelés sont-ils non solubles ? Les cas du Karabakh et de l'Abkhazie', in A. de Tinguy (dir.), *Regards sur l'Eurasie, l'année 2016*, Paris: Etudes du CERI.

Merlin, Aude and Serrano, Silvia (eds), 2010. *Ordres et désordres au Caucase*, Brussels: Editions de l'Université de Bruxelles, pp. 125–143.

Minassian, Gaidz, 2008. 'Armenia, a Russian Outpost in Caucasus?', Paris: IFRI. https://www.ifri.org/sites/default/files/atoms/files/ifri_RNV_minassian_Armenie_Russie_ANG_fevr2008.pdf.

Mouradian, Claire, 1990. *De Staline à Gorbatchev: histoire d'une République soviétique, l'Arménie*, Paris: Ramsay, p. 475.

Münkler, Herfried, 2005. *The New Wars*, Cambridge: Polity Press.

Papazian, Taline, 2010, 'Nœud gordien ou rocher de Sisyphe? Le conflit du Karabakh dans la vie politique arménienne', in Aude Merlin and Silvia Serrano (dirs), *Ordres et désordres au Caucase*, Brussels: Editions de l'Université de Bruxelles.

Papazian, Taline, 2016. *L'Arménie à l'épreuve du feu. Forger l'Etat à travers la guerre*, Paris: Karthala.

Paris, Roland, 2004. *At War's End: Building Peace after Civil Conflict*, Cambridge: Cambridge University Press.

Richards, Paul, 2005. *No Peace No War: An Anthropology of Contemporary Armed Conflicts*, Athens (OH): Ohio University Press.

Schwartz, David and Panossian, Razmik, 1994. *The Politics of Nation-Building in Post-Soviet Armenia, Azerbaijan and Georgia*, Toronto: University of Toronto Centre for Russian and East European Studies, p. 149.

Stedman, Stephen, 1997. 'Spoiler Problems in Peace Processes', *International Security*, 22(2), 5.

Stedman, Stephen John, Rothchild, Donald S. and Cousens, Elizabeth M., 2002. *Ending Civil Wars: The Implementation of Peace Agreements*, Boulder (CO): Lynne Rienner Publishers.

Tilly, C., 1984. *War Making and State Making as Organized Crime*, in P. B. Evans, D. Rueschmeyer and T. Skocpol (eds), *Bringing the State Back In*, Cambridge: Cambridge University Press, p. 170.

8 'Exorcism of cultural otherness'

Refugee women in post-Soviet Armenia

Eviya H. Hovhannisyan

In the last few decades the concept of 'refugee' has become a popular subject for researchers and policy makers. Numerous academic papers and official reports have tried to define the 'refugee' concept and a number of them have focused on its impact on the host country's socio-economic life and politics (Wahlbeck, 2002; Jackson, 1999). Up until now, it seems as if the study of refugee behavior is dominated by a negative categorization of its subjects. Refugees have not only experienced a myriad of difficulties in the country they left but were also subject to discrimination in the country where they sought a new life. Recently, the interest in investigating the refugee experience has shifted to another level.

The socio-cultural image of refugees, the host community and their everyday practices of interaction have come to constitute the focus of our research. The chapter first introduces a theoretical background on the issue of refugee stereotyping and then reviews some of the negative stereotyping models and prejudices that refugees encounter when resettling in Armenia. In particular, it deals with certain findings of research into the process of the construction of refugee women's stereotyping after their forced relocation to Armenia, and the process of deformation of this stereotype influenced by the local discourses. The empirical material for this research was collected in the Vardenis district of Armenia, which is populated by two socio-cultural groups of Armenians, that is, the local inhabitants and refugees from the Azerbaijan Soviet Socialist Republic (SSR). The research is based on the analysis of the social and cultural dichotomy of these two groups. Our challenge is to understand the reasons for and the patterns of the construction of the refugee women's negative image in the post-Soviet Armenia and to identify the impact of the stereotypes on marital relationships with the locals, as well as the lengthy process of leveling cultural 'otherness' between the different socio-cultural groups. Based on the refugees' life stories, documented through a combination of qualitative methods, this paper outlines how experiences of stereotyping could categorize refugee women as 'other', regardless of their ongoing efforts to navigate a range of situations while resettling to Armenia. The topic of negative stereotyping and abuse of refugee women is taboo in the Armenian society. Therefore, relatively few articles are written on this theme.

168   *Eviya H. Hovhannisyan*

The empirical material generated by the research adds to the evidence reported in the literature to date about the refugee alienation practices.

Historical review of the issue

From the late 1980s to the early 1990s Armenia and Azerbaijan underwent major socio-demographic transformations. The Nagorno-Karabakh conflict (from 1988 to 1994) forced hundreds of thousands of people to flee their homes. Fearing for their lives, Armenians living in Azerbaijan fled the country – about 360,000, according to available statistics (De Waal, 2013). In turn, the vast majority of ethnic Azerbaijanis left Armenia and Nagorno-Karabakh. A portion of the deported Armenians later settled in the abandoned former Azerbaijani villages in Armenia, occupying the houses formerly owned by Azerbaijanis that were left in the process of forced relocation.

Mostly these were Armenians who had managed to exchange their property (flats, houses, orchards) in Azerbaijan with the Azerbaijani refugees from Armenia (Huseynova et al., 2008). The phenomenon of property exchange during the first years of Armenian-Azerbaijani mutual resettlement definitely facilitated the whole process, as many families knew beforehand where they would have to move to. The resettlement process was gradual: representatives of both parties were travelling from Azerbaijan to Armenia and vice versa during for about three years, carrying their possessions, selling their houses, drawing up the documents and so on. This lasted until both republics had almost completely rid themselves of the representatives of the 'undesirable' ethnic group.

These historic events left a deep imprint on the consciousness of the two societies, changing the entire pattern of socio-cultural institutions and inter-ethnic relations in the two countries (Shahnazarian, 2014). The structure and hierarchy of the socio-cultural institutions changed radically in several regions of Armenia (Syunik province, Vardenis district, Masis district) after a complicated process of replacement of the dominant ethnic contingent. These changes entailed a new type of relationship between the local Armenian population and the Armenian refugees from Azerbaijan, which forms the subject of the research for this chapter.

We will start by considering some aspects of group conflict theory, in which we will place our reflections on refugees as an economic and moral threat to society. Then we will proceed to a discussion of the stereotypes of refugee women in everyday discourses in the Vardenis district of Armenia, which is populated by both refugees and local Armenians. We will end with the notion about the homogeneity of the Armenian society analyzing a question regarding the various relationship types between the two groups of Armenians in this small district.

We should note that many of the refugee families (especially in the large cities of Azerbaijan such as Baku and Kirovabad) had a high social status in their former places of residence and the education, employment and property to match their status. They were mostly petroleum engineers, chemists and shipbuilders who used to work at the industrial plants in the large cities of Azerbaijan. After the resettlement, even given the successful transportation of almost their entire property, the refugees were unable to occupy a matching social niche in Armenian society and to find a suitable application of their knowledge in the rural areas of Armenia. Partly for this reason and partly because of the lack of knowledge of Armenian (as the mother tongue or the language of communication for the refugees was Russian), and also because of the complex socio-cultural relations with the local Armenian population, a large number of refugees left Armenia in the first years of resettlement. Those families who had no opportunity to emigrate (there were also those who refused to move again and live in a foreign country) gradually began to integrate into Armenian society, but already with a 'defective' social status. Only a small number of the refugees managed to adapt to the new social environment. Having made the change from urban to rural life, a few refugee households have acquired some knowledge in farming, though the majority of refugees were by no means farmers. Nevertheless, they managed to use their level of education (for example as doctors or teachers) and consolidate a middling social status within particular settlements.

Refugee stereotypes and attitudes towards the 'other'

Attitudes toward refugees tend to vacillate over time, with several factors influencing public attitudes towards migration, including both economic and non-economic factors. Taking a more recent review of the literature and mass media, we can state that the beginning of the 1990s represents the moment when the image of refugees began to be characterized by negative features in Armenia (Yalçın-Heckmann et al., 2010). Historically, this moment coincides with the collapse of the Soviet Union in 1991, the Nagorno Karabakh War in 1992–1994 and the consequent economic decline in Armenia. Newly arrived Armenian refugees from Azerbaijan were perceived as a threat to the country's economic situation by the host community. The local authorities faced with the issues of the shelter providing, distribution of humanitarian aid, health assistance, naturalization policies, and so on. The poor prevailing economic conditions potentially affected intergroup relationships. The various versions of group conflict theory share a central premise, that the negative attitudes of group members towards other social groups are mainly rooted in perceived intergroup competition for economic resources and scarce goods (Jackson, 1993). The portrayal of refugees as an economic threat is a frequent image used in everyday discourses, media and political debates where the arrival of people seeking asylum is associated with socio-economic changes and with the fluctuation of the labour market (Billiety et al., 2014).

During our research we were faced with a number of everyday circumstances in which the refugees were presented as lazy, insane, licentious,

170   *Eviya H. Hovhannisyan*

reinforcing their exclusion from the host society. In this line of thinking, anti-refugee attitudes stem from the perception that refugee groups pose a threat to certain interests and values of the indigenous social group. Moral (Zárate et al., 2004) or symbolic threats (Stephan et al., 1999) refer to the perception that outgroups adhering to different cultural traditions and value systems pose a threat to one's own value system, which is believed to be morally right. The formation of stereotypes based on refugees' relaxed morals and the looseness of their women is a common element in a moral threat syndrome discernible in many societies (Kontogiorgi, 2006, p. 186).

Perceived value differences due to culture or religion are considered symbolic threats that are seen as threatening to the social fabric of the host community. Though perceived realistic threats, more than perceived symbolic threats, predicted prejudicial attitudes and beliefs about refugees (Mayda, 2006; Pereira et al., 2009). Each type of threat may embody unique aspects of threat and should be considered in models of prejudice and perceived threat (Stephan et al., 1999; Ceobanu et al., 2010).

The development of perceived threat models is conceived as a fundamentally collective process, through which a particular social group comes to define other groups (Blumer, 1958). It is essentially through these definitions that intergroup stereotypes are constructed. Perceived realistic and symbolic threats increase anxiety and influence intergroup tensions, and this may culminate in conflict or discrimination (Kamans et al., 2011; Riek et al., 2006). Therefore, an additional factor to consider in models of prejudice and threat is the affective dimensions associated with intergroup relations. The majority of research has focused on cognitive processes, whereas affective components have been relatively absent. Nonetheless, more recent research has increasingly incorporated affect into models and analyses of intergroup conflict (Mackie et al., 2002). Stephan and colleagues (Stephan et al., 1999) focus on the role of intergroup anxiety as another aspect of threat, in addition to perceived realistic and symbolic threat and negative stereotypes, which contribute to prejudice. This attitude, together with the state's policy, contributes to creating myths and stereotypes concerning refugees and projecting distorted images of people that seek protection from persecution in their home country.

This theoretical section also considers the issue of Armenian refugee identity within the overall problematique of intergroup conflicts. On the one hand, it is the process of the construction of a new social and ethnic identity by the refugees themselves in a new place of living. On the other hand it is the process of constructing the refugee images by the host society (and vice versa), through these images the host society constructs itself. In third all these processes and mechanisms of identity construction are influenced by the political and international discourses. The main specificity of our case is the fact that these are not just refugees, in the sense of 'others', but are returnees to their historical homeland and co-ethnics. The intrigue is in how the uncertainty arises about the 'refugee' concept and how it is discussed and filled with everyday practices. Are the Armenian refugees from the Azerbaijan SSR co-ethnics who have the right to return home or are they 'others', unwelcome foreigners? The few existing studies on this topic claim that local Armenians preferred to coexist with their 'own' local Azerbaijanis rather than with the refugees, in other words 'other' Armenians from Azerbaijan (Huseynova et al., 2008, pp. 8–9). Both the local Armenians and the Armenian refugees from the Azerbaijan SSR found themselves thrust into a relationship full of unknowns, and this is one of the major reasons why each respective group began to file individuals of a particular socio-cultural group under labels. Therefore, after moving to Armenia, Azerbaijani Armenians found themselves 'others' in their ethnic homeland.

The identity of the Armenian refugees who migrated to the former Azerbaijani settlements in Armenia is complex and multifaceted. It was formed in close relation with the Azerbaijani cultural environment, and after the resettlement to Armenia it was faced with the local Armenian cultural tradition, which had a lot of differences in language, religion and social structure. These identity markers are deeply embedded in the past experience of the refugees and in the existing socio-cultural differences with the host community (Shnirelman, 2000, p. 5). The views, character traits, stereotypes and qualities ascribed to them by the locals, their stance and the way they behaved in their everyday lives led to the creation of two groups, and the imposition of serious limits on their social interactions.

I conducted ethnographic fieldwork over approximately five months in 2014 and 2015, seeking contextual understandings of stereotype concepts in the Vardenis district of Armenia. A combination of participant observation, in-depth interviews and visual ethnography was used to explore the refugee women's strategies employed to survive in the host society. An ethnographic approach was used to contextualize the everyday experiences of this group of refugees and allowed for detailed descriptions of gender-specific discourses. I particularly focus on the women stereotypes because the main scope of the contradiction between co-ethnics and 'others' is best seen through this focus. Observations of their homes, community gatherings and workplaces in the Vardenis district were recorded regularly to complement data collected through interviews and photos. Such observations focused on the women's interactions with family members, neighbors, local community members and colleagues. These methods were not only chosen to convey the depth and richness of themes, which could at times be of a sensitive nature, but also because they are particularly appropriate for collaborating with marginalized groups like refugee women (Harper, 2002; Lenette et al., 2013). The biographies, recorded more than two decades after moving to a new territory, not only shed light on the past of these people but also demonstrate the complicated process of their integration into a new society. The fieldwork reveals a relationship structure between newcomers and the local population, resulting in the formation of

172 *Eviya H. Hovhannisyan*

kinship and social solidarity networks that lie at the basis of the new economy and social structure of the region.

The process of stereotyping between local Armenians and Armenian refugees

To explore the larger role stereotypes play in the lives of societies, we must understand why people turn to stereotypes in the first place, how certain labels applied to or held by specific groups can determine individuals' decisions and how failing to remain cognizant of the fact that stereotypes do not define every individual within a particular population leads to societal conflict. For a more detailed analysis of the refugee stereotypes we decided to appeal to the various patterns of the integration process: a) the initial juxtaposition; b) the economical distancing; c) the moral distancing; d) the gradual alienation vs. fusion (Markina, 2015; Groenewold et al., 2006). During the time the relationship and socio-cultural boundaries between the two groups are fluctuating from the gradual disintegration to the coalescence. On the one hand the various mechanisms designed to strengthen the oppression of refugees were involved at each of these stages. On the other hand the socio-economic boundaries between the two different groups of Armenians were quite flexible. The different patterns of integration and grassroots practices of mutual alienation of refugees and local Armenians remind us of the establishment of a new majority-minority dynamic between local Armenians and newly arrived diasporan *aghpar*[1] population by the late 1940s in Soviet Armenia (Abbasov et. al., 2016, p. 190). As a result, between 1946 and 1949 more than 100,000 Armenians left their homes in the Middle East, Greece, the Balkans, France and the US in order to resettle in Soviet Armenia. The harsh post-war conditions and unintelligible social norms were as much an obstacle to the repatriates as their reception by the locals. After the resettlement they faced with the problems in housing, such as limited amount of living space, inequalities between the different sectors of Soviet society, lack of facilities and poor sanitation. *Aghpars* faced discrimination, alienation and a big cultural chasm with the local Armenians, whose thinking and way of life juxtaposed with theirs.

During the first years, the period between 1988 and official recognition of Armenia as an independent nation state on 21 September 1991, the focus of government programs was mainly to provide shelter for the large number of refugees that had fled from Azerbaijan (Groenewold et al., 2006, p. 4). We can qualify the initial juxtaposition between the host society and refugees as relatively neutral. The reaction the host community had to the refugees reflects the predisposition to fear anything that is not familiar to it – anything that disrupts the patterns it is accustomed to seeing is often perceived as a threat.

During the second stage, between 1991 and 1995, a public policy on the integration of refugees into Armenian society was complicated by the economic consequences of the disintegration of the USSR system (Groenewold et al., 2006, p. 4). The newcomers were no longer the only vulnerable group in the country, as most people in the country now faced unemployment and deteriorating living conditions, leading to a situation whereby more than half of the population lived below the national poverty level. Economic and environmental resource burdens (perceived or actual) led to resentment by locals, resistance to integration and pressure on authorities to segregate refugees. The economic relationship between the host society and the refugees was constructed on the principle of domination-subordination during the entire time after resettlement. In the rural areas of Armenia, social stratification is primarily determined by the transmission of economic and social capital from generation to generation. In the early 1990s, local residents of the Vardenis district were able to redistribute the whole agricultural property left over from the *kolkhozes* (land, livestock, agricultural machinery), not allowing the refugees to access this source of capital. The locals privatized the most fertile lands, the highest-quality cattle and almost all equipment (tractors, combines). Most workplaces in the state institutions of the district were occupied by the locals. All attempts of the refugees to set up their own business (a private ambulance, a dental clinic, a shop) were either 'stifled' or taken under the authoritarian control of the local Armenians. This fact became the basis of the initial economic superiority of the locals with regard to the refugees. Thus, the refugees had very few opportunities to penetrate the dominant social groups in their new place of residence. This unequal distribution of labour affects the further development of the social hierarchy and the emergence of a few groups of influence (the local administration, the local criminal elites) that consist exclusively of local residents. The refugees generally occupy the middle and lowest rungs in the employment hierarchy (Hovhannisyan, 2016).

A large number of refugee families were not able to adapt to the living conditions (for economic, social and cultural reasons) in the rural areas of Armenia. They sold their lands and houses for a paltry price to the local residents and went abroad (mostly to the Russian Federation) in the first years of resettlement. These were mainly former urban dwellers who had neither the knowledge and skills in agriculture, nor did they speak Armenian or know the Armenian traditions. One man commented:

> The locals always oppose themselves to the refugees. They call them 'galma' [Turkish word for the newly arrived people] in an pejorative manner. The local men hardly ever marry the refugee women and vice-versa. Even in everyday life, for example at the doctor, the locals are always served out of turn, while the refugees are left at the end of the queue.
>
> (local man, 54 years old, Mets Masrik, 15 August 2014)

174   *Eviya H. Hovhannisyan*

The process of moral distancing was implemented through cultural expectations and stereotypes, that includes knowledge about the local 'traditionalism and morality'. Various characteristics (differences) in education and in appearance, and language differences (Armenian/Russian) given to each group increased the distance between the two categories. The host community dominates the process of social elimination of the resettlers by constructing the image of the foreigner as a threat and depriving his initial equivalent status (Markina, 2015, p. 52):

> The refugee women strongly stood out from the host population in the early years of the resettlement. The local Armenians were shocked when they saw women with dyed blonde hair. They freely communicated with the men on the street or at work. The local Armenian women didn't dye their hair and didn't wear pants in the late eighties. Nobody denies that they were beautiful, feminine, in comparison to the local Armenian women, but they were not like us.
> (local woman, 34 years old, Mets Masrik, 11 August 2014)

The process of contraposition and 'production of otherness' was directly implemented in everyday interaction and discourses. The most pronounced markers of otherness were the visual image of the refugee women and the behavioral image of refugee men who did not comply with the traditional notions of local Armenians. The refugee women looked very different from the women of the host community. Many of them, having resettled from the cities of Azerbaijan, seemed well-groomed, educated and free in communication with men:

> All that I was aware of and was able to do during my life in Baku was to go to work in the morning and to return home in the evening, take a shower and lie down to have a rest. That's all! We communicated with men freely, we used to go to the theatre and cinema, we drove with families to the seashore. It was urban culture. We were accustomed to that kind of life in Baku.
> (refugee woman, 52 years old, Mets Masrik, 25 August 2014)

Such an unusual image of a woman does not meet the local standards of the patriarchal wife, mother of a large family and keeper of the hearth and was thus unacceptable for the local Armenians (Shahnazarian, et. al., 2014, p. 29). This fact strongly influenced the stereotyping of the refugee women's image and the construction of the main discourse against them:

> The local Armenian women were extremely backward in comparison with the refugee women. The refugees considered the locals as unenlightened, illiterate and uncouth. The local Armenians considered the refugee women

as prostitutes, and the refugee men as flabby and spineless people who had lost the image of the traditional Armenian man. We hardly met refugee men, because most of them left to earn money in Russia soon after resettlement.

(local woman, 34 years old, Mets Masrik, 11 August 2014)

The social distance between the represented groups is usually accompanied by emphasizing the differences between the person depicted and the speaker (Braidotti, 2000 p. 222).Additionally, in the same way that the Vardenis residents constructed stereotypes of the refugees based on their own cultural values, some of the refugees further validated their generalizations about local Armenians based on traditions valued in their respective settlements (Baku, Kirovabad, Khanlar and so on). In their turn, the refugees behaved with a certain arrogance to the host community. Distancing through cultural differences led to the gradual opposition of the two groups.

This linear manner of stereotyping is entirely based on observing behavior that appears common among a group of individuals with certain identifiable physical characteristic. So at first sight, the production of otherness took place through rather transparent and primitive, binary oppositions (Spivak, 1999, p. 22): traditional / non-traditional, moral / immoral, masculine / feminine. Such a dualistic way of thinking determines the structure of the hierarchical power relations (Braidotti, 2000, p. 228).

It is particularly important that there was increasing interest in the refugees as women and vulnerable victims. The culmination of this interest was an increasing number of abductions of refugee women by the local men and a significant number of forced marriages in the early years of the resettlement. Such marriages often disintegrated after a few years. The reason for divorce was the mutual intolerance towards the cultural differences of the opposite group. A local woman commented:

The refugee women were unable to put up with the harsh treatment of our local men. Quite often the husbands beat their refugee wives following jealous accusations. They were not accustomed to the free urban manners of their wives. The refugee men are much more gentle and kind, and they respect their women.

(local woman, 34 years old, Mets Masrik, 11 August 2014)

The discursive oppression of the refugees was pronounced with a strong feminine bias. The host community opposed the morality (traditionality) of the local Armenian women and the immorality (licentiousness) of the refugee women. As an object of the discursive representation, the image of the 'foreigner' does not depend on its real properties, but on the position of the representing group. The representations are embedded first in the language and then in the culture, institutions and political ambience of the representor (Said, 1977, p. 248). Therefore, the negative representation of the refugee

176 *Eviya H. Hovhannisyan*

women was primarily produced by the local Armenian women. Their social authority implied dominance in the local discourses:

> There were a lot of cases when local Armenians were married to the refugee women after abducting them in the first years of resettlement. Those were the lowest strata of the local population - the drug addicts, the alcoholics. Around 70 percent of these marriages broke up subsequently. A lot of divorced refugee women were left alone with their children in the early 1990s. There was a very difficult economic situation in the district in the postwar period. Quite often these single mothers (the divorced refugee women) were not able to feed their children. These hard conditions led them to prostitution in exchange for grain or other products. They are forced to trade sex for food for their children. These practices and negative attitudes were based precisely on the treatment of the local Armenians.
>
> (local woman, 57 years old, Mets Masrik, 13 August 2014)

The representations of refugees are overwhelmingly feminized and infantilized images as against the images of locals as harsh, authoritative people. Stereotypical feminization is a part of the colonial discourse. In our case, the local population acts as a colonizer suppressing the refugee community through the feminine markers in order to show its weakness and social subordination. Both refugee women and men were attributed the common feminine features (gentle, beautiful, well-groomed, feminine, soft by their nature, kind). The host community has suppressed this feminine portrait of the foreigner in a metaphorical and literal sense during the whole time since their resettlement. Sexual harassment by the local men and the construction of the prostitute image of the refugees by the local Armenian women were the basic mechanisms of subordination of the 'others'. Many refugee women felt they were excluded or stigmatized within their host communities because of their marital status. The locals attributed to the refugee women, and in particular the refugee ex-wives of local Armenians, the stereotype of the prostitute. This theme represents a significant aspect of resettlement discourses, which to date has been largely absent in the literature. A key implication that informs nuanced understandings of the refugee women experiences in resettlement is that women raising children alone, and whom their community as well as broader host society did not fully respect, could face significant hardships, thus increasing their vulnerability and keeping them at the margins of their communities:

> Once, in summer, I came to visit my neighbours. I wore a dress of medium length with open knees and with short sleeves. After my visit the lady of the house called me individually and said: 'My husband does not like it when a woman walks around with a naked body. Please, cover up your legs and arms, and don't dye your hair anymore, because there are a lot of men in the village who look upon you as a prostitute!'. I replied to

her: 'Let them look if there is something interesting to look at!'. According to the local Armenian proverb 'When you come into the house as a daughter-in-law and see that the relatives of your husband are blind, you have to gouge out your eyes too; if they are bald, you have to cut your hair too'.

(refugee woman, 56 years old, Mets Masrik, 25 August 2014)

The desire of the authoritative subject to subdue the 'foreigner' through the practices of destroying the otherness and standardizing society through discursive influence is the major problem and cause of hatred within a culture (Baudrillard, 1997 p. 113). The refugee women were stereotyped as the 'other', but this did not lead to their exclusion and abuse in the sense of cleansing, but rather to a special type of violence in the sense of, subordination and assimilation. Here again, the intrigue is that they are simultaneously compatriots and 'others'. At the level of self-identification both groups consider themselves Armenians, but at the level of socio-cultural practices and previous social context they are significantly different.

The representation of the 'Other' is always more or less deformed, it cannot be neutral. The discourse reflects the social structure which stands behind it (Dorogavtseva, 2008 p. 31).Therefore individual, sometimes apparently insignificant elements of the discourse – visual forms, behavioural images and verbal texts – created a powerful set of stereotypes. From the abovementioned passages from the interviews, we can notice both the whole process of the construction of the refugee women images – pretty, well-groomed, educated, free, and also the process of their deformation through the cognitive practices and local discourses – the licentious women with their free manners. We can claim that refugee women were especially vulnerable to gender-based violence during the resettlement to the host countries. An analysis of the refugee stereotypes reveals that the prevailing images are those representing the stereotype of the 'young female', whereas refugee men are rarely represented. This is due to the fact that refugee men left to earn money in the first years of the resettlement, which would not contribute to the representation of them as a social and economic threat in the host country. On the other hand, the stereotypes of the local population show that the prevailing images are those representing the image of a 'rough young man', whereas the local women are not represented at all. We can state that the main body of stereotypes in the region were produced by the local women. The various forms of sexual harassment and torments in the light of the stereotypes of immorality were used routinely in order to shame and demoralize individuals, families and communities who are considered as others. These were the practical and discursive mechanisms for the destruction of the other as a potential social threat.

The last stage in the process of alignment of the social boundaries between the two groups of Armenians was the longest and the most controversial.

178 *Eviya H. Hovhannisyan*

During this stage, the otherness of the refugees was gradually reduced to the 'merge of the two groups', or it was constituted as controversial and completely contrasting to the norms and values of the host community:

> I have married a refugee. Up to now, people from our village say that my husband is 'gyalma'. The same attitude is in our culture when somebody marries a person of a different nationality or faith – Yazidis, Assyrians, Muslim. Even in the local schools the teachers treat the refugee children with disdain. They draw a clear boundary between the local children and the refugee children.
>
> (local woman, 34 years old, Mets Masrik, 11 August 2014)

The fluidity of the socio-cultural borders between two groups means that refugees are never fully separated from the local community. Despite the construction of the mutual hetero-stereotypes there are many examples of mixed marriages of refugees and local Armenians. The process of alienation gradually shifted to the deconstruction of the discourse, or rather, to its partial subversion (Butler, 1990 p. VII). In this process of the gradual merging of the two groups, the local Armenians can be identified as the dominant group, dictating the local rules not only in the economic, administrative and political sphere but in matrimonial relations as well. This is determined by the previous stages of building a hierarchy between the two groups. The emphasis was put on the masculinity of local men as aggressors and on the femininity of refugee women as victims of this aggression. The power imbalance of gender relations in most societies generates cultures of masculinity prone to violence:

> With time local Armenians have had families with the refugees. They marry refugee women and men. It's easy to be a godfather at the wedding of the refugees. They do not know our cultural traditions and local customs. In our tradition, if someone is chosen the godfather at the wedding, all wedding expenses must be paid by him. The refugees do not know our traditions. They are much more pragmatic than the town resident.
>
> (local man, 46 years old, Mets Masrik, 13 August 2014)

The shifting boundaries between the two groups through the matrimonial relationship can be primarily explained by everyday pragmatism. Refugees and locals mix together for purposes of trade, marriage, seasonal work and so on. The cases when a local Armenian woman marries a refugee man are significantly fewer. This is partly due to the fact that part of the refugee men left in the early years of resettlement. On the other hand, as representatives of the hierarchically dominant group the local Armenian women did not seek to bind their lives with the men from the oppressed social group.

The children born in mixed marriages are mostly ranked as locals. This is due to the fact that on the one hand the dominance of the locals in the social

Refugee women in post-Soviet Armenia 179

hierarchy is transferred onto their family relations. On the other hand, the second generation of the resettlers is already the culture-bearer of the host community.

Conclusion

In light of the matrimonial relationship (with the expressed dominance of the local Armenians) the multifaceted stereotyping of both groups reveals the trajectory of the changing social boundaries, from neutrality to total exclusion, or gradual involvement. This suggests that the aforementioned two groups can be conventionally divided into several sub-groups of actors (local men / local women, refugee men / refugee women, children). Each sub-group plays an important role in the process of relation construction during the last quarter century. At the discursive and symbolic level each of the sub-group is represented by the strong stereotypical characteristics (traditional / non-traditional, moral / licentious, masculine / feminine, cultural / rough (uncouth), beautiful (well-groomed) / ugly and so on).

The conventional stereotyping and negative attitudes towards the refugees are based on the common notion of 'imagined communities', that implies the myth of cultural homogeneity of the nation. We pose the question on how these two groups can reach the common perception of the community. The problem with the stereotyping of the refugees is that they do not belong to any society: they had to flee their home country, the Azerbaijan SSR, which makes them 'outsiders' of the country of exodus, while they also do not belong to the society of the host country, Armenia, despite the fact that they are ethnically Armenians. In the case when the heterogeneous social groups are perceived as a homogeneous 'imagined community', the gradual templating and stereotyping occurs.

However, the findings discussed in this chapter contribute to debunking the 'myth' of homogeneity in relation to the refugee and local Armenian groups and demonstrates the diversity of everyday practices and experiences among their sub-groups. The position of the majority of refugee families is inherently precarious even after 28 years of resettlement because of the trauma of exclusion from their initial community as well as their exclusion from the host community and its social structure. The socio-cultural exclusion of the refugees can be considered mainly as a lack of participation in social institutions during the course of distribution of economic and symbolic resources, as an exception of social structures and discourses, the isolation of individuals from the 'moral resources' provided by concrete group that are criteria of 'insider-ness' (Ban'kovskaya, 2002, p. 6). The discourse on the refugees is largely blind to refugees in denying them a place in the discourse. Discursive strategies that deny any otherness deprive the 'other' of the opportunity and even the capacity for the articulation of his interests, the expression of his cultural identity and the formation of his positive image. Refugees are de facto integrated when

180 *Eviya H. Hovhannisyan*

they are able to sustain livelihoods, through access to land or employment, and can support themselves and their families, when they have access to education and health facilities, when they are socially networked into the host community, so that intermarriage is common, ceremonies like weddings and funerals are attended by everyone, and there is little distinction between the refugees' and hosts' standard of living (Jacobsen, 2001, p. 9). The social integration of the refugees is the result of the interplay of numerous factors. Of particular importance are the mixed marriages between refugees and members of the local population. Inter-marriage is one of the most effective means of bringing about social integration. With a few exceptions, it can be assumed that the children of such marriages will be integrated.

A more critical analysis considers that stereotypes are often constituted through the value difference (Innes, 2010). The stereotyping of refugees as traumatized victims, vulnerable women identifies them with the subjects who are voiceless, passive, politically innocent, untainted by communal ties or economic self-interest. The problem with refugees is that the 'other', represented by the host community, moves to be physically inside the ethnic state, which means that the values, culture and identity of society are reinforced through the stereotypes and state policy within this context. Thus, refugees appear not simply as a potential threat to the host community's values and economics, but mainly as a mass of humanity in need of the social and moral security.

Note

1 *Akhpar* is both a pejorative term for diaspora Armenians and a slight corruption of *akhper*, the Armenian colloquial word for 'brother' but also meaning 'trash' (Astarjian, 2010).

References

Abbasov, I., Delihuseyinoglu, H., Pipia, M., Rumyansev, S. and Sanamyan, E. (2016). 'Ethnic Groups and Conflicts in the South Caucasus and Turkey', *The Caucasus Edition: Journal of Conflict Transformation*, July.

Alexander, M., Brewer, M. and Livingston, R. (2005). 'Putting Stereotype Content in Context: Image Theory and Interethnic Stereotypes', *Personality and Social Psychology Bulletin*, Vol. 31, 781–794.

Astarjian, H. (2010). 'National Schizophrenia: the Grey Genocide', *The Armenian Weekly*, 19 February. Retrieved from: http://armenianweekly.com/2010/02/19/astarjian-national-schizophrenia-the-grey-genocide/.

Ban'kovskaya, S. (2002). 'Chuzhak i igranici: k ponyatiyu socialnoi marginalnosti' ['Strangers and Boundaries: The Notion of Social Marginality'], *Otechestvennye Zapiski*, Vol. 6, 457–467.

Baudrillard, J. (1997). 'The City and the Hatred', *Logos*, Vol. 9, 107–117.

Billiety, J., Meulemanz, B. and De Witte, H. (2014). 'The Relationship Between Ethnic Threat and Economic Insecurity in Times of Economic Crisis: Analysis of European Social Survey Data', *Migration Studies*, Vol. 2, 2, 135–161.

Blumer, H. (1958). 'Race Prejudice as a Sense of Group Position', *The Pacific Sociological Review*, Vol. 1, 3–7.

Braidotti, R. (2000). *Sexual Difference as a Nomadic Political Project in Feminist Reader*, in Zdravomyslova, E. and Temkina, A. (eds), *Feminist Reader*. St. Petersburg: Dmitriy Bulanin (in Russian).

Butler, J. (1990). *Gender Trouble: Feminism and the Subversion of Identity*. New York: Routledge.

Camino, L. and Krulfeld, R. (1994). *Reconstructing Lives, Recapturing Meaning: Refugee Identity, Gender, and Culture Change*. Philadelphia: Gordon and Breach.

Ceobanu, A. and Escandell, X. (2010). 'Comparative analyses of public attitudes toward immigrants and immigration using multinational survey data: a review of theories and research', *Annual Review of Sociology*, Vol. 36, 309–328.

De Waal, Th. (2013). *Black Garden: Armenia and Azerbaijan Through Peace and War*. New York: NYU Press.

Dorogavtseva, I. (2008). 'Universal'nye zakonomernosti reprezentatsii Drugogo v literaturnykh i neliteraturnykh tekstakh' ['Universal Patterns of Representation of the Other in Literary and Non-Literary Texts'] *Gumanitarnyy vector [Humanities Vector]*, Vol. 3, 31–36 (in Russian).

Groenewold, G. and Schoorl, J. (2006). 'The Living Conditions of Refugees in Armenia: Millennium Development Indicators and Coping Behaviour', country report. The Hague, NIDI. Retrieved from: www.unhcr.org/statistics/STATISTICS/45adf1132.pdf.

Harper, D. (2002). 'Talking about pictures: a case for photo elicitation'. *Visual Studies*, Vol. 17, 1, 13–26.

Hovhannisyan, E. H. (2016). 'Elitism among Refugees in the Rural Environment: Authority, Kinship, Social Networks and Economic Survival', in Y. Antonyan (ed.), *Elites and 'Elites': Transformations of Social Structures in Post-Soviet Armenia and Georgia*. Yerevan: YSU Publishing House, pp. 49–70.

Huseynova, S., Akopyan, A. and Rumyantsev, S. (2008). *Kizil-Shafag and Kerkenj: History of Villages Exchange in Situation of Karabakh Conflict*. Tbilisi: Heinrich Böll Stiftung South Caucasus.

Huseynova, S. and Rumyantsev, S. (2010). 'New Life in Old Galoshes. The Space Mastering of The Village in a Situation of the Collective Resettlement', *Laboratorium. Journal of Social Research*, Vol. 1, 28–49 (in Russian).

Innes, A. (2010). 'When the Threatened Become the Threat: The Construction of Asylum Seekers in British Media Narratives', *International Relations*, Vol. 24, 4, 456–477.

Jackson, I. (1999). *The Refugee Concept in Group Situations*. The Hague, London and Boston: Martinus Nijhoff Publishers.

Jackson, J. (1993). 'Realistic Group Conflict Theory: A Review and Evaluation of the Theoretical and Empirical Literature', *The Psychological Record*, Vol. 43, 3, 395–413.

Jacobsen, K. (2001). 'New issues in refugee research: the forgotten solution: local integration for refugees in developing countries', Working Paper No. 45. Retrieved from: www.unhcr.org/research/RESEARCH/3b7d24059.pdf.

Kamans, E., Otten, S. and Gordijn, E. (2011). 'Power and Threat in Intergroup Conflict: How Emotional and Behavioral Responses Depend on Amount and Content of Threat', *Group Processes and Intergroup Relations*, Vol. 14, 293–310.

Kontogiorgi, E. (2006). *Population Exchange in Greek Macedonia: The Rural Settlement of Refugees 1922–1930*. Oxford: Clarendon Press.

Lee, J. (1991). 'Social Perception and Social Reality: A Reflection-Construction Model', *Psychological Review*, Vol. 1, 54–73.

182 *Eviya H. Hovhannisyan*

Lenette, C., Brough, M. and Cox, L. (2012). 'Everyday resilience: narratives of single refugee women with children'. *Qualitative Social Work*, June.

Mackie, D. and Smith, E. (eds). (2002). *From Prejudice to Intergroup Emotions: Differentiated Reactions to Social Groups*. Philadelphia: Psychology Press.

Markina, V. (2015). 'Mekhanizmy proizvodstva inakovosti v diskurse: teoriya i metodologiya analiza (na primere odnogo kinoteksta)' ['The Process of Othering in Discourse: a Case of Subordination of or Disengagement from the Other?'] *The Journal of Social Policy Studies*, Vol. 13, 49–64 (in Russian).

Mayda, A. (2006). 'Who is Against Immigration? A Cross-Country Investigation of Individual Attitudes Toward Immigrants', *The Review of Economics and Statistics*, Vol. 88, 510–530.

Ministry of Territorial Administration and Development of Republic of Armenia, the State Migration Service (2014). 'The Number of the Armenian Population in the Major Cities and Regions of the Azerbaijan Soviet Socialist Republic', 18 April. Retrieved from: http://smsmta.am/.

Pereira, C., Vala, J. and Costa-Lopes, R. (2009). 'From Prejudice to Discrimination: The Legitimizing of Perceived Threat in Discrimination Against Immigrants', *European Journal of Social Psychology*, Vol. 40, 1231–1250.

Riek, B., Mania, E. and Gaertner, S. (2006). 'Intergroup Threat and Outgroup Attitudes: A Meta-Analytic Review', *Personality and Social Psychology Review*, Vol. 10, 336–353.

Said, E. (1977). *Orientalism*. London: Penguin.

Schweitzer, R., Melville, F., Steel, Z. and Lacherez, P. (2006). 'Trauma, post-migration living difficulties, and social support as predictors of psychological adjustment in resettled Sudanese refugees', *Australian and New Zealand Journal of Psychiatry*, Vol. 40, 2, 179–188.

Shahnazarian, N. and Ziemer, U. (2014). 'Emotions, Loss and Change: Armenian Women and Post-Socialist Transformations in Nagorny Karabakh', *Caucasus Survey*, Vols 1–2, 2, 27–40.

Shnirelman, V. (2000). 'Cennost' proshlogo: etnocentristskie istoricheskie mifi, identichnost' i etnopolitika' ['Value of the past: ethnocentric historical myths, identity and ethnic policies'] in Olkott, M. and Malashenko, A. (eds), *Realnost' etnicheskikh mifov* [*Reality of Ethnic Myths*]. Moscow: Moscow Carnegie Center, pp. 12–33 (in Russian).

Spivak, G. (1988). 'Can the Subaltern Speak?' in Nelson, C. and Grossberg, L. (eds), *Marxism and the Interpretation of Culture*. London: Macmillan.

Spivak, G. (1999). *A Critique of Postcolonial Reason: Toward a History of the Vanishing Present*. Cambridge: Harvard University Press.

Stephan, W., Ybarra, O. and Bachman, G. (1999). 'Prejudice Towards Immigrants', *Journal of Applied Social Psychology*, Vol. 29, 2221–2237.

Wahlbeck, Ö. (2002). 'The concept of diaspora as an analytical tool in the study of refugee communities', *Journal of Ethnic and Migration Studies*, Vol. 28, 2, 221–238.

Yalçın-Heckmann, L. and Shahnazarian, N. (2010). 'Experiencing Displacement and Gendered Exclusion: Refugees and Displaced Persons in Post-Socialist Armenia and Azerbaijan', *Caucasus Edition: Journal of Conflict Transformation*, 1 November. Retrieved from: http://caucasusedition.net/analysis/experiencing-displacement-and-gendered-exclusion-refugees-and-displaced-persons-in-post-socialist-armenia- and-azerbaijan/.

Zárate, M., Garcia, B., Garza, A. and Hitlan, R. (2004). 'Cultural Threat and Perceived Realistic Group Conflict as Dual Predictors of Prejudice', *Journal of Experimental Social Psychology*, Vol. 40, 1, 99–105.

Index

Abdulatipov, Ramazan 46
Abkhaz diaspora 64
Abkhaz-Georgian war 1992–1993 110
Abkhazia 1, 4, 6, 8, 14, 16, 24;
    as *de facto* state 105, 106, 107;
    democratisation 66; and EEU 111;
    ethnic divisions 112–115; and EU 57,
    58; Inguri River checkpoint 109–112;
    and Russia 58, 60–61, 64, 67–71;
    tourism in 63; war veterans 153
ABLs *see* administrative boundary lines
adats 93, 95, 96
Adjara 102
administrative boundary lines (ABLs) 24,
    110, 113
Afghanistan 19, 24
aghpar population 172
agricultural economy 133
agricultural products 63, 109
agriculture 89, 173; modernization
    of 86–87
Ajaria 63
Alasania, Irakli 21
alims 96
Aliyev, Heydar 123
altruism 82
ancestral solidarity 82
'anchor' projects 7
ANM *see* Armenian National Movement
Annual National Programs (ANPs) 19
ANPs *see* Annual National Programs
anti-clanship campaign 43
anti-corruption campaign 43
anti-corruption policy 95
anti-terrorist operations 15
Arabic countries 80
archaization 81
Armenia: Association Agreements
    106–107; and EEU 4–5, 8, 104;
and EU 23, 106–107; and
    Nagorno-Karabakh 69–70;
    national borders 102; refugee women
    in 167–180; and Russia 59, 64;
    war veterans 9–10; *see also* Armenian
    Army; Armenian diaspora; Armenians
Armenian Army 154–156
Armenian diaspora 64, 69
Armenian National Movement
    (ANM) 148
Armenians: genocide of 150; in
    Nagorno-Karabakh conflict 146–160;
    relocation to Armenia from
    Azerbaijan 10
Arms Trade Treaty (ATT) 30
arms transfers 30
army service 84; *see also* military service
arson 40
ATT *see* Arms Trade Treaty
authoritarianism 1
Autonomous Oblasts 102
Autonomous SSR 102
Azerbaijan: Association Agreements
    106–107; and EU 23, 57, 106–107;
    migration from 9, 121–139; national
    borders 102; public health 125; public
    spending 125; relocation of Armenians
    from 10; and Russia 59; social sector
    125; social security 125; *see also*
    Azerbaijanis; Azeri diaspora; Azeris
Azerbaijanis 132–135, 138
Azeri diaspora 122, 123
Azeris 122, 129, 137

Balkars 88
bank loans 83
Barinov, Igor 41
Belarus 106
Belarusians 132

184 *Index*

Belaventsev, Oleg 41, 45
Belya Rechka 88
Beslan 45
Bibilov, Anatoly 68
birth rates 79
Bishkek Protocol 59
black markets 63
Black Sea 63
borderlands 108–109
borders: creation of 103; *de facto* 106;
  hardening and softening of 108; as loci
  of power 107–109; mobility through
  108; permanence and legality 107;
  role of 108; *see also* boundaries
boundaries: cleavages between 114;
  commercial 104; creation of 103–104;
  de facto 104; hardening and softening
  of 108; as loci of power 107–109; of
  security structures 104; territoriality
  of 109–112; *see also* borders;
  'boundary activation'
'boundary activation' 108
Bourdieu, P. 103
bribery 94, 95
business: and economic development 89;
  family 92; local 91, 92; relationships 62

'Canadianisation' 126
CAR *see* Central African Republic
CASCADE project 6, 8
CBMs *see* confidence-building measures
ceasefire agreements 105
ceasefire lines 105, 109;
  Abkhaz-Georgian 109, 113
Central African Republic (CAR) 13, 24
Central Asia 9, 16, 120, 123, 127–128,
  136–137
Chechen rebels 16
Chechnya 37–44; development model 85;
  federal transfers in the budgets 88;
  Muslim tradition in 80; policy of
  political participation 44–46;
  social exclusion from Russia 47, 49;
  war veterans 153
children: number of 82; of refugees 178
Circassian activists 47
CIS *see* Commonwealth of
  Independent States
civil insecurity 138
civil society 2, 7, 29–30, 67, 70, 104
clan-based networks 62
cleavages 7–8; between boundaries 114;
  ethnic 102; production of 103
clientelism 9, 62–63, 69, 82

Cold War 57
combatants 152–153
Common Security and Defence Policy
  (CSDP) 2, 13, 23–24, 26–31
Commonwealth of Independent States
  (CIS) 105, 111, 135
confidence-building measures (CBMs)
  23–24, 29
conflict: 'frozen' 106, 145, 153;
  protraction 104; resolutions 95;
  in South Caucasus 105–106;
  'unresolved' 105, 145, 153–154;
  see also conflict-affected areas
conflict-affected areas 8, 23;
  see also conflict
coping strategies 8
corruption 43–44, 62, 69, 94
Cossacks 41
counter-modernization 79
counterterrorist campaigns: in Chechnya
  37–39, 47; and Islamic State 41;
  and radicalisation 41; and social
  exclusion 47–48
courts 96
Crimea 41, 48
criminal groups 63
crisis management 2, 5, 23–24, 26–28, 32
CSDP *see* Common Security and
  Defence Policy
cultural identity 42
cultural 'otherness' 10, 167–180
customs: in Dagestan 84–85;
  differentiated from traditions 84
cyber security 30

Dagestan 38–41, 43, 46; education 83;
  family and society 82; immigration 79;
  land issues 87; mobility 83; Muslim
  tradition 80; people's views on the
  future 85–86; perception of success
  83–84; survey on modernization
  process 81–86; traditions and
  customs 84–85
DCFTA *see* Deep and Comprehensive
  Free Trade Agreement
decision-making 3
Deep and Comprehensive Free Trade
  Agreement (DCFTA) 8, 104,
  106–107, 111
Defence and Security Committee (DSC)
  17, 20, 30
democracy 1–4; 'exclusive' 67; promotion
  by EU 1–3; and security governance
  4–6; 'symbolic' 67

Index 185

democratisation 3, 7; and dependency 65–72; fast-track 57; and Georgian Armed Forces 13–32; limitations on 62–65; in South Caucasus 57–73
demodernisation 7, 78
demographic changes 79
dependency: and democratisation 65–72; economic 3
depopulation 6, 127
desertion 15
diaspora associations 135, 138
diasporas 64; Abkhaz 64; Armenian 64, 69; Azeri 122–123; Ossetian 64; Uzbek 135; *see also* diaspora associations
djogad 148–150, 153
Dombai 91
draft: in Dagestan 84; in Georgia 15
drugs 62
DSC *see* Defence and Security Committee
Dudinka 125

EaP *see* Eastern Partnership
Eastern Partnership (EaP) 1–2, 23, 27–28, 58, 59, 106
EC *see* European Commission
economic dependence 3
economic deprivation 64
economic development 42–44; and business 89
economic dislocation 8
economic modernisation 43
economic sanctions 62, 64
economy: agricultural 133; criminalisation of 63; Dagestan 83; fragmented 103; higher 83; North Caucasus 86–96; parallel 63; planned 63; shadow 62–63, 88–90
education 64, 81, 85, 123, 125, 133, 169, 174; higher 83; military 159; 'patriotic' 158; secular 83
educational support 64
EEAS *see* European External Action Service
EEU *see* Eurasian Economic Union
embezzlement 95, 97
employment 89, 94, 136–137, 173
ENP *see* European Neighbourhood Policy
environmental degradation 7
ESS *see* European Security Strategy
ethnic cleavages 102
ethnic diversity 82
ethnicity 112–115
ethnic mobilization 93

ethnic structure 7
ethno-cultural diversity 79
ethno-politics 102
EU *see* European Union
EUBAM Libya 24
EUCAP Nestor 24
EUFOR RCA 24, 31
EU-Georgia Association Agreement 8
EUJUST THEMIS 23–24
Eurasian Economic Community 106
Eurasian Economic Union (EEU) 2, 4, 106; and Abkhazia 111; and Armenia 4–5, 8, 104
European Commission (EC) 22
European External Action Service (EEAS) 26–27
European integration 13–32
European Neighbourhood Policy (ENP) 1–2, 22–23, 27–28, 58, 59
European Security Strategy (ESS) 22, 26
European Union (EU): and Abkhazia 57, 58; Association Agreements 106; and Azerbaijan 57; conflict prevention and resolution 57–58, 63; and Georgia 8, 13, 22–32, 57, 58; 'liberal peace-building' model 57; Monitoring Mission (EUMM) 24, 27, 28; and NGOs 29; and peacebuilding process 6; and promotion of democracy 1–3; and South Caucasus 22–23, 57–59, 106; and South Ossetia 57; Special Representatives (EUSRs) 23, 27
executive accountability 18

Facebook 137
family 82; businesses 92; networks 7; weddings 84–85
farmlands, depletion of 87
Federal Agency for Nationalities Affair 41
Federal Security Service 41
feminization 176
forced marriages 175
FPAs *see* Framework Partnership Agreements
Framework Partnership Agreements (FPAs) 24
France 64
free movement facilities 64
fundamentalism 80

Gali district 112–114
Gamsakhurdia, Zviad 13, 14
GC *see* Group of Confidence

186   *Index*

gender-based violence 177
Geneva International Discussions (GID) 23, 106
Georgia 1, 2, 4; armed forces 13–32; Association Agreements 106; DCFTA agreement 104; and EU 8, 13, 22–32, 57, 58, 106; Inguri River checkpoint 109–112; national borders 102; and NATO 5, 16–17, 24–25, 29–31; and OSCE 106; parallel economy 63; political system 17–18, 20–21; and Russia 59; security sector reform 5; *see also* Georgians
Georgians 105, 113–115
Georgia Train and Equip Program (GTEP) 15
GID *see* Geneva International Discussions
globalisation 109
Global North 57
'good authority' 95
Granovetter, M.S. 138
grassroots corruption 94–95
Group of Confidence (GC) 17
groups: conflict theory 169–172; making and unmaking of 103; solidarity 82
Grozny 40, 45, 153
GTEP *see* Georgia Train and Equip Program
Guseinov, Afil 135

hajj 80
Hobsbawm, Eric 84
Horn of Africa 24
Hovanisyan, Artur 158
human rights: abuses in Georgia 15, 18, 19–20; in the armed forces 30; promotion of 57; and security sector reform 14
human security 29–30
human trafficking 16
hybrid regimes 67
hydrocarbons 121, 125

ID *see* Intensified Dialogue
identity 8, 103; ethnic 48, 80, 113–114; group 47–48; national 47, 70; North Caucasus 46–50; religious 80; self-identification 113; Russian 48
IDPs *see* internally displaced persons
illegal substances 16
imams 96
IMF *see* International Monetary Fund

immigrants 79
independence: limitations on 62–65; and modernity 97
individualism 81
Individual Partnership Action Plan (IPAP) 16
Inguri River 104, 109, 112, 115
Ingushetia 38–41; federal transfers in the budgets 88; Muslim tradition 80
Intensified Dialogue (ID) 16
interdependence 69
intergroup anxiety 170
intergroup conflict 170
internally displaced persons (IDPs) 23
International Monetary Fund (IMF) 15
international security 17
International Security Advisory Board (ISAB) 18
International Security Assistance Force (ISAF) 19, 24, 31
Internet 83
investment projects 90–92
IPAP *see* Individual Partnership Action Plan
Iraq 17
ISAB *see* International Security Advisory Board
ISAF *see* International Security Assistance Force
Islam 7, 40, 47, 97; 'new' 98; radical forms 79; 'renaissance' of 79–81; Salafi 41; and social community 50; as source of identity 50; Sufi 40; and young people 80, 97
Islamic State 39, 41
Islamism 6, 7; insurgency 1
Italy 92

jamias 88, 96

Kabardino-Balkaria 38, 39, 41, 43, 46, 88; Muslim tradition 80
Kadyrov, Akhmed 38, 40, 44
Kadyrov, Ramzan 38, 40, 41, 44–5, 47, 48
Karachai-Cherkessia 38, 41; Muslim tradition 80
Kazakhstan 106
Khajimba, Raul 67, 68
Khasan'ya 88
Khloponin, Aleksandr 41, 42, 43
kindred relations 82, 83
kinship-based networks 62
Kokov, Yurii 46

Kola Peninsula 126, 135–138
kolkhozes 86
kolkhoz-sovkhoz system 86
Koltso 152
korenizatsiya 102
Kosovo 17, 60, 71–72
Kozak, Dmitry 42
Krasnodar krai 87
Kumyks 87, 88
Kusumkent 82, 83
kutan lands 87

labour migration 8–9, 120–139
land: market 87; ownership 88, 89;
    privatization 87; shares 86; survey 89;
    transfer 87; use rights 86; use
    system 88
legal frameworks 8
legal institutions 95–96
legal systems 93
Libya 24
Lisbon Treaty 26, 27, 28
local businesses 91, 92
local development 92–96

Magomedov, Magomed salam 39
Mahabart batallion 156
Makhachkala 82, 83, 88
Mali 24
malnutrition 15
Manukyan, Vazgen 156
MAP *see* Membership Action Plan
marital relationship 10
marketisation 57
mass migration 79
material wealth 83
medical services 15
Medvedev, Dmitry 42
Melikov, Sergei 41, 45–46
Membership Action Plan (MAP) 16, 25
mercantilism 82
migration 8–9; and diaspora associations
    135; generational angle 128; labour
    8–9, 120–139; mass 79; for military
    service 128–132; polar 9, 122–139;
    policy 8; 'shuttle' 133–134; and social
    ties 132–133; for work 131–132
military bases 128
military service: migration for 128–132;
    and social status 131; *see also*
    army service
Military Strategy 18
minefields 87
Mingrelians 113–114

Ministry of Defence (MOD) (Georgia)
    14–17, 19, 20, 25, 29, 31
Ministry of Internal Affairs 41
Minsk peace process 59, 61
mobility: in Dagestan 83; partnerships 8;
    social 8, 82, 86, 97–98; in Soviet
    times 120
mobilization 93
modernity 83–84, 97
modernization 7, 78; forms of 96;
    Islamic 79–81; in the North Caucasus
    78–99; socioeconomic 79–81;
    and technological innovations 92;
    tools of 94
Moldova 28
money laundering 62
monocities 126, 127
mosques 40, 42
multiculturalism 79
Murmansk 122, 125–138
Muslim brotherhood 81
Muslim clothing 83
Muslims 47–48, 50, 80
mutiny 15
mutual aid 82

Nagorno-Karabakh 1, 6; aftermath of
    conflict 10; and Armenia 4–5, 69–70;
    Armenian diaspora 64, 69; as *de facto*
    state 105, 106, 107; democratisation
    66; economy 69; and EEU 4–5;
    'Four-Day War' 146–160; and OSCE
    58, 59, 60, 105; and Russia 59, 61, 64,
    151–152
Nal'chik 88
Nasirova, Paridokhon 135
Nasyr-Kort 40, 41
national cohesion 70
National Guard, Georgia 14
national identity 47, 70
National Security and Crisis
    Management Council (NSCMC) 20
National Security Concept 16, 18–19
National Security Council (NSC) 14,
    17, 20
NATO *see* North Atlantic Treaty
    Organization
NATO-Georgia Council (NGC) 18–19
NCFD *see* North Caucasian Federal
    District
NCOs *see* non-commissioned officers
networks: clan-based 62; criminal 108;
    family 7; kinship-based 62; *see also*
    social networks

188 Index

New Force party 48
NGC *see* NATO-Georgia Council
NGOs *see* non-governmental organizations
Nogais 87
non-commissioned officers (NCOs) 18
non-governmental organizations (NGOs): Abkhazia 58; and EU 29, 58; Georgia 14, 16, 18
Norilsk 122, 125–137
Norilsk-Nickel Kombinat 126
North Atlantic Treaty Organization (NATO): and Georgia 5, 16–17, 24–25, 29–31; 'liberal peacebuilding' model 57; Membership Action Plan (MAP) 16, 25; Parliamentary Assembly (PA) 21, 29; Partnership for Peace (PfP) programme 14, 22; *see also* NATO-Georgia Council (NGC) 18–19
North Caucasus 5–7; demographic changes 79; economy 42–44, 86–96; financial basis 88–90; identification and belonging 46–49; investment projects 90–92; land issues 86–88; modernization 78–99; policy of force 38–42, 49; political participation 44–46; Russian governance 37–51; shadow economy 88–90; traditionalism 81–82
North Caucasus Federal District (NCFD) 7, 42, 78–79, 88, 89, 90, 93
North Caucasus Federal Military District 38
North Ossetia–Alania 88
Northern Fleet 126
NSC *see* National Security Council
NSCMC *see* National Security and Crisis Management Council

oil industry 89, 123
Organization for Security and Cooperation in Europe (OSCE) 22, 57–60; and Georgia 106; Minsk Group 105, 145; and Nagorno-Karabakh 58, 59, 60, 105
Orthodoxy 80
OSCE *see* Organization for Security and Cooperation in Europe
Ossetian diaspora 64

Pankisi Gorge 16
PAP-DIB *see* Partnership Action Plan-Defence Institution Building

parallel economy 63
Partnership Action Plan-Defence Institution Building (PAP-DIB) 16
Partnership and Cooperation Agreement (PCA) 22
Partnership for Peace (PfP) 4, 22
PCA *see* Partnership and Cooperation Agreement
PDO *see* Public Defender's Office
peacebuilding 6, 57–62, 105, 111; 'liberal' model 57
peacekeeping missions 105, 111
pensions 64
personnel management 18
PfP *see* Partnership for Peace
planned economy 63
pluralisation 7
pluralism 70, 82
political participation 44–46
polyjuridism 93, 95, 96, 97
post-authoritarian societies 25
post-colonial studies 9
prejudice 170
presidentialism 9
prisons 19
private-enterprise economic projects 78
private entrepreneurship 7
private initiative 92
property letting 90
Psou River 112, 115
public benefits 94
Public Defender's Office (PDO) 30
public health 125
public spending 125
Putin, Vladimir 5, 37, 43, 45, 49, 106; on ethnic state identity 48

radicalisation 41
reciprocity 138
refugees 137; definition 167; stereotypes and attitudes towards 169–179; women 10, 167–180
regional development 92, 96–97
regional security 3, 4, 6, 106
religious authorities 96
religious identity 42
religious revival 79–81
rents 69
Resolute Support 24
restaurants 134
Rose Revolution 16, 23, 29
Russia: and Abkhazia 58, 60–61, 64, 67–71; and Armenia 59, 64; and Azerbaijan 59; and the 'Four-Day

Index 189

War' 151–152; and Georgia 59; governance of the North Caucasus 37–51; and Nagorno-Karabakh 59, 61, 64, 151–152; 'passportisation policy' 64–65; as patron state 64, 70; and South Ossetia 58, 60–61, 64, 65, 67–71
Russia-Abkhaz Treaty on Alliance and Strategic Partnership 4, 8
Russian citizenship 64
Russian Civil Union 48
Russian Platform 48
Russian Public Movement 48
Russia-South Ossetia Alliance and Integration Treaty 4

Saakashvili, Mikheil 16, 17, 23
Salafi communities 39–40, 47; *see also* Salafism
Salafism 40, 41, 42, 80; *see also* Salafi communities
Samegrelo 113
Samstkhe-Javakheti 102
SAO *see* State Audit Office
Sargysan, Vazgen 148, 156
SDR *see* Strategic Defence Review
secular law 96
secular state 81, 97, 98
security governance 4–6, 13, 19, 28, 31
security sector reform (SSR) 5, 13–14, 26; and crisis management 28; and promotion of democracy 28
self-determination 59
self-employment 90
self-expression 84, 97
self-identification 113
self-realization 84, 97–98
self-sufficiency 43
service sector 134
Seventh Framework Programme 3
sexual harassment 176
shadow economy 62–63, 88–90
share privatization 86
Sharia law 88, 95, 96
Shevardnadze, Eduard 14, 15
Shoigu, Sergei 41
shopping centres 134
siloviki 46
Sochi Olympics 40, 48
social benefits 64
social capital 98
social change 3
social cohesion 47
social contract 42, 43
social deprivation 64

'social embeddedness' 138
social exclusion 47–48
social insecurity 138; *see also* social security
social instability 7, 78
social mobility 8, 82, 86, 97–98
social networks: and diaspora associations 135; and military service 131; participation in 137; and principle of reciprocity 138; *see also* networks
social polarisation 6
social sector 125
social security 81, 125; *see also* social insecurity
social status 82, 84; and military service 131
social tension 92
social ties 8, 132–133
socio-economic development 6, 37, 44, 78, 93
socio-economic reform 2
soft power tools 64
South Caucasus: arctic labour migration 120–139; borders and boundaries 107–109; cleavages 7–8; and EU 22–23, 106; European Neighbourhood Policy 27–28; migration from 9; peacekeeping missions 105, 111; regional dynamics 104–107; regional security 4; unrecognized states 56–73
Southern Federal District 42
Southern Federal Military District 38
South Ossetia 1, 4, 6, 14, 16, 18, 23, 24; as *de facto* state 105, 106, 107; and EU 57; and Russia 58, 60–61, 64, 65, 67–71
Soviet boundaries 102–104
Soviet Socialist Republics (SSR) 102
SSOP *see* Sustainment and Stability Operations Program
SSR *see* security sector reform
stalemates 95
State Audit Office (SAO) 19, 21, 29
Stavropol krai 78, 79, 89; federal transfers in the budgets 88; share privatization 86
stereotyping 169–179
Strategic Defence Review (SDR) 16
stroiotryadi 132
success 83–84
Sufi 40–41
Sufi Brotherhood 95
Sumgait 147–148

190 *Index*

Sustainment and Stability Operations
Program (SSOP) 17
Svaneti 102
Sweden 23
Syria 39

Tajiks 133, 136
Taliban insurgency 24
tampering 95
tax 63, 89–90
technological innovations 92
territorial development 93
territorial integrity principle 59–60
terrorism 30, 41, 42, 45
Tibilov, Leonid 68
top corruption 94
tourism 63
tourism–recreation cluster 90
traditionalism 81–82
traditional values 7
traditions 84–85
transnational criminal networks 108
transparency 92
Trasdniestria 106
trust 94, 96, 98
Turkey 24, 59, 70; Abkhaz diaspora 64
Tuybe 82, 83

Ukraine 2; European Neighbourhood
Policy (ENP) 28; migrants 132, 137
unemployment 89
United National Movement (UNM) 19, 23
United Nations: 'liberal peacebuilding'
model 57; Military Observer
Mission 105; Monitoring Mission
(UNOMIG) 111
UNM *see* United National Movement

UNOMIG *see* United Nations
unrecognised states 56–73; adjustment
towards recognition 65–72;
normalisation without recognition 66
urbanization 6, 79, 81; and family size 82
USA 62
Uzbek diaspora 135
Uzbeks 133, 136

value systems 170
visas 8
V kontakte 137
VOMA 159

Wahhabism 80
war veterans 9–10
wealth 83–84
weapons: illegal trafficking 62; of mass
destruction 22
weddings 84–85
welfare state 138
well-being 14, 86, 92; material 84
'westward drift' 127
Wider Europe Communication 22–23
women: and education 83; refugee 10,
167–180; and secular state 98
workplace 85

xenophobia 48, 137

Yerevan 106
Yerkrapah Union 148, 153, 156–159
Yevkurov, Yunus-Bek 39, 40
young people 80, 97

Zmeva, Elena 136
Zmeva, Olga 136